Ubuntu Linux® For Du[mmies]

BESTSELLING
BOOK SERIES

CW00922936

Using Help

Ubuntu offers a straightforward, simple-to-use boot-time help system. The section "Using the Boot Prompt Function Keys" describes how to use the system and what information it provides.

You'll want to use the command-line more often to perform simple and complex system administration tasks as you become more skilled using Ubuntu. The second section "Knowing Some Useful Commands" describes some useful command-line examples.

Some Useful Commands

The following list provides some straightforward, useful command-line examples. Click the Gnome Applications menu and select Accessories ➪ Terminal to open a terminal emulator window, then use these commands:

- ✔ `clear` Clears the current screen of all text.
- ✔ `ls` Lists the current directory.

   It's like the MS-DOS `dir` command.
- ✔ `ls dir` Lists the specified directory.
- ✔ `cat file` Concatenates (adds) the contents of the file to your screen.

   It's like the MS-DOS `type` command.
- ✔ `more file` Displays the file one page at a time.
- ✔ `tail file` Displays the file one page at a time from the end of the file.
- ✔ `pwd` Shows name of the current directory.
- ✔ `cd dir` Changes to the specified directory.

   It's like the MS-DOS `chdir` command.

For Dummies: Bestselling Book Series for Beginners

Ubuntu Linux® For Dummies®

Cheat Sheet

Using the Boot Prompt Function Keys

When booting from an Ubuntu CD-ROM you're given the chance to select several options to control the startup process. You can optionally select an option when you see the Ubuntu startup menu (the first menu option is Start or install Ubuntu).

The following lists provide a summary of those codes.

Using the F1 Help Menu

Press the F1 function key and the Welcome to Ubuntu help menu opens. You can then press the following function keys to get specific information.

- **F1:** The main F1 menu
- **F2:** Minimum hardware requirements
- **F3:** Several methods you can use to start Ubuntu.

  For instance, you can turn off power-saving mode if you're having problems getting Ubuntu to boot and suspect that option is causing the problem.
- **F4:** Additional boot methods.
- **F5:** Special boot parameters overview (why you might use boot parameters and where to find them)
- **F6:** Hardware-specific special boot parameters (examples of boot parameters for specific devices)
- **F7:** More hardware-specific special boot parameters (more examples of boot parameters you might use for specific devices)
- **F8:** Debugging-oriented special boot parameters.
- **F9**: Describes how you can get help from Ubuntu.
- **Esc**: Exits the Help menu

F2 Language Menu

Pressing the F2 function key opens an extensive language support menu. Use the Up and Down cursor keys to navigate the menu and select a language.

F3 Key Map Menu

Pressing the F3 function key opens an extensive keyboard support menu. Use the Up and Down cursor keys to navigate the menu and select the mapping that matches your keyboard.

F4 VGA Menu

If you're not satisfied with your computer screen's resolution, press the F4 function key. A menu displays a selection of screen resolutions. Use the Up and Down cursor keys to select a resolution from the menu.

F5 Accessibility Menu

This menu provides options to help access your computer for those who need extra help. Use the Up and Down cursor keys to select an assistant option. For instance, select the High Contrast option if you need a brighter screen.

F6 Others Menu

This menu opens a one-line text editor showing the Ubuntu kernel boot options. You can modify any options that are

- Fed to the Linux kernel
- Used by the kernel to start your Ubuntu computer

Getting a Virtual Terminal

Linux provides six virtual consoles (text-based command-line interfaces). Simultaneously press the Control (Ctrl) and Alternate (Alt) keys with any of the functions keys from F1 through F6. For example, press Ctrl-Alt-F1.

Return to the graphics screen by pressing Ctrl-Alt-F7.

Ubuntu® Linux®

FOR

DUMMIES®

Ubuntu® Linux®
FOR
DUMMIES®

by Paul G. Sery

Wiley Publishing, Inc.

Ubuntu® Linux® For Dummies®

Published by
Wiley Publishing, Inc.
111 River Street
Hoboken, NJ 07030-5774
www.wiley.com

WILEY

About the Author

Paul Sery is a systems administrator employed by Sandia National Laboratories in Albuquerque, New Mexico. He's currently working on creating a centralized log event collection and analysis system and using open source public key encryption to build inexpensive two-factor authentication systems.

In his spare time, he and his wife Lidia enjoy riding their tandem through the Rio Grande valley. They also enjoy traveling throughout Mexico. Paul is the author of *Linux Network Toolkit, Knoppix For Dummies* (both through Wiley Publishing), and several other Linux books. He has a bachelor's degree in electrical engineering from the University of New Mexico.

Dedications

To my wife, Lidia.

Author's Acknowledgments

Mark Richard Shuttleworth created Ubuntu, without which this book would be impossible. Ubuntu has added to the productivity and creativity of the world, and I thank him for his creation.

I want to especially thank Kyle Looper and Pat O'Brien, who gave me so much help with this project. I'd also like to thank the staff at Wiley Publishing — they continue to give me great assistance.

I also want to thank my wife, Lidia, for her good advice, support, and encouragement. Without her, I would still be the pocket-protector-wearing, busted-eyeglasses-fixed-with-tape, *Star Trek*-costume-wearing, Saturday-night-hacking, sorry sorta guy. Well, I was never into *Star Trek*, but I am a geek and I'm lucky to have met her.

Publisher's Acknowledgments

We're proud of this book; please send us your comments through our online registration form located at `www.dummies.com/register/`.

Some of the people who helped bring this book to market include the following:

Acquisitions, Editorial, and Media Development

Project Editor: Pat O'Bren

Acquisitions Editor: Kyle Looper

Copy Editor: Heidi Unger

Technical Editors: Joe Brockmeier, Jason Luster

Editorial Manager: Kevin Kirschner

Media Development Specialists: Angela Denny, Kate Jenkins, Steven Kudirka, Kit Malone

Media Project Supervisor: Laura Moss

Media Development Manager: Laura VanWinkle

Editorial Assistant: Amanda Foxworth

Sr. Editorial Assistant: Cherie Case

Cartoons: Rich Tennant (www.the5thwave.com)

Composition Services

Project Coordinator: Erin Smith

Layout and Graphics: Jonelle Burns, Joyce Haughey, Stephanie D. Jumper, Heather Ryan, Ronald Terry

Proofreaders: Aptara, Melanie Hoffman

Indexer: Aptara

Anniversary Logo Design: Richard Pacifico

Publishing and Editorial for Technology Dummies

Richard Swadley, Vice President and Executive Group Publisher

Andy Cummings, Vice President and Publisher

Mary Bednarek, Executive Acquisitions Director

Mary C. Corder, Editorial Director

Publishing for Consumer Dummies

Diane Graves Steele, Vice President and Publisher

Joyce Pepple, Acquisitions Director

Composition Services

Gerry Fahey, Vice President of Production Services

Debbie Stailey, Director of Composition Services

Contents at a Glance

Table of Contents

Introduction

∙∙

*U*buntu *Linux For Dummies* tells you how you can use the fastest growing Linux distribution on the planet. Ubuntu Linux is very easy to use (even if you've only used Windows before) and provides a powerful platform on which to get your work done. Ubuntu is also fun to use!

You can use Ubuntu Linux as fast as you can rip the companion CD out of its plastic sleeve in the back of the book, pop it into your CD-ROM drive, and reboot your computer. Ubuntu Linux is available as a *live* Linux distribution, which means it boots directly from the CD-ROM included with this book, and you can start using it right away.

When you get the feel for Ubuntu Linux, you can install it on your computer from the *Ubuntu Linux For Dummies* CD-ROM. One of Ubuntu's strengths is — in my opinion — its easy-to-use installation system. Answer a handful of questions, and you've got yourself a full-blown Linux computer. Easy.

You'll also find that Ubuntu Linux works great as your everyday computer workstation. Ubuntu is designed to help you perform all of your primary tasks, such as word processing and Web browsing — and most of the other things you might want to do, such as instant messaging. If you've got a job for a PC, Ubuntu can do it for you.

About This Book

I wrote *Ubuntu Linux For Dummies* to help you get started using Ubuntu Linux and have some fun along the way. First, the book helps you get started using Ubuntu by covering the essentials, such as booting Ubuntu live and then installing it on your computer. After getting started, I explain how you can use Ubuntu's major components, such as networking, office productivity tools, and such. I use extensive examples to show exactly how to install, configure, and use the included software.

What's in This Book

For Dummies series books are organized into independent parts, and this one is no exception. You can read the chapters of *Ubuntu Linux For Dummies* in any order. You can even read the paragraphs backwards, if you're so inclined — although that might not be the best way to go. Whatever your inclination, I intend this to be easy to read in any direction.

- ✔ If you want a complete course in using Ubuntu Linux, you can read the whole book from beginning to end and follow along with your computer. The book shows you how to

  - Start Ubuntu directly from the CD.

  - Permanently install Ubuntu on your computer.

  - Connect to the Internet.

  - Use the basic operating system features.

  - Perform cool, specialized Ubuntu tasks.

- ✔ If you just need an answer to a specific question or instructions for performing a specific task, you can look it up and follow the instructions without reading the whole book. For example, you might be a Linux veteran who just needs to find information on performing a special Ubuntu task. Find the topic you're interested in, in the Table of Contents or Index, and flip directly to that portion of the book.

The following sections tell you how you can navigate each part of *Ubuntu Linux For Dummies.*

Part I: Starting Fast

Part I describes what Ubuntu Linux is and how you can get started using it. Chapter 1 describes Ubuntu's philosophy and architecture. Chapter 2 introduces the live nature of Ubuntu and tells you how you can use it without touching your existing operating system. Chapters 3 and 4 cover preparing a computer for a new (or additional) operating system and permanently installing Ubuntu. Finally, Chapter 5 provides some of the simple essentials you need to start using Ubuntu as your workstation.

Part II: Networking and the Internet

Part II focuses on connecting your Ubuntu workstation to networks and the Internet. There's a special chapter for each kind of network or Internet connection you might have. Chapter 6 describes connecting to a private network via Ethernet. Chapter 8 moves on to using high-speed broadband Internet connections. Chapter 9 reverts to using old-school dialup modems, and Chapter 10 provides the essential network security ingredient, the firewall.

Part III: Working with Ubuntu Workstation

Part III gets to work by acquainting you with the primary Ubuntu desktop applications, such as word processing, Internet browsers, and e-mail clients. Chapters 11 and 12 look at the GNOME graphical desktop environment and its features. Chapter 14 covers using the ground-breaking Mozilla Firefox Web browser. In Chapter 15, I tell you about using the Evolution e-mail client. Chapter 16 is close to my heart, as it describes using the Microsoft Word–compatible OpenOffice.org Writer, as well as other programs that come with Ubuntu.

Part IV: Multimedia Ubuntu

Part IV gets back to having some fun by describing how to use Ubuntu's communication and multimedia applications. You learn how to make phone calls to other computers and telephones using Ubuntu. I also show how to remotely work on and remotely manage Microsoft Windows servers. The remaining chapters describe how to use Ubuntu as a multimedia entertainment center to play music, make audio CDs, edit photographs, and more.

Part V: The Part of Tens

For Dummies books love to give top ten lists. This book includes chapters showing how and where to find information about and help for using Ubuntu. You also learn how to keep your Ubuntu computer secure.

Part VI: Appendixes

The appendixes introduce other Ubuntu flavors: Kubuntu, Edubuntu, and Xubuntu. Kubuntu is nearly the same as Ubuntu but is based on the KDE desktop manager. (Ubuntu uses the GNOME desktop manager.) Edubuntu is nearly the same as Ubuntu but provides additional educational applications and uses a fun, colorful, customized GNOME desktop. Xubuntu uses a lightweight desktop manager — Xfce — that uses fewer computer resources and can be used on older, slower computers. You can download and use any of these Ubuntu variations from www.ubuntu.com. You'll also find guidance on SSH, and a brief summary of the *Ubuntu Linux For Dummies* CD-ROM.

Foolish Assumptions

My job in writing this book is to make using Ubuntu Linux as easy as possible. To that end, it's a good idea to convey some of my assumptions about my readers. I assume that you

✔ **Are curious about Linux in general and want to see what it's about.**

Great! That's what this book is all about. Sure, it's oriented around learning the Ubuntu Linux distribution, but most of what you read here is applicable to any version of Linux.

✔ **Want an alternative to commercial software.**

That's what Linux, open source software, and Ubuntu are all about. Linux (and Ubuntu Linux, which combines the various aspects and components of the Linux world together in its own, unique way) provides a great alternative to huge, monolithic operating systems.

Open source software is copyrighted like proprietary software. However, open source software is licensed in a way that permits you to freely use, modify, and distribute the software as long as you don't prevent anyone else from doing the same. Open source software can be sold or given away.

✔ **Have a computer.**

Unfortunately, Ubuntu Linux doesn't run on an abacus, TV, or coffee maker. However, it runs on most home computers, including PCs and Macintoshes.

The *Ubuntu Linux For Dummies* CD-ROM runs on 32-bit PCs (most PCs made in the last 20 years). If you have a hot new 64-bit PC or a PowerPC-based Mac, you can download Ubuntu and use this book to run it.

You might not want to read *Ubuntu Linux For Dummies* if you're looking for the following:

✔ **A book about wine tasting.**

In that case, read *Wine Tasting For Dummies* or rent the movie *Sideways*.

✔ **Ubuntu Linux reference material.**

This book concentrates on the more basic aspects of the system and doesn't delve into the more complex.

✔ **Information on building an Ubuntu Linux server.**

Ubuntu Linux comes in two flavors: Desktop and Server. Rather than trying to become the jack-of-all-trades — but an ace of none — Ubuntu decided to dedicate separate editions to the Linux desktop and Linux server. This book uses the Desktop version of Ubuntu Linux — surprise, surprise — and concentrates on helping you use it.

✔ **Details on becoming a professional system administrator.**

Being a system administrator myself, I would love to write more about the job. I could fill books about it — actually, I have. System administrators are suave, sophisticated, talented, extremely well-paid professionals who are always good looking and have good people skills. Or is that the other way around? I always forget. Anyway, as wonderful as the profession is, there isn't enough room to do it justice here. So this book provides just enough system administration material to efficiently run your Ubuntu Linux computer.

Conventions Used in This Book

I confess, I love conventions. I love going to them and learning more about computers. I even love the social aspects of computer conventions: Borg-like kids encrusted with wearable computers; pale, computer-room-generated skin, and so on. Total nerd-dom. I like to fit in.

On the other hand, I don't like book conventions of the nit-picking kind. However, conventions are necessary whether they have something to do with Star Trek or how instructions are written in a book.

The following sections describe the methods I use in the text to get you through the book quickly and easily so that you can spend more time with your new operating system.

Italics

Terms that might be unfamiliar to you often appear in italics and are followed by a helpful definition or explanation of the term. Also, you'll find place-holder text in italics.

Special font

You'll see some words in this book in a special font that looks like this:

```
monofont
```

Here are the types of things that you will find in this special font:

- ✔ Web addresses look like this: `www.dummies.com`.
- ✔ When I ask you to type something, it appears in `monofont`.
- ✔ Filenames, directory names, and file paths appear in `monofont`.
- ✔ Certain terms that are specific to Linux appear in `monofont`. (If you're new to Linux, don't worry. I explain everything along the way.)

Command paths

Throughout the text you see *command paths,* which are instructions for navigating menus within menus within menus. A command path can look something like this:

Choose Applications⇨Accessories⇨Terminal from the GNOME menu bar.

What that means is that when you click the Applications menu that appears in the GNOME menu bar along the top of your computer monitor, a menu appears, from which you should choose the Accessories option, and another menu appears, from which you should choose the Terminal option.

Ubuntu provides shortcuts for several menu selections. For instance, clicking the blue globe icon in the GNOME menu bar near the top, center of the screen opens the Firefox Web browser. Clicking the Firefox icon is a shortcut for choosing Applications⇨Internet⇨Firefox Web Browser from the GNOME menu bar.

What to use, click, or run

Throughout the book, I'm specific about what objects are important when specifying instructions. Instructions tell you exactly — step by step — what you need to do to accomplish a task. I often provide a picture to better illustrate the task at hand.

Understanding URLs

URLs (Uniform Resource Locators) are Web addresses. They're what you use in Web browsers and file managers to locate Web pages on the Internet or files and directories on your computer.

URLs use the form of `protocol://address` and appear in monofont format, like this: `www.wiley.com` or `www.google.com`.

Ubuntu Linux Is Ubuntu

Ubuntu Linux is a Linux distribution. It's common practice in technology to shorten phrases, and this is no exception. Rather than writing *Ubuntu Linux* when describing the Ubuntu Linux distribution, I just say *Ubuntu*. Either way — *Ubuntu* or *Ubuntu Linux* — it means the same thing.

Icons Used in This Book

I make extensive use of icons in this book. Using icons helps to identify useful information.

Some sage words can save you time, trouble, or money. This icon is a handy highlighter.

Using Ubuntu Linux is almost always a fun and carefree process. However, there are times when performing a function can cause unwanted results that you can't easily fix. This icon warns you when there's a possibility of a negative outcome if you don't follow the instructions precisely.

If you have *Ubuntu Linux For Dummies,* you don't need to memorize the book. But some concepts are used so frequently that they're worth the trouble. This icon marks them for you.

I use the Technical Stuff icon to identify extra information that might be interesting but might not be absolutely necessary.

Part I
Starting Fast

AFTER INSTALLING UBUNTU NED AND LORETTA SELECT THE COMPUTER'S BACKGROUND

© RICHTENNANT

"Oh — I like this background much better than the basement."

In this part . . .

Chapter 1 describes the philosophy behind Ubuntu and what Ubuntu is. In this part, I describe how to start using Ubuntu out of the box.

Chapter 2 shows how to boot your computer — or any computer! — directly from the companion Ubuntu CD-ROM.

Chapter 3 describes how to prepare a Windows computer to install Ubuntu alongside Windows in a dual-boot configuration.

Chapter 4 shows how to install Ubuntu on a computer with or without Windows.

The final chapter of Part I shows how to do some basic Linux computer tasks.

Chapter 1

Ubuntu and U

*T*he Ubuntu Linux distribution is the fastest-growing Linux distribution on the planet. It's designed to provide powerful functionality, and yet it's easy to use, no matter where in the world you live.

One of the most difficult balancing acts in the Linux world is deciding how much stuff (applications such as the Firefox Web browser and the Openoffice.org office productivity suite) to provide users. Some Linux distributions provide too little, and most provide too much. Ubuntu, however, has learned how to balance both sides very well.

Ubuntu is well supported by its user community, as well as commercially. This is important because different people and organizations need different levels and types of support.

All these factors add up to its exploding popularity, which is based on its ease of use, usefulness, and support.

Ubuntu, say what?

Ubuntu (pronounced *oo-BOON-too*) is a Zulu word that translates to "humanness."

Used as a verb, *Ubuntu* describes the practice of respecting one's family and neighbors — or more broadly, the community at large.

At its core, *Ubuntu* means that the members of a community take care of each other and the community itself. The creators of Ubuntu Linux took this philosophy of commitment to community to drive their creation. Ubuntu Linux (many people pronounce it *LIN-icks*) is designed for the community of Linux users — all of us.

Introducing Ubuntu Linux

Ubuntu is a Linux distribution. Linux distributions take the Linux *kernel* (the *kernel* is the software that orchestrates the interaction of programs and applications with computer hardware) and add an installation system, administration software, productivity applications, and other parts to make it possible for people to use their computers. Putting the parts together creates a sum that is greater than the pieces themselves.

I often use the word *Linux* as shorthand for *Linux distribution.* Depending on the context, Linux can mean just the software system that allocates resources on a computer; the Linux kernel is a computer operating system that humans use to interface with the bits and bytes that computers understand. But more frequently, Linux means the sum total of parts that we interact with. I also use the term *Ubuntu* to refer to *Ubuntu Linux,* which is the Linux distribution created by the Ubuntu organization.

Beyond the bits and pieces that make up your average Linux distribution, Ubuntu Linux is dedicated to the following principles and capabilities:

- ✔ **Free and open source:** Every application, utility, and program in Ubuntu is *open source,* which means it's designed and written to be freely used — and even modified if you want to modify it. Ubuntu collects the applications and adds additional value by combining them into a lean but usable package.

- ✔ **Extensive language and assistive technology support:** It's almost impossible to find a language or keyboard that Ubuntu doesn't support (work with). Ubuntu also specializes in providing software aids to assist all people to use Linux, regardless of physical ability.

- ✔ **Based on Debian Linux:** Debian is a very stable Linux distribution that is completely community based. (Debian developers design and test the changes and upgrades they make to the distribution so that it works well and doesn't cause unintended problems; this philosophy makes Debian stable and reliable.) Because no commercial entity owns any part of the distribution, the community can control and improve it as it desires.

- ✔ **Clean, usable interface:** Ubuntu uses the GNOME (pronounced *guh-NOME* or *nome,* whichever you prefer) desktop. They tweak the desktop so that it balances ever so well between providing all the applications and tools you like to use, but not so many that it becomes cluttered. Ubuntu is a lean, mean, fighting machine!

When free means free

Linux is a free operating system. It's licensed under the open source GNU (pronounced *guh-NEW*) General Public License, or GPL for short. (There are other open source licenses similar to GPL.) Any software published under an open source license, basically, can be used for any purpose the software's author desires.

GNU (which stands for GNU's not UNIX — seriously) is an acronym designed for and by computer geeks. Geeks like myself spend all our time working and playing on computers. When we aren't fooling around with computers, we think up stuff, such as recursive acronyms. (Actually, I wish I was smart enough and clever enough to combine concepts like recursion and the need to come up with acronyms, but I'm glad someone else can.)

✔ **Live media:** By *live*, I mean that you can use Ubuntu directly from the disc. You can experiment with it without affecting or changing your computer — or someone else's — at all. No installation required.

Chapter 2 shows how to run live Ubuntu from the CD included with this book.

✔ **Predictable, regular releases:** Ubuntu releases an updated version every six months. This makes it easy to plan when, if at all, to upgrade your computer.

✔ **Commercial and community support:** You can purchase support anywhere in the world. You can also get community-based support from user groups, online documents, and so on.

This dedication to all the things that make Linux and the greater open source system of creating and distributing software makes Ubuntu an outstanding Linux distribution.

Choosing a Version of the Operating System

Ubuntu is lean. Many Linux distributions (other versions of Linux) try to fit everything — including the kitchen sink — into their editions. That requires at least three CD-ROMs for the installation files! Very few people ever need anything close to that much software.

To avoid distribution bloat, Ubuntu created two distribution versions. Here's the story.

Ubuntu Desktop

The Ubuntu Desktop distribution creates a very clean, usable, graphical desktop for you to use as your desktop computer. By *graphical,* I mean that you see pretty icons that you can click (like in Windows and Macintosh), not ugly code that you have to read through and talk back to (like in DOS and UNIX).

The Desktop distribution is on the CD that comes with this book. You get applications such as the OpenOffice.org word processor, spreadsheet, and multimedia. OpenOffice.org is like, and compatible with, Microsoft Office and includes the stuff we like to use on our home and work computers or workstations. I tell you a little bit about using those programs in Chapter 16.

The Desktop version can be called a *workstation* version.

Ubuntu Server

The Ubuntu Server distribution is oriented to, well, *servers.* It isn't people friendly. It throws all the fun stuff out the window and concentrates on adding software that's oriented toward getting the job done. Web servers, e-mail services, and all that good nerd software go into this distribution.

You can download the server version from www.ubuntu.com.

The Ubuntu philosophy

The Ubuntu Web site describes the Ubuntu philosophy as follows:

Ubuntu is a community driven project to create an operating system and a full set of applications using free and open source software. At the core of the Ubuntu Philosophy of Software Freedom are these core philosophical ideals:

1. **Every computer user should have the freedom to run, copy, distribute, study, share, change and improve their software for any purpose, without paying licensing fees.**

2. **Every computer user should be able to use their software in the language of their choice.**

3. **Every computer user should be given every opportunity to use software, even if they work under a disability.**

The Canonical Source

Canonical Ltd. is a company that develops, distributes, and promotes open source software. Ubuntu is one of the projects it sponsors. It doesn't — and won't ever — charge for Ubuntu Linux.

Canonical embraces the open source ethic and doesn't own the software it produces. It could — but doesn't — sell software, like Ubuntu. Rather, it sells support services to those who want the assurance that they can use Ubuntu professionally and always be able to get a level of service necessary to run a business.

You can find more information about Canonical at www.canonical.com, which outlines the company's products, goals, and philosophy.

The genesis of Ubuntu

Mark Richard Shuttleworth founded a company called thawte in 1995. thawte's business is providing the means that helps make Internet commerce secure. The company is a digital *certificate authority* (CA), which is responsible for creating a chain of trust that enables us to shop, bank, and send our sensitive personal information on the Internet.

Every Web browser — such as Mozilla Firefox, Internet Explorer, and the like — comes installed with certificates created by major CAs like thawte; the certificates are digitally signed (endorsed) by the CA. Web sites that deal with sensitive information, such as Internet commerce, create their own certificates and pay to have companies like thawte digitally sign them. So browsers have client certificates, and Web servers have server certificates.

Both sides — the browser clients and the Web servers — use their certificates to set up encrypted communication channels; the clients also use the certificates to verify that the server is who it's supposed to be — not someone pretending to be the server. The beauty of this system is that the client doesn't need to know anything about the server before striking up

communication. The handshake, or *dance* might be a better description, depends on the certificates and allows both sides to communicate securely. The protocol (handshake) is called the Secure Sockets Layer (SSL) and when in use, is designated by the httpd:// in the browser's Location text box and padlock icon in the lower-left corner.

Mr. Shuttleworth sold thawte to another CA and security company, VeriSign, in 1999 and formed HBD Venture Capital, which helps startup companies get . . . well, started. thawte went on to become a very successful and prominent company.

Mark Shuttleworth has also been involved as a Debian Linux developer for several years. Debian is a completely noncommercial Linux distribution, and it's considered to be technically advanced. He took his commercial success and combined it with his interest in open source and formed the Shuttleworth Foundation in 2001, which funds educational projects in South Africa. In 2004, he funded the start of the Ubuntu Linux project through Canonical Ltd. In 2005, he founded the Ubuntu Foundation, which oversees Ubuntu Linux development.

Getting Started

Ubuntu Linux For Dummies guides you through all three ways you can use Ubuntu on a PC:

- ✔ Run live Ubuntu *directly from the CD* without permanently installing it on a computer.

  Chapter 2 shows you the startup steps for live Ubuntu.

- ✔ Permanently install Ubuntu on a PC without keeping Windows.

  Chapter 4 guides you through the Ubuntu installation.

- ✔ Teach Windows and Ubuntu to live in harmony on the same PC.

  - • Chapter 3 shows how to make room for Ubuntu on a Windows PC.

    You'll also need to refer to Chapter 2 to start live Ubuntu so you can use some system tools that aren't included in Windows.

  - • Chapter 4 guides you through the Ubuntu installation.

Ubuntu provides all the features you need to use Linux as your everyday workstation. It's free, reliable, full of features and applications, and easy to use. Ubuntu literally works out of the box — or in software terms, on the disc — so you can use it before installing it. You get a wonderful combination of stuff.

Sound good? Let's get started!

Chapter 2

Live Ubuntu

*O*ne of the reasons Ubuntu is so popular is that it's so easy to use. Ubuntu is distributed live on either a CD-ROM or DVD. By *live,* I mean that Ubuntu can be booted (started) directly from that disc. Forget about spending a long afternoon installing it — you can use it right now.

How can Ubuntu be alive? Well, it's not *alive,* it's *live.* That's "live" in terms of being directly bootable from read-only media. To reach its live status, Ubuntu is constructed in such a way that it can start from the disc and then use your computer's RAM (random access memory) to store files. This memory isn't saved when you reboot your computer.

Ubuntu Linux For Dummies includes a live Ubuntu CD-ROM that works with most Windows PCs.

Making Sure You Can Use Ubuntu on Your Computer

Here's what you need to run live Ubuntu:

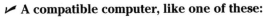

✔ **A compatible computer, like one of these:**

- *Intel/AMD-compatible 32-bit PC (typical Windows computer)*

  Most PCs made in the last 20 years use 32-bit processors.

  This book's companion CD runs on 32-bit PCs.

- *Intel/AMD-compatible 64-bit PC (the latest, fastest Windows machine)*

Windows computers using the Advanced Micro Devices AMD64 (Athlon64 and Opteron) or Intel EM64T (Xeon) processors are 64-bit.

This book's companion CD doesn't work on 64-bit computers. You can download a 64-bit Ubuntu CD from `http://releases.ubuntu.com/6.10`. Ubuntu provides instructions for burning the CD at `http://help.ubuntu.com/community/BurningIsoHowto`.

- *PowerPC-based Apple Macs:* This book's companion CD doesn't work with PowerPC-based computers. You can download a PowerPC-compatible CD from `http://releases.ubuntu.com/6.10`. Ubuntu provides instructions for burning the CD at `http://help.ubuntu.com/community/BurningIsoHowto`.

Ubuntu Linux For Dummies doesn't provide instructions for installing Ubuntu Linux on Macs.

✔ **CD-ROM or DVD drive:** Your computer must have a CD-ROM or DVD drive that you can boot Ubuntu from.

✔ **An Ubuntu CD-ROM or DVD:** In the back cover of this book, you'll find an Ubuntu CD for 32-bit PCs.

If you want to connect your Ubuntu computer to a network or the Internet, Chapters 6 through 9 describe how to configure Ubuntu to use various networks and Internet connections after you start it. When you're finished, you can just eject the disc and reboot the computer, and it will work exactly as you found it. You will leave no tracks in the rice paper, Grasshopper.

Less talk, more rock! Let's start using Ubuntu.

Running Live Ubuntu

Follow these steps to run live Ubuntu from this book's companion CD-ROM:

1. **Insert your Ubuntu CD-ROM in your CD-ROM or DVD drive.**

   After you eject any disc that might already be inserted, of course.

2. **Start or reboot the computer.**

   If you're running Microsoft Windows XP or Vista, follow these steps to reboot:

a. Click the Start button in the lower-left corner of your screen.

The Start menu pops up.

b. Click the Turn Off Computer option (or it might say Shut Down) in the lower-right side of the menu.

The Turn Off Computer (or Shut Down Windows) window opens.

c. Click the Restart option.

Restart might be a button, or it can be an option in the drop-down menu, depending on how your computer's set up.

Windows shuts itself down and then restarts your computer.

Always use the Microsoft Windows restart process to reboot your computer. Shutting off your computer by pressing the power button — or by pulling the plug — can damage the computer's _file system_ (the internal organization of your data). If you're really unlucky, Windows sometimes can't repair damaged file systems.

3. If necessary, tell the PC to boot from the CD or DVD drive.

If your computer checks the CD or DVD drive for an operating system _before_ it boots from the hard drive, it will automatically boot from the Ubuntu disc. You can go directly to Step 4 now.

If your computer doesn't automatically boot from its CD-ROM or DVD drive before it looks at the hard drive, you need to tell the computer what you want it to do when it starts rebooting. The sidebar "Booting from your CD-ROM or DVD drive" gives you a couple of options.

4. Press the Enter key to select the Boot from CD-ROM option.

Ubuntu automatically boots from the CD-ROM after 30 seconds if you do nothing.

As Ubuntu boots, numerous subsystems are started for such jobs as

- Finding available hardware

- Starting networking

- Mounting file systems

Mounting is a Linux term for making storage devices such as your hard drive, CD-ROM/DVD, and USB drives available for use.

Ubuntu's process is clean, quick, and displayed graphically, as shown in Figure 2-1.

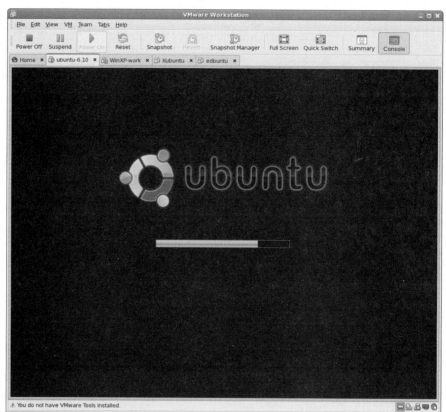

Figure 2-1:
Ubuntu
starts each
subsystem.

Booting from your CD-ROM or DVD drive

If your PC doesn't automatically try booting from the CD or DVD drive by default, you have a couple of options to force it.

Some computers let you specify what device to boot from *just this time.* If you don't want to change the default boot, try these steps as your computer begins to boot:

1. **Press F12 or the Escape key if and when you see the one-time boot menu prompt.**

   The one-time boot menu appears.

2. **Press the appropriate key for booting from your CD-ROM or DVD drive.**

   Your PC boots from the indicated device. Next time, the PC will boot from its default.

If you want the computer to check the CD or DVD drive every time it reboots, you can change the default. Try these steps as your computer begins to boot:

1. **Press the BIOS configuration key.**

   Most computers use the F2 key to start the BIOS configuration editor. Other common keys are F1, the Escape (Esc) key, and the Delete (Del) key. Read the screen carefully as the computer boots to find out which key to press.

The BIOS configuration screen opens.

2. **Select the Boot option when the BIOS editor starts.**

3. **If necessary, use the BIOS editor menu to make your CD-ROM or DVD drive bootable.**

The appropriate key is typically the plus (+) or space key to make a device bootable.

4. **Use the appropriate key to move the CD-ROM or DVD drive above the hard drive.**

Usually, the up- and down-arrow keys move a device up and down the list.

5. **Press the Escape key to exit the boot menu.**

6. **Press the Escape key to exit the BIOS configuration.**

7. **Select the Save and Exit option.**

When your computer boots from your Ubuntu disc, you'll quickly see the screen shown here.

When Ubuntu finishes checking, starting, and mounting, it's ready to use, as shown in Figure 2-2.

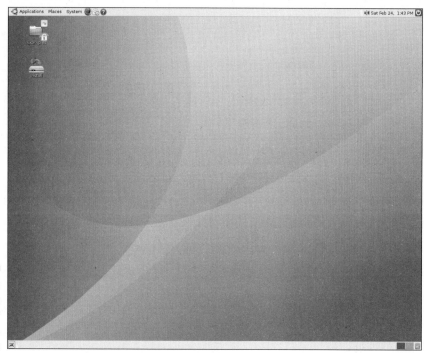

Figure 2-2:
Ubuntu is
ready for
use.

The Graphical Environment

The underlying graphical system is based on the X Window System, also known simply as X (but not the *X-Files*), maintained by the X.Org Foundation. The *graphical desktop environment* — the look and feel — is based on the GNOME (pronounced *guh-NOME*) system. Both X and GNOME are open source software, of course, and I describe them in more detail in Chapters 11 and 12. For now, all you need to know about X and GNOME is that they give you an attractive and functional place to work.

GNOME is attractive, highly customizable, and provides links to all of the software described in this book. I describe and explain the applications in later chapters.

There's plenty more to discover about Ubuntu, and the rest of this book is dedicated to showing how.

   ✔ If you want to use live Ubuntu now, Chapter 5 starts with the basics.

   ✔ If you want to *permanently* install Ubuntu on a hard drive, Chapters 3 and 4 show you how to prepare a PC and install Ubuntu.

It's your choice. Read on!

Chapter 3

Preparing to Install Ubuntu

In This Chapter

▶ Evaluating how much space you need for Ubuntu

▶ Backing up your Windows computer

▶ Removing unnecessary files

▶ Organizing the files you want to keep

▶ Creating a partition for Ubuntu to live on

A s shown in Chapter 2, Ubuntu works very nicely from a CD-ROM or DVD as a *live* (meaning that you don't have to install it) operating system. But if you want to make Ubuntu a permanent part of your computing life, you'll find the installation process to be very easy. Installation is one of Ubuntu's many strengths.

The Ubuntu installation process is the easiest of all Linux distributions.

This chapter describes how to prepare your computer to install Ubuntu alongside Windows. When you're finished, you'll have a *dual-boot computer* — meaning that you can boot into either Ubuntu or Windows. Because most current useful computers have Microsoft Windows XP installed, I describe how to make Windows behave and play nice with its soon-to-arrive little brother. Don't worry, they won't fight.

If you don't want to keep your current Windows — or Linux — installation and files, you don't have to worry about making nice with it. You can skip to Chapter 4 and install Ubuntu over the existing operating system. *Windows, you are the weakest link. Goodbye.*

Preparing to Make Room for Ubuntu

A dual-boot system with Ubuntu and Windows requires enough hard drive space for both Windows and Ubuntu. I recommend a hard drive with

✔ A bare minimum of 3GB of *unused* capacity to install Ubuntu on. This amount of unused space will let you install Ubuntu and have almost 1GB of unused space to work with when running Ubuntu. This type of Ubuntu installation will mostly be good as a platform for learning and experimenting with Ubuntu. However, the small amount of storage space will prevent you from using the Ubuntu installation as a typical workstation on which you store information such as word processing files, music files, and so on.

✔ Preferably 10GB of *unused* capacity on which to install Ubuntu and create a practical workstation you can use as an everyday computer.

You can determine the amount of free space on your Windows computer by double-clicking the My Computer icon and right-clicking the Local Disk (C:) icon. In the My Computer window that opens, select the Properties option. The Local Disk (C:) Properties window opens, showing the used and unused space on your disk.

Introducing file systems and partitioning

It's common to think in terms of an operating system being installed on a hard drive. (Hard drives are also referred to as *hard disks* or just *disks*.) Hard drives ultimately do store information, such as applications, files, and folders. However, it's a little more complicated than that.

Hard drives by themselves can store only single bits of information. They store information in a useful way — information that you can easily store and retrieve — only if they're formatted. *Formatting* organizes the raw storage space of a disk so that data can be stored on the disk. An operating system, such as Ubuntu or Windows, can then read and write files to the formatted disk.

But a hard drive must first be partitioned before it can be formatted. *Partitioning* a hard drive allocates chunks of the drive that themselves can be formatted; partitions can be viewed as independent, *logical hard drives*. PC hard drives can have between one and four partitions.

PCs generally (but not always) come formatted with one or two partitions on which Microsoft Windows is installed:

✔ One partition has Windows XP or Windows Vista installed on it.

✔ The second partition contains *system recovery files*. (They're used to help fix Windows when necessary. For instance, if you accidentally delete files that the Microsoft Windows operating system needs to run.)

If you want to install Ubuntu Linux alongside Windows on the same hard drive, you have to

1. **Back up your files and folders.**

2. **Create an additional partition.**

3. **Format the new partition.**

4. **Install Ubuntu.**

The Ubuntu file system repartitioning utility works with either of these common Windows PC hard drive formats:

- ✔ **NTFS:** If your PC came from the factory with Windows Vista, Windows XP, Windows 2000, or Windows NT, the hard drive probably is formatted with Microsoft's NT File System (NTFS).

  NT stands for New Technology (which it was, when Windows NT was introduced in 1993). NTFS is much more secure and reliable than FAT.

- ✔ **FAT:** If you have an older PC that came with Windows Me, Windows 98, or an earlier, non-NT Windows version, your computer's hard drive might be formatted with Microsoft's old file allocation table (FAT).

  FAT isn't generally used on new computers, except occasionally to host Windows recovery system files.

If you don't want to keep Microsoft Windows on your computer, skip reading this chapter and go directly to Chapter 4, which provides an option for completely overwriting your Windows installation.

Installing Ubuntu alongside Windows

Installing Ubuntu alongside Windows requires you to perform the following general steps, as shown in detail in this chapter:

1. Make a backup of your personal files and computer settings.

   The repartitioning process is safe but not absolutely so. Whenever you perform a job like this, you run the risk of accidentally losing information. That isn't good, so plan for the unexpected.

2. Remove temporary and unnecessary files.

   Using your Windows computer for everyday tasks such as Internet browsing creates temporary files. Those files build up over time and take up space. You should remove those files to open up space for Ubuntu.

3. Defragment your C drive (C:\).

   Microsoft Windows has to find space to save your files. Whenever you create or save a file, your computer looks for and finds an unused portion of your hard drive (the C drive on Windows systems). This process tends to scatter the information, data, and so on that comprises files. Over time, that scattering (or *fragmenting*) process can get messy. Defragmenting your drive reorganizes your data and frees up space that you need for Ubuntu.

4. Repartition your C drive (C:\).

   Repartitioning squeezes your Windows partition into a smaller space. The freed-up space is where you install Ubuntu (which is covered in Chapter 4).

Backing Up Your Data

"Life is unfair," goes the "They Might be Giants" tune. How true. Well, fair or unfair, you have to be ready for unexpected events — like accidentally losing your files and folders from your Windows computer. Backing up your Windows computer prepares you for life's vagaries.

In this section, I describe how to back up Windows XP and Windows Vista computers. Both Windows XP and Windows Vista provide backup utilities that, for our purposes, differ in one major respect. Windows XP can't directly back up to a CD or DVD writer, but Windows Vista can. You can indirectly back up to a writable CD or DVD from Windows XP, however, and I show you how.

Creating your backup plan

Before you decide where to save your files, you need to decide what files to save. Microsoft's backup utility gives you the option of either

- Saving everything on the hard drive — from the Windows startup screen to your most recent files.

- Saving just your personal files and configuration settings.

  This option doesn't save files that comprise the Windows operating system. You can usually restore the Windows operating system and applications from its original installation media.

When backing up your computer, you might not need to save everything. It might be fine to just

- Back up your personal files.

- Skip backing up software that you can reinstall directly from the original discs, such as the following:

    • Applications (such as Word and Photoshop)

    • The Windows operating system

If you have your original Microsoft Windows disc(s) and your application media, you can probably save just your personal files and settings (such as your Internet Explorer bookmarks). If you ever need to reinstall all the files for your Windows computer, you can

  1. Rebuild the operating system from the original disc(s).

  2. Reinstall your applications from the original disc(s).

  3. Restore the personal files that you backed up.

Microsoft will replace lost Windows installation disc(s) if you can prove you have a valid license. Proof can be in such forms as a sales receipt, the license itself, or even packaging material that contains the correct markings. Microsoft's replacement policy is on the Web at

```
http://support.microsoft.com/default.aspx?scid=kb;[ln];326246
```

Considering storage devices

The following list describes all the possible backup devices you might be able to use:

✔ **External hard drive:** This is the best option, in my opinion. External hard drives connect to your computer via USB or FireWire cables. These devices are reasonably inexpensive and easy to use. Just plug one in and you're ready to go. Between backups, you can easily store an external hard drive in a safe place.

You can purchase hard drives attached to a USB connector. These devices look like overfed USB flash drives. Instead of containing an electronic flash chip, these devices use a microdrive hard disk.

✔ **Second partition on your primary hard drive:** Many Windows computers come with one physical hard drive divided into two partitions. (Partitions look like individual hard drives to the computer and can be thought of as *virtual hard drives*.) The second partition uses a small fraction of the total hard drive space and is used to recover your operating system in case your Windows operating system is accidentally erased or corrupted. In case of such a disaster, you can restore your computer to its original state (how it was configured at the time of purchase) using the software stored on the second partition. Your primary partition is named the C: drive and the second partition, if you have one, is labeled the D: drive.

Both Windows Vista and Windows XP let you make backups to the second partition. You should only back up to the second partition if using it as a temporary holding area to make a permanent backup to a writable CD or DVD; I use this method when backing up Windows XP to a CD or DVD because Windows XP doesn't let you back up directly to those devices.

✔ **Second internal hard drive:** You can install a second hard drive inside your computer next to your primary disk and use it like an external one. Internal disks are less expensive than external ones because they don't require the case and power supply.

Internal backup hard drives have a couple of drawbacks:

• They aren't as easy to connect as an external device. You have to open your computer, install the drive, hook it up to a control cable and power supply, and then button the computer back up.

- • If your computer is stolen or destroyed, your backup is stolen or destroyed, too.

✔ **USB flash drive:** These devices are inexpensive and very easy to use. Simply plug your USB flash drive into your computer. Windows recognizes the device, and you can start using it.

  Lower-priced USB flash drives might not have enough storage space to fully back up your computer. Current technology provides very inexpensive one-half to one gigabyte (GB) of space. (You can purchase flash drives with up to 4GB USB for approximately $100.) Technology marches forward, and you'll soon be able to purchase 8GB and higher devices.

✔ **Writable CD/DVD:** These are the most commonly available external storage media in use today. Writable CD/DVDs are nearly ideal for backup purposes because they're common, cheap, and easy to store.

  Both CDs and DVDs have limits on how much they can store. CDs have a limit of about 740MB, and DVDs can store up to 4.7GB of data; newer, dual/double-layered DVDs can store up to 8.5GB of data.

Figure 3-1 shows an internal hard drive on the left, a USB flash drive in the middle, and an external and a USB hard drive on the right.

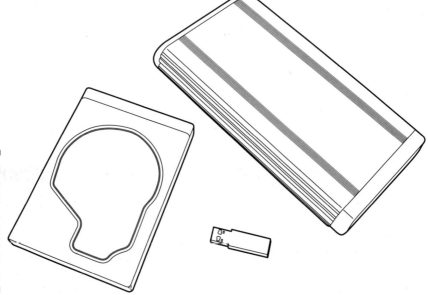

Figure 3-1:
Left to right:
an internal
hard drive,
USB flash
drive, and
USB hard
drive.

Storing data in a flash

USB flash drives are also called *USB pen drives* or *USB memory sticks.* These drives use flash memory technology. Like a hard drive, flash memory is *nonvolatile,* which means that it doesn't need electrical power to save data. Other computer memory — referred to as RAM (random access memory) — needs to have constant power to retain data. Your computer forgets what you've been doing when you shut it down, so you have to save your work on a nonvolatile device like a flash drive or a hard drive.

Flash memory's small size and big capacity makes it ideal for backing up your files.

Flash has the advantage over media such as writable CD-ROMs for saving information because you can easily rewrite to it, and it's very portable. But it isn't good at acting as your computer's main memory.

- ✔ **Tape devices:** Tape devices are expensive and not widely used for consumer-level data backups. Tapes are great for making backups if you have a tape drive. Otherwise, I recommend using the preceding methods.

- ✔ **Networked file shares:** You can back up to a file server over a private network. If the server provides you with a network file share, you can use that share in place of local media. A network file share looks like a locally attached disk drive but is actually located on another computer and accessible via a network.

Unfortunately, you can't back up directly to a writable CD-ROM or DVD with Windows XP. You can, however, use the utility to back up your files to the D: drive if you have one. The files are saved to a single file that you can then burn to a CD.

Backing up Windows XP with a wizard

No need to conjure up Harry Potter to save your Windows files. In this chapter, I describe how to use the Microsoft Windows Files and Settings Transfer Wizard to back up your computer. This utility is designed to help you transfer data between old and new computers, but you can also use it to back up your data. It provides the following options to back up:

- ✔ **User account personal data:** Your word processing, spreadsheet, music, video, and any other files you've created.

✔ **User accounts settings:** The preferences and configurations you've saved. For instance, e-mail account settings.

✔ **The entire computer:** All the files on your computer, including personal data, account settings, applications, and the files that comprise the Microsoft Windows operating system.

It's possible — although unlikely — to unintentionally destroy your valuable files and settings while installing Ubuntu, so this chapter shows you how to back up user account personal data and settings.

You can find out how much free space you have for installing Ubuntu on your Windows hard drive (the C: drive) by completing these simple steps:

1. **Double-click the My Computer icon on your desktop.**

   The My Computer window opens. (Alternatively, you can click the Start menu and select the My Computer option.)

2. **Right-click the C: drive and select Properties.**

   The Local Disk (C:) Properties dialog opens, showing the amount of used and unused disk space.

Windows XP can write backups directly to internal and external hard drives, floppy disks, network file shares, and USB flash drives. Windows XP can't write backups directly to CDs and DVDS, but the sidebar "Backing up your backup to CD" shows how to save a backup from your C: drive to a recordable disc.

Start preparing your Windows hard drive for Ubuntu by making sure the proper backup media is installed and ready to use.

1. Select (and if necessary, obtain) your backup media as described in the "Considering storage devices" section.

2. Connect your backup device to your computer.

   If you're using an external device, follow these steps:

   a. Plug the USB or FireWire connector into your computer.

   b. Power on the device — external hard drive — if necessary.

Installing an internal device (such as a second internal disk drive) can be a difficult task. Check the manufacturer's manual for specific instructions. In general, installing an internal hard drive follows these steps:

1. Insert the drive into a disk bay.

2. Fix the device to the disk bay with screws.

3. Connect the drive to the computer motherboard with an IDE cable.

4. Plug a power cable into the drive.

When you have your backup media in place, you can start backing up. Here's how you can do that:

1. **Reboot, if necessary, into Microsoft Windows.**

2. **Log in to your computer as a user with administrator privileges.**

   The Owner user account has administrator capability by default.

3. **Choose Start⇨All Programs⇨Accessories⇨System Tools⇨Files and Settings Transfer Wizard.**

   The transfer wizard dialog opens.

4. **Click Next.**

   The transfer wizard asks you which computer you're on, as you see in Figure 3-2.

   - *New Computer:* Choose this option if you're copying files to a new computer.

   - *Old Computer:* Choose this option if you're copying files from the old computer.

   Use the Old Computer option — radio button — to save your files and settings before installing Ubuntu.

Figure 3-2:
Tell the wizard what computer you're on.

5. **Select Old Computer and click Next.**

   After you make your choice and click Next, the Windows Security Alert dialog opens (if you've installed Windows XP Service Pack 2 and are running its firewall). Figure 3-3 shows the dialog.

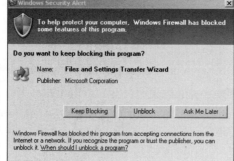

Figure 3-3:
Respond to
the
Windows
firewall.

6. **Click the Unblock button.**

   • *Keep Blocking:* Select this option if you're using a local backup device (such as a hard drive or a USB flash device).

   • *Unblock:* Select this option if you're using a network-based backup device (such as a Windows file share).

   • *Ask Me Later:* Leave the current firewall settings in place and make the decision about whether to unblock or keep blocking until later.

7. **Select the appropriate transfer method and click Next.**

   The wizard dialog asks you to select the transfer medium from the following options.

   • *Direct Cable:* You can use a serial cable or USB (or ancient RS232) to connect one computer to another. You can back up your first computer to the second when they're connected.

   • *Home or Small Office Network:* Back up your computer to a network file share. This option frees you from having to obtain and attach physical devices such as USB flash drives and external or internal hard drives.

   • *Other/Floppy Drive or Other Removable Media:* Select this option when using USB or FireWire hard drives or flash drives; also use this option for internal hard drives, tapes, or floppy disks. I use the Other option in this example.

   Use the Other option if you want to resave the backup to a writable CD or DVD when this backup process is finished. You must use this method if you want to use a CD or DVD as you back up media because Windows XP's backup utility can't use those devices directly.

   The Select a Transfer Method dialog opens.

8. **Select the appropriate transfer option for your backup media and click Next.**

   Figure 3-4 shows the Floppy Drive or Other Removable Media selection.

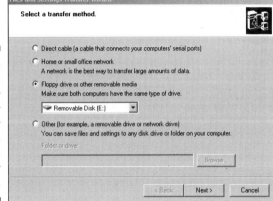

Figure 3-4: Selecting the Floppy Drive or Other Removable Media transfer method.

   • *Other:* Select this option if saving to a folder on your Windows C: drive, a floppy disk, or removable storage media such as a USB flash drive.

   After you specify the storage media, you're offered several backup options, as shown in Figure 3-5.

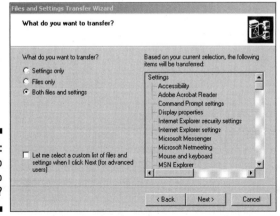

Figure 3-5: What do you want to transfer?

9. **Select the Both Files and Settings radio button.**

   - *Settings Only:* Only save Windows settings like your network configuration.

   - *Files Only:* Only save your personal files.

     If you don't care about saving your configurations and settings, you only need to save files.

   - *Both Files and Settings:* Save both your Windows settings and personal files.

     If you want to save both personal files and settings, you need to save both your files and your Windows settings.

10. **Click the Next button.**

    The Collection in Progress dialog opens (shown in Figure 3-6) and shows the progress of the utility as it locates files and settings to back up.

    When the utility finishes locating everything, it displays one more dialog, asking whether you'd like to continue.

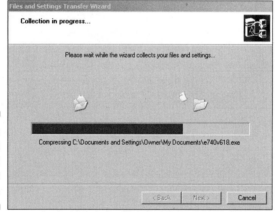

Figure 3-6: The Collection in Progress dialog.

11. **Click OK in the dialog that opens.**

    Your files and settings are saved.

12. **Click Finish when the backup finishes.**

Your important files and settings are saved for posterity. You can use the backup wizard's restore function if you ever need to retrieve any or all of your backed up files.

Backing up your backup to CD

If you use Windows XP and want to use a CD as your backup media, you can't use it directly. You must first use the Files and Settings Transfer Wizard to make a backup to your C: drive and then burn the backup to a CD.

The following instructions show how to burn a backup image you make in the "Backing up your Windows XP computer to a writable CD" section. (You can also use a writable DVD if you have purchased commercial DVD burner software.)

1. Use the Windows XP Files and Settings Transfer Wizard to create a backup of your files, settings, and data to the My Documents folder on your C: drive.

   The backup is written to a file called USMT2.UNC in the specified folder.

2. Click the My Documents icon on your desktop.

   The My Documents window opens.

3. Insert a writable CD into your CD burner.

   The CD drive window opens.

4. Click the OK button.

   The Windows Explorer dialog opens.

5. Right-click the USMT2.UNC file in the My Documents window and select the Copy option.

6. Right-click the CD drive window and select Paste.

   The USMT2.UNC file icon appears in the CD drive window.

7. Click the Write these Files to CD option in the options on the left, middle side of the window.

   The CD Writing Wizard dialog opens.

8. Click the Next button.

The CD Writing Wizard dialog displays a progress bar while it writes your backup file to the CD. The CD Writing Wizard closes when it completes the write process. Your backup is secure on the CD.

Your files and settings are stored in a file called USMT2IMG.DAT on the storage device. The backup wizard compressed all the files and stored it in this one file.

Backing up Windows Vista

Except for Home Basic, all versions of Windows Vista — Home Premium, Business, Ultimate, and Enterprise — provide a utility designed to automatically back up your computer on a daily or weekly basis. You can use the backup utility to back up your Windows Vista computer to prepare to install Ubuntu.

Windows Vista can write backups directly to internal and external hard drives, floppy disks, network file shares, and CDs and DVDs. Windows XP can't back up directly to flash drives.

The following instructions show how to back up your Windows Vista computer using a writable CD or DVD disc:

1. **Click the Start button and choose All Programs⇨Accessories⇨System Tools⇨Backup Status & Configuration.**

   The Backup Status & Configuration dialog opens.

2. **Click the Set Up Automatic File Backup option.**

   The User Account Control dialog opens.

3. **Click the Continue button.**

   The Back Up Files dialog opens with the On a Hard Disk, CD or DVD radio button selected. The radio button controls a drop-down menu that is set by default to DVD RW Drive (D:).

4. **If you want to save to a network file share, select the On a Network radio button.**

   A network file share looks like a local drive but is really another computer that you can store files to over a network. The Back Up Files dialog allows you to back up to a network file share instead of a CD/DVD writer.

5. **Click the Next button.**

   The Back Up Files dialog displays a list of check boxes and options describing the type of files to be saved; each option is selected by default. To be safe, you should accept the default to save each type of file.

6. **Click the Next button.**

   A notification icon — File Backup Needs Attention — pointing to an icon on the Windows menu bar. (The File Backup Needs Attention icon has an exclamation mark inside a yellow triangle.)

7. **Click the File Backup Needs Attention icon.**

   The Back Up Files dialog opens telling you it's about to back up your files.

8. **Click the Save Settings and Start Backup button.**

   The Back Up Files dialog asks you to insert a writable CD or DVD in your computer.

9. **Insert a blank CD or DVD in your computer's writable CD or DVD drive.**

   A second dialog, named Back Up Files, opens and asks you if you want to format the disc.

10. **Click the Format button.**

    The disc is formatted and the second Back Up Files dialog closes. When the disc is formatted, the backup process begins, and a progress dialog opens, showing the backup progress. When the backup completes, the progress dialog closes, and control returns to the original Back Up Files dialog.

11. **Click the Close button.**

The Back Up Files dialog closes, and you have your files backed up.

Prepping your Hard Drive

After you back up your computer, you need to get your hard drive ready to install Ubuntu.

The rest of this chapter describes how to organize and format the space for Ubuntu.

Removing unnecessary files

Everyday activities like Web browsing build up temporary files on your computer. The temporary files store information that helps the computer do its job or speed up processes like browsing.

For instance, browsers save the actual Web pages that you visit for possible later use. When you return to a Web page you've visited before, the browser tries to reuse the *cached* (saved) Web page file rather than reload it via the Internet. This works only if the Web page hasn't changed between the first and subsequent visits; your browser fetches the Web page from the Internet if the page has changed. Reusing a locally stored file saves time because retrieving the information from your computer is faster than retrieving it through the Internet connections.

However, the dynamic nature of Web pages means that cached files soon go out of date, and you can delete them if you'd like. Removing them and other temporary files can free up significant amounts of disk space but don't affect your ability to access any Web page. The process is simple:

1. **Choose Start➪All Programs➪Accessories➪System Tools➪Disk Cleanup.**

The Disk Cleanup dialog opens, as shown in Figure 3-7.

2. **Click OK if you want to delete all temporary files from your Windows computer.**

Another dialog opens, asking if you want to continue.

3. **Click OK.**

The utility proceeds to remove unnecessary and temporary files.

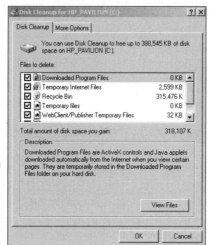

Figure 3-7:
Get rid of
files you
don't need.

Organizing your files with Disk Defragmenter

Microsoft Windows provides a defragmenting utility that consolidates files into adjacent spaces on your hard drive. (See the nearby sidebar, "Fragments of knowledge," if you'd like to know more about how defragmenting works.) Defragmenting a drive makes more space available for the stuff you want to store on your computer — such as Ubuntu.

The Windows defragmenting utility is easy to use. Follow these steps to organize the files saved on your hard drive:

1. **Choose Start⇨All Programs⇨Accessories⇨System Tools⇨Disk Defragmenter.**

   The Disk Defragmenter dialog, shown in Figure 3-8, opens. The dialog shows the drives available on your computer.

   The C: drive is generally your primary hard drive.

2. **Click your primary hard drive.**

   For example, in the Disk Defragmenter window in Figure 3-8, I clicked HP PAVILION (C:).

3. **Click the Defragment button near the bottom-left side of the window.**

   Another window opens, showing the defragmenting progress. Figure 3-9 shows an example dialog at the very beginning of the process.

   The process takes at least a few minutes.

Fragments of knowledge

The information contained in computer files is stored in what are known as *binary bytes* on a disk drive. The computer operating system decides exactly where to store the bytes on the disk. The computer tries to store the bytes consecutively — first, second, third, and so on — if it can. It's somewhat analogous to storing pieces of paper, from the same document, on your desk.

Over time, the many files of the operating system, applications, and user files tend to fill and clutter up the disk, and they're no longer stored consecutively. When the computer can't store the contents of files in adjacent spaces, it just puts them wherever they'll fit — which isn't organized or efficient. Files become *fragmented,* which creates a couple of problems:

✔ **Scattering bytes across a disk drive slows the computer slightly.** A drive's magnetic head must be repositioned to read data in different places. That extra movement takes extra time.

However, only when a disk drive becomes very fragmented will you likely notice a severe performance hit.

✔ **Fragmentation limits the space available for other stuff on your computer.** Files that aren't saved in an orderly fashion tend to take up more space than they really need. It's like that car in the mall parking lot that someone has parked crooked, taking up more than one spot. The car is only one parking space wide, but its placement actually makes two or three spaces unusable for other regular-sized cars. The same thing happens on your hard drive. Technically, you have space to save files, but they aren't big enough spaces.

Returning to the pieces of paper analogy, you can free up desk space by sorting and stacking the scattered pieces in one pile or placing them in a folder.

Figure 3-8: The Disk Defragmenter window.

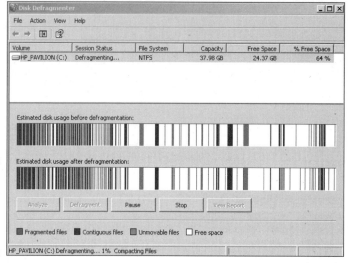

Figure 3-9:
The Disk
Defrag-
menter in
action.

You see the Disk Defragmenter dialog when the process finishes. Figure 3-10 shows the successful conclusion to the process. Compared to Figure 3-9, a lot of space has been freed; the dialog shows much more white space (free space) after the process finishes.

4. Click the Close button (the X in the upper-right corner of the dialog).

5. Select File⇨Exit to quit the disk defragmenting utility.

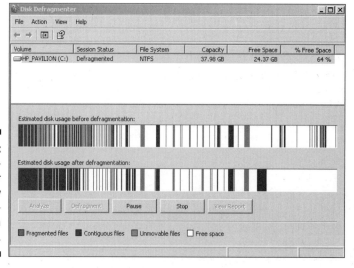

Figure 3-10:
Disk Defrag-
menter
successfully
defrag-
ments a
hard drive.

Repartitioning Windows: Scootch Over and Let Ubuntu Sit Here!

Computer hard drives include at least one partition. A *partition* is a virtual (or logical) drive within a physical hard drive.

Computer operating systems such as Windows or Ubuntu Linux see partitions, not hard drives. For instance, your Windows C: drive is really a partition of the physical hard drive. If you have a D: drive, the D: drive is a second partition on your hard drive.

Adding an additional partition to your Windows hard drive allows you to install Ubuntu alongside Windows.

On a typical PC, the default Windows partition takes up the entire hard drive, even though it probably isn't using all the space. After backing up your Windows files and settings, you can make a place for Ubuntu, too.

You can shrink the Windows partition to make space for a permanent Ubuntu installation.

The rest of this chapter uses live Ubuntu. Chapter 2 shows how to start live Ubuntu from the CD that comes with this book. (If you need to use Chapter 2 now, go ahead. I'll wait here until you start Ubuntu.)

Resizing your Windows partition

You can make room for Ubuntu by shrinking the existing Windows partition. Ubuntu provides an easy-to-use tool called GParted.

The following instructions free up space for a permanent Ubuntu installation on a Windows XP PC. After you boot Ubuntu from the Ubuntu CD-ROM, follow these steps:

1. **Click the System menu at the top of the window and select Administration⇨Gnome Partition Editor.**

   The GParted window, shown in Figure 3-11, opens.

2. **Select the first NTFS partition shown in the GParted window.**

3. **Click the Resize/Move button.**

   The Resize dialog opens, showing the amount of free space on the partition. Figure 3-12 shows an example dialog.

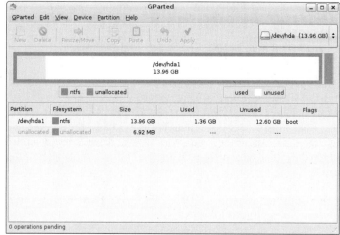

Figure 3-11:
Scootch
Windows
over to
make room
for Ubuntu.

Figure 3-12:
The Resize
window.

4. **Drag the black arrow immediately to the right of the green border to resize the Windows NTFS partition.**

   You must decide how to reallocate your hard drive. The trick is to leave enough to meet both your Windows and Ubuntu needs. For instance, if you expect you'll need 10GB more of storage space for your Windows document and media files, leave that much free space on your Windows partition. (Of course, you aren't allowed to make the Windows partition smaller than its *current* data.)

   You can also type in the amount of space in MB you want to free up in the Free Space Following (MB) text box. For instance, 10000 to create a 10GB partition to install Ubuntu onto.

   You need at least 3GB to install Ubuntu.

5. **Click the Resize button.**

   Figure 3-13 shows the newly sized partition-to-be.

   You exit from the Resize window and return to GParted.

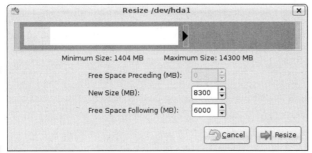

Figure 3-13:
Looking at a
shrunken
partition.

6. **Click the Apply button.**

   The Apply Operations to Hard Disk dialog opens.

7. **Click Apply.**

   The Applying Pending Operations dialog opens and shows the progress of the resize operation.

Control returns to the GParted window when the disk is repartitioned.

The rest of this chapter shows how to format the partition.

Formatting the new partition

The following instructions continue using GParted in Ubuntu to format the empty space you created in this chapter into a new partition. *Formatting* essentially puts navigation markers on the hard drive that computer operating systems use to store files and folders. You can install Ubuntu onto the new partition when it's formatted. Follow these steps:

1. **In the GParted window, click the unallocated item in the list in the lower part of the dialog to select the new, empty space.**

   The new space is shown as unallocated.

   Figure 3-14 shows

   - *The original NTFS partition:*

     This is the NTFS partition used by Windows.

     Don't select the partition labeled Filesystem NTFS (or FAT on older computers)! This is where Windows works from.

   - *The unallocated space:* This is the unused space that was created in the preceding section.

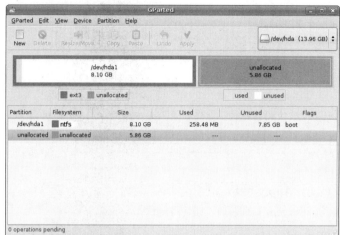

Figure 3-14:
The NTFS
and unused
partitions.

When viewed on a color monitor, the NTFS partition is shown in color, but the unused space isn't.

2. **From the toolbar at the top of the GParted window, choose Partition⇨New.**

   The Create New Partition dialog opens, showing your new partition. Figure 3-15 shows an example dialog.

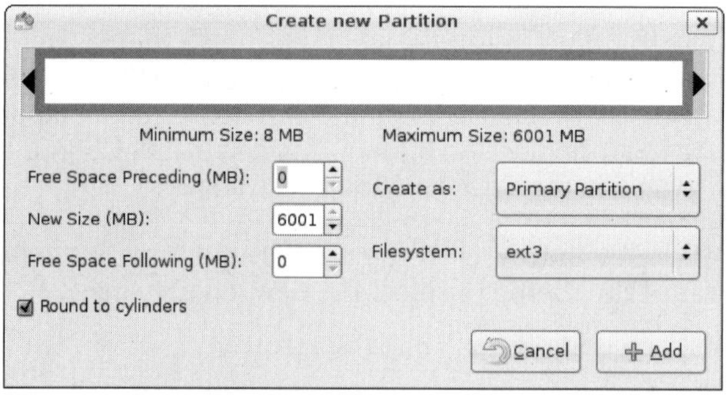

Figure 3-15:
Add a
partition.

3. **Click the Add button.**

   You exit the Create New Partition dialog and return to the GParted window, shown in Figure 3-16.

4. **Click the Apply button.**

   The Apply Operations to Hard Disk dialog opens.

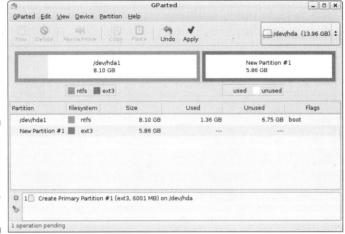

Figure 3-16:
GParted is
ready to
format the
new
partition.

5. **Click Apply.**

   The Applying Pending Operations dialog opens while the partition is created. When the dialog exits, your new partition is created.

   The space you stole from Windows is now partitioned and formatted. You can use this space to install Ubuntu Linux. Chapter 4 walks you through the process.

Chapter 4

Installing Ubuntu Linux

· ·

In This Chapter

▶ Evaluating what you need

▶ Selecting settings: Language and time zone

▶ Defining your user account

▶ Configuring a file system to install to

▶ Installing Ubuntu Linux to your hard drive

▶ Finishing the installation

· ·

You can install Ubuntu to your hard drive if you have space alongside Microsoft Windows, intend to erase a current Windows installation entirely, or are using a new hard drive.

If you don't want to completely erase Windows, Chapter 3 shows how to free up space from your current Windows installation.

This chapter is divided into sections describing each stage of the permanent Ubuntu installation process on a hard drive.

This chapter is only a fraction of the length of other installation chapters I've written — which shows how straightforward installing Ubuntu is.

Stage 1: Gathering Your Resources

In general, Ubuntu Linux is easy to install. Use the following checklist to make sure you have everything you need for the installation:

✔ **A compatible computer**

Ubuntu can run on

- *Intel/AMD-compatible 32-bit PCs:* This book's companion CD runs on 32-bit PCs.

Almost all PCs made in the last 20 years use 32-bit processors.

- *Intel/AMD-compatible 64-bit PCs:* This book's companion Ubuntu CD does not work on 64-bit computers. You can download a 64-bit Ubuntu CD from `http://releases.ubuntu.com/6.10`. Ubuntu provides instructions for burning the CD at `http://help.ubuntu.com/community/BurningIsoHowto`.

Many of the newest, fastest PCs use 64-bit processors. Computers using the Advanced Micro Devices AMD64 (Athlon64 and Opteron) or Intel EM64T (Xeon) processors are 64-bit.

- *PowerPC-based Apple Macs:* This book's companion CD does not work with PowerPC-based computers. You can download a PowerPC-compatible CD from `http://releases.ubuntu.com/6.10`. Ubuntu provides instructions for burning the CD at `http://help.ubuntu.com/community/BurningIsoHowto`.

Before you attempt to install Ubuntu on a computer, make sure that you save every file from the computer that you might need later. Chapter 3 covers Windows backup options.

✔ **CD-ROM or DVD drive**

Your computer must have a CD-ROM or DVD drive that you can boot Ubuntu from.

If you plan to use the disc that comes with this book, you can use a CD or DVD drive.

✔ **A hard drive with enough empty disk space**

You need one of the following devices:

- *A new, empty hard drive*

- *A used hard drive you can completely erase*

    You don't need to prepare the hard drive before installing Ubuntu if you don't wish to save the *operating system* that's on it (for example, Windows), installed *applications* (such as Word and Photoshop), and any *data* (word processor files, pictures, e-mail messages, bookmarks, and so on).

    You will erase the operating system and any data on the disk, if any exist, using this option. You should back up all of your personal files, settings, and data before using this option. Chapter 3 shows how to back up files.

- *A used hard drive you can repartition*

    If you need Windows, you can repartition your computer to make a place for Ubuntu, too. Chapter 3 describes how to free up space from a Windows partition and format it for use by Ubuntu.

    You can repartition a hard drive that contains other operating systems. *Repartitioning* simply means that you shrink the space allocated to an existing operating system and create unused space that you can use to install Ubuntu.

✔ **An Ubuntu DVD or CD-ROM**

We supply an Ubuntu CD for 32-bit PCs in the back cover of this book.

You don't need a network connection to install Ubuntu. You can proceed through the installation now if you don't have a network connection and install and configure a network connection later. Chapters 6, 7, 8, and 9 describe how to configure Ubuntu to use various networks and make an Internet connection.

Stage 2: Starting the Install

Follow these steps to start the installation process:

1. **Boot Ubuntu from the DVD or CD-ROM.**

   Chapter 2 walks you through this process.

   You see the screen shown in Figure 4-1 when Ubuntu is up and running.

   The Install icon, near the upper-left side of the screen, indicates that Ubuntu wants to make the installation process as simple as possible.

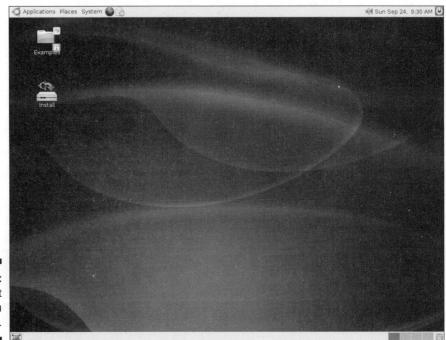

Figure 4-1:
Looking at
the Ubuntu
desktop.

2. **Double-click the Install icon (or right-click and select Open).**

The Welcome screen, shown in Figure 4-2, opens.

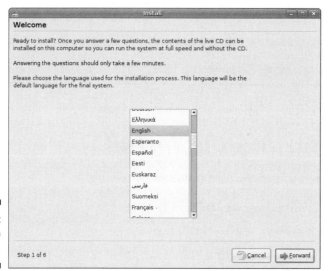

The welcome screen really, really wants to get started, so it's really a Welcome, welcome, yeah, yeah, yeah, please pick your language.

3. **Click to select the language of your choice and click Forward.**

So far, so good, eh? You're ready to move on to Stage 3.

Stage 3: Selecting Your Time Zone

The next steps ask you some straightforward questions about sundry items such as your time zone. Here's how you can move through quickly:

1. **Select the *general area* near your time zone.**

The Ubuntu installation displays a world map, shown in Figure 4-3. Click anywhere near where you live — you don't have to be precise.

You can select the city closest to your residence:

   a. Click the Selected City drop-down menu below the map.

   b. Scroll through the list and select your city.

2. **Select your time zone.**

When you click your general geographical area, the map zooms in on that area. You then click the city closest to where you live and your time zone is selected.

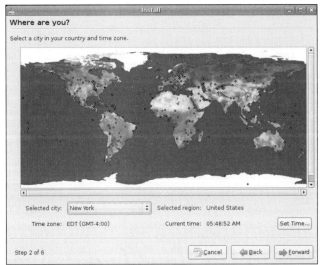

Figure 4-3: Set up your time zone.

You can use this window to

- *Correct your clock.*

  Click the Set Time button near the lower-right side of the window and the Time and Date Settings window opens. You can change the time and date as desired.

- *Tell your computer to synchronize itself with time servers using the NTP (Network Time Protocol) system.*

  Click the Synchronize Now button, and your computer synchronizes itself automatically. Click the OK button in the Date/Time Properties dialog when finished.

3. **Click the Forward button.**

The Keyboard Layout window opens. Figure 4-4 shows the Keyboard Layout dialog.

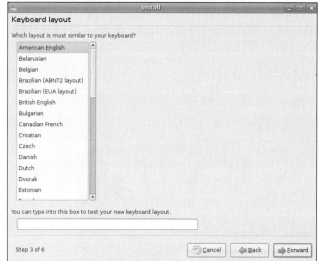

Figure 4-4:
What
keyboard
are you
using?

Good job! Now you can move on to Stage 4.

Stage 4: Setting Up Your Login Account

The section describes how to select a username, a password, and (optionally) a name for your computer. Follow these steps:

1. **Click the Forward button.**

   The Who Are You? window opens.

   I wonder if Pete Townshend uses Ubuntu.

   Figure 4-5 shows the initial screen.

2. **Type your name in the What Is Your Name? text box.**

3. **Type the username in the What Name Do You Want to Use to Log In?
   text box.**

4. **Type a good password in the Choose a Password to Keep Your
   Account Safe text box.**

Figure 4-5:
Who are
you? Who
who?

Step 4 of 6

Selecting a good password is critical to maintaining good security. Consider these important points:

- *Pick a password that you can remember without writing it down.*
- *The password should never use words that can be found in a dictionary.*
- *The password should be at least eight characters long.*

    The longer the better, as long as you can remember it.

Practice using a new password several times immediately after creating it to ensure it sticks in your memory.

I find the best compromise is to pick a phrase you like and change it. For instance, take *The kids are alright* and change it to *da kids okay,* which becomes *d@k1dsokay*. That's a very good ten characters long, and I can remember it without writing it down.

5. **Type your computer's name in the What Is the Name of This Computer? text box.**

    This is the name your computer will be known as on the network.

    Figure 4-6 shows an example of the fictitious user Joe Computer's account.

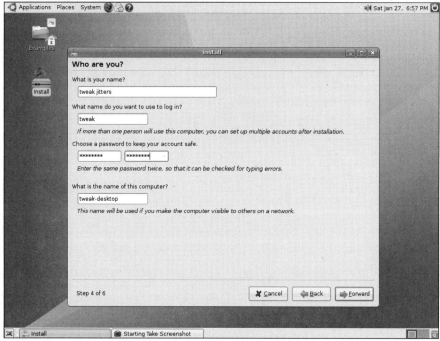

Okay, enough about you. Click the Forward button and move on to Stage 5.

Stage 5: Selecting a File System

The most difficult part of the Ubuntu installation process actually isn't difficult at all. This part of the installation process requires you to select the hard drive partitioning onto which Ubuntu will be installed.

The Select a Disk window opens as the Ubuntu installation system searches for and finds a hard drive (disk) to use. When the search process finishes, the Prepare Disk Space window, shown in Figure 4-7, opens.

I recommend using one of these options:

- ✔ **Resize Partition and Use Freed Space:** Select the largest existing, unused partition space.

  The following section, "Selecting an unused partition," shows the steps.

- ✔ **Erase Entire Disk:** Erase an entire hard drive and use it to install Ubuntu onto.

  The section "Erasing an entire disk" shows the steps.

Figure 4-7:
Tell the
installer
how to
partition the
disk.

I don't recommend using the Manually Edit Partition Table option unless you're already an expert Ubuntu Linux user.

Selecting an unused partition

Ubuntu can live side by side on the same hard drive with Microsoft Windows, in a *dual-boot configuration* (which means that you can install two operating systems on one computer).

If you need to set up Ubuntu on the same hard drive as Windows, Chapter 3 describes how to free up space from a Windows partition and format the partition for use by Ubuntu.

When you have the partition you need for Ubuntu, follow these steps:

1. **Select the Resize SCSI1 (0,0,0), partition #1 (sda) and Use Freed Space: radio button.**

   At this point, you've selected the option to delete all files on your Windows hard drive. You haven't actually erased anything yet.

2. **Proceed to the section "Stage 6: Installing Ubuntu Linux" to complete the Ubuntu installation process.**

Erasing an entire disk

Erasing a disk is easy. Just take a hammer and smash the hard drive.

However, if you want to erase the hard drive and then use it for Ubuntu, the Ubuntu installation system can do the job.

This is the option that deletes everything from your computer, including Microsoft Windows. If you want to keep what's already on your computer, follow the steps in the "Selecting an unused partition" section and continue on with "Stage 6: Installing Ubuntu Linux."

If you want to connect Ubuntu to wireless networks, you might need your Windows driver and information file for your wireless network card. Chapter 7 shows how to find them. Save these files somewhere else (like on a CD) before you wipe out Windows.

Follow these steps to erase Windows:

1. **Click the Erase Entire Disk radio button in the Prepare Disk Space dialog.**

   At this point, you've select the option to delete all files on your Windows hard drive. You haven't actually erased anything yet.

2. **Proceed to the section "Stage 6: Installing Ubuntu Linux" to complete the Ubuntu installation process.**

Stage 6: Installing Ubuntu Linux

All that remains now to finish installing Ubuntu Linux on your computer is to install Ubuntu Linux to your hard drive. So take a deep breath and follow the instructions in this section.

This is the point of no return for your computer:

✔ If you intend to install Ubuntu alongside Microsoft Windows — without erasing Windows, you might unintentionally erase files, folders, or Windows itself — before you complete the installation, you should be sure that

   • You've backed up your *files*.

   • You have the original software to reinstall your *Windows operating system* and *programs*.

If you haven't backed up your computer, you should click the Cancel button. Check out Chapter 3 for backup instructions and advice.

✔ If Ubuntu will be the only operating system on your PC, this is the point where the old operating system and *all your old files* will be obliterated. Last chance to click Cancel and change your mind!

If you've been following the installation instructions in this chapter, here's how to format your Linux partitions and install Ubuntu onto them:

1. **Click the Forward button.**

   The Ready to Install dialog opens.

   • The dialog shows all the selections you've made so far during the installation process.

   • The dialog shows the partitions it will create within the space you allocated in Chapter 3.

   Figure 4-8 shows an example Ready to Install dialog.

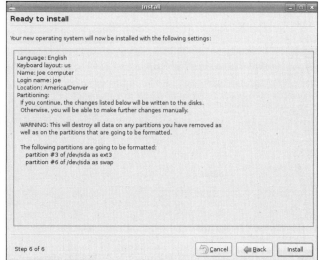

Figure 4-8:
The Ready to Install dialog shows all of your installation choices.

All changes that you've made so far, while preparing to install Ubuntu, aren't permanent. If you continue from here, the changes will be permanent.

   • *Your disk will be formatted.*

   • *Ubuntu files will be installed.*

You can go back to any previous menu by clicking the Back button.

2. **Click the Install button.**

   The Installing System dialog opens, displaying

   - *A graphical progress indicator*
   - *A short description of the function being performed*

   The installation process will take at least a few minutes while Ubuntu

   - *Formats its partition on your hard drive*
   - *Copies itself from the DVD or CD-ROM to its partition on your hard drive*

This is a good time to get another cup of coffee, tea, tequila, or whatever. When you get back, you'll probably be ready for the next section of the chapter.

Stage 7: Finishing the Installation

After Ubuntu finishes installing itself, it opens the Installation Complete dialog shown in Figure 4-9.

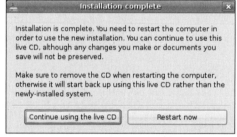

Figure 4-9:
The
Installation
Complete
dialog.

You're given the option to either

- ✔ **Continue Using the Live CD:** Clicking this button puts your computer back into the state it was in before starting the installation process. You can continue to use the live CD instance. (The information you entered during the installation configuration is saved. You can reuse the information you previously entered if you start the installation process again.)

- ✔ **Restart Now:** Clicking this option restarts your computer. During the reboot, you should eject the Ubuntu CD-ROM or DVD (in Step 2 of the list that follows) and you'll reboot into the permanently installed version of Ubuntu Linux.

If you've been following the instructions in this chapter, here's how to reboot to the Ubuntu Linux installation on your hard drive:

1. **Click the Restart Now button.**

    Live Ubuntu starts shutting itself down and prompts you to press the Enter key, as shown in Figure 4-10.

Figure 4-10: Ubuntu prompts you to finish the shutdown process.

2. **Remove the Ubuntu disc and press the Enter key.**

    Ubuntu restarts your computer and displays a boot option menu, as shown in Figure 4-11.

Figure 4-11: Boot that baby up!

3. Press the Enter key to continue the boot process.

By default, Ubuntu will boot itself after ten seconds if you do nothing. (Pressing the up- or down-arrow key moves the menu cursor and prevents any action until you press the Enter key.)

Ubuntu boots and displays a login screen, as shown in Figure 4-12.

4. Type your username and password.

If you've followed the instructions in this chapter, use the name and password you created in the "Stage 4: Setting Up Your Login Account" section.

Ubuntu authenticates you and drops you into a GNOME window, shown in Figure 4-13. (GNOME is pronounced *guh-NOME*. Don't worry about what that *guh-means* right now. It's pretty much just your desktop. I tell you more about it in Chapters 11 and 12.)

Figure 4-12:
Come on in!

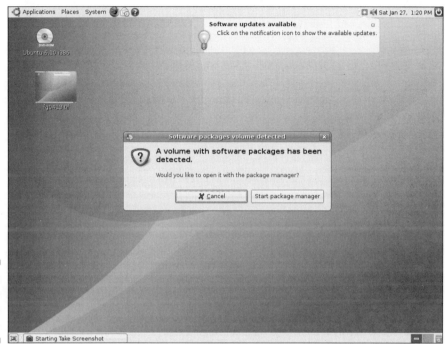

In the GNOME window, you see the following:

- *An icon pointing to your installation CD-ROM or DVD, if present.*

  If you're using the CD that comes with this book, the icon says
  `Ubuntu 6.10 i386`.

- *A dialog informing you that updates are available.* If you're connected to a network with Internet access or directly to the Internet,
  your Ubuntu computer is, too. (Installing Ubuntu doesn't change
  any devices — such as a DSL or cable modem — that you've
  already configured. Ubuntu will automatically connect to your network or Internet connection.)

  The Updates Available window means that there are newer versions available for software installed on your computer.

- A dialog named Software Packages Volume is detected, if your
  Ubuntu CD is still in place.

This GNOME window is similar to the live disc default window, but the
Examples and Install icons from the live disc version are missing.

Running the Package Manager

After logging into your Ubuntu user account on a computer with an Internet connection, Ubuntu looks for software package updates. If Ubuntu detects any updates, it opens a notification icon informing you of their availability. The following instructions describe how to install updates.

To use the Package Manager, follow these steps:

1. **Click the notification icon, pointed to by the Software Updates Available notification icon.**

   The Software Updates dialog opens, showing the available updates.

2. **Click the Install Updates button.**

   The Enter Your Password to Perform Administrative Tasks dialog appears.

3. **Type your password in the Password text box.**

   The Downloading Package Files dialog opens, showing the progress of the package download and installation process. When the packages are downloaded and installed, the Changes Applied dialog opens.

4. **Click the Close button in the Changes Applied dialog.**

   The Changes Applied dialog closes, and you return to the Software Updates dialog.

5. **Click the Close button in the Software Updates dialog.**

   The Software Updates dialog closes, and you're finished with the update process.

Congratulations! You're now the proud owner of a permanent Ubuntu installation. Unlike live Ubuntu, any changes you now make to the installation are saved.

Chapter 5 describes how to get started using Ubuntu Linux.

Chapter 5

Ubuntu 101

The rest of this book shows how to use and master Ubuntu. Before proceeding, however, I'd like to introduce several essential Linux concepts and systems that will serve as an underpinning for the topics to come.

This chapter helps you get started with Ubuntu and the Linux operating system in general. I introduce the technologies underpinning Linux and Ubuntu; this information is essential to understanding how Ubuntu and computers in general work. I also describe the basics of using and operating your Ubuntu computer. This information gives you a working knowledge of fundamental Linux tools that will help you use the rest of this book.

Understanding the Linuxisms

The word *Linux* has different meanings, depending on the context in which it's referred to:

✔ **Linux kernel:** Linux is the operating system that controls everything you do on your Ubuntu computer; this is technically the Linux kernel. The Linux kernel controls who can use resources like memory, disk space, and time allocated on the central processing unit (CPU).

Linus Torvalds started writing the Linux kernel in 1991 because he wasn't satisfied with any of the operating systems he had access to. Early on, he released his work to the nascent Internet and immediately hit a nerve. The power of communication and the need for such an operating system resulted in many talented people helping to make the project a success. Linus also licensed his work under the GNU General

Public License (GPL), which allowed people to use, modify, and distribute his work as long as they allowed others to do the same. Using the Internet and GPL, Linux quickly exploded into worldwide use and today is second only to Microsoft Windows in use.

✓ **Linux distribution:** Linux is also the overall system that consists of the Linux kernel and all the supporting systems. Ubuntu Linux is an example of this. Ubuntu is a Linux distribution that contains the Linux kernel, GNU applications, the Linux file system, a graphical environment, and many other subsystems.

✓ **Multiuser:** Linux is a multiuser operating system. People can share a Linux computer. You assign separate user accounts to each person, which limits one person from interfering with another.

✓ **Multitasking:** Linux is a multitasking operating system. You can run multiple programs at the same time.

Each program gets a slice of time to perform its task before being forced into the background, so that the next program in line can get its slice. Computers operate so quickly, however, that all processes appear to be running at once.

✓ **GNU:** GNU is a comprehensive and free operating system project that was started in 1983 by Richard Stallman. It consists of a kernel, system utilities, libraries, compilers, and system administration programs.

GNU is a recursive acronym for GNU's Not UNIX.

The kernel wasn't released until recently, but the other parts have been very widely used for decades. Linux wouldn't be a popular operating system today if not for GNU. Many people reasonably refer to GNU Linux when talking about Linux. That makes sense because Linux, as I just mentioned, originally was just the operating system kernel. When the Linux kernel was released in 1992, it was quickly combined with GNU software to create a usable operating system. However, the powerful forces of popular lexicon, branding, and pure inertia set using the single word *Linux* into place.

✓ **GPL:** The GNU General Public License (also referred to as the *GNU Public License*) was created by Richard Stallman. There are other similar licenses in use, but the GPL is their ancestor. GPL is the reason that Linux, Mozilla Firefox, and many other applications exist today.

Thinking about processes and programs

Processes are programs in motion, so to speak. A *program* is a sequence of instructions that perform some job or function. Everything you do on a computer is performed by a program.

Firefox, OpenOffice.org, and even Linux itself are all programs.

Programs are stored in files on the Linux file system (which is described in this chapter). When you run (or start) a program — for instance, click a program icon — Linux reads the contents of the program file into memory (RAM) and starts executing the instructions contained in the file.

Once the program is loaded and started, it's called a *process* and is controlled by the Linux kernel.

When you start a program, whether a complex one such as Mozilla Firefox or a relatively simple one such as GNOME calculator, the Linux kernel loads the contents of the corresponding program file into memory and starts running it. The program startup process — no pun intended, but I'll take it anyway — is more complicated than that, but that's the gist of it.

Getting to know the Linux file system

Everything that you use or save on a computer is stored as a file on disk drives of some sort. Programs are stored as files. Other types of information, such as word processing files, spreadsheets, and photographs, are stored as files, too. In fact, Linux organizes every resource (except network connections) as a file. All of these resources together are considered a *file system*.

Linux interacts with all devices as if they are files. For instance, your hard drive is viewed as the file /dev/hda or /dev/hdb. Each file is actually the IDE interface of the first and second hard drive, respectively.

Directory rules

Files are stored inside directories. *Directories* are actually files themselves whose sole purpose is to allow files to be logically organized.

Linux directories are like Windows *folders*.

There's no requirement that any particular files have to be located in any particular directories. However, all Linux computers adhere to conventions that provide these general organization rules:

- ✔ **Directories can contain directories.** There is no practical limit to the number of directories within directories.
- ✔ **A directory that contains another directory is called the *parent*.**
- ✔ **The directory inside a directory is the *child* of the parent.**
- ✔ **The slash (/) character separates directories.**

Microsoft Windows uses backslashes (\), rather than forward slashes (/), to separate directories.

✔ **The `root` directory is the home location of all other directories.**

✔ **`Root` is designated by the first slash in any directory list.** For instance, if you want to see the contents of the `etcetera` directory, where configuration files are stored, you type the command `ls /etc` at the command prompt. (See the "Using the Shell" section in this chapter for information about typing commands.) Using the slash character tells the command to look in the root directory for the `etc` directory. (Linux's `root` directory is equivalent to the Windows C:\ drive.)

✔ **A *path* is a list of one or more directories.** You specify a path when describing where to find a file or directory. For instance, the path to the file containing this chapter on my computer is `/home/paul/doc/ulfd`. Each directory — `home`, `paul`, `doc`, `ulfd` — is part of the path; the first slash (/) is the `root` directory.

You can see an example of a directory path by clicking the Places menu in the GNOME menu bar — towards the top-left side of the screen — and selecting the Desktop option. A window opens, showing the contents of your home folder (directory). You see the name of your home directory below the Up button, near the top-left side of the window. Click the left-facing arrow button immediately to the left of your home directory name. The window shows a series of buttons representing the directory path to your `Desktop` directory. The example shown in Figure 5-1 shows the directories leading to my `Desktop` directory: `home`, `paul`, `Desktop`.

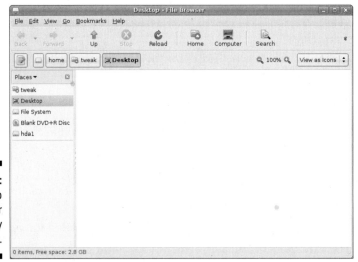

Figure 5-1:
The Desktop folder directory path.

Common directories

In the future, if and when you start to perform more Linux administration, it's useful to know what and where some of the common Linux directories are. The following list introduces the location and purpose of some of the common Linux directories; all of the directories are created and populated by default when you install Ubuntu (or run Ubuntu from a live CD-ROM):

- ✔ /boot   Linux kernels and their supporting files. After you install Linux, you'll find the Linux kernel saved in /boot.

- ✔ /dev   Device files. Physical devices are represented as files by the Linux kernel. The kernel reads and writes to devices through files contained in this directory. So is your hard drive, and if you have a printer or a USB memory disk connected to your computer, for example, you'll find a corresponding device file in this directory.

- ✔ /etc   System configuration files. Files in this directory allow your computer to automatically use networking, printers, and other devices when they've been configured.

- ✔ /home   User account directories. Your user account home directory, created during the installation process described in Chapter 4, lives here. For instance, if you created a user account called heidi during the Ubuntu installation, that account will have a home directory /home/heidi created for it.

- ✔ /proc   A pseudo directory. This directory is not physically located on any disk drive but is a view into the Linux kernel itself. Linux allows you to view certain internal data structures, and in some cases, control them via files found here.

  It isn't necessary to use the /proc file system unless you're performing very advanced system administration tasks. Ubuntu makes the everyday management of Ubuntu very easy by providing utilities that make it unnecessary to use the /proc file system.

- ✔ /tmp   Temporary files that can be deleted after you've used them. For instance, there are many files that Linux creates to manage or facilitate running utilities and applications that are stored temporarily in this directory.

- ✔ /usr   Additional directories that store system and application programs, libraries, and supporting files.

  Libraries are small pieces of software — called *subroutines* or *functions* in programming speak — that perform simple, common tasks and are shared by multiple programs and applications. Programmers use libraries when writing an application so they don't have to "reinvent the wheel" every time they need to perform some common task; for instance, a Web browser and e-mail client application and word processor all use the same library function to read and write files on a Linux file system.

✔ /usr/bin   User applications and utility programs. /usr/bin contains applications like the Firefox Web browser and Evolution e-mail/calendar, and utilities like the ls command. Most applications and utilities are stored here by default.

✔ /usr/sbin   System applications and utility programs. /usr/sbin is similar to /usr/bin/, but it stores applications and utilities used for system administration. /usr/sbin is not accessible by users unless they use sudo to gain superuser privilege.

✔ /usr/local   Third-party or user-supplied applications, utility programs, configuration files, databases, and so on. You typically use this directory structure to store applications and utilities that aren't part of the Ubuntu installation. For instance, if you download a beta version of Firefox, you should install it in /usr/local/bin so as not to overwrite the production version found in /usr/bin — and also to reduce confusion about what version resides where.

✔ /var   Files that vary with time. This directory contains files that the operating system creates, deletes, reads, and writes to. For instance, when you print a document, a temporary file holding the formatted text gets written to the /var/spool directory. It's deleted when the print job finishes.

For instance, when you print a document, Linux creates an output file to send to the printer — but first it stores, temporarily, the output in /var/spool/lp. After the document is printed, Linux deletes the temporary file.

Differences between Linux and Windows

Linux files and directories are similar to Windows files and folders, but there are a few differences:

✔ Linux uses different names — forward slashes, backward ones, — but the concept is the same.

✔ The Linux root directory / is replaced by a drive symbol, such as the common C:\ drive.

✔ You also have to explicitly mount a file system to use it in Linux. Linux must *mount* a file system before it can start using the file system.

Linux has gotten very good at hiding such processes. For instance, plug your USB flash memory device into your Ubuntu computer, and you'll see a window showing its contents in a few seconds. Ubuntu detected and mounted the device without intervention.

Using the shell

Ubuntu provides a powerful and useful graphical interface. You can perform every type of task, such as finding and opening files and setting up network interfaces, using Ubuntu's graphics. (Chapters 6 through 21 describe using the Ubuntu graphical utilities and GNOME graphical interfaces.) However, Linux also provides a non-graphical and very powerful interface where you type commands at the keyboard instead of clicking a mouse. Microsoft Windows, as a matter of fact, is trying very hard to catch up with Linux and provide non-graphical commands.

Linux computers make extensive use of shells. *Shells* are programs that provide text-based user interfaces to the Linux operating system. When working in a shell, the user enters a command plus optional arguments, and the shell *parses* (separates the various parts of a command into usable parts) and then executes the command. Because shells are used to launch commands (programs), they're often referred to as the *command line interface* (CLI).

Shells provide both the platform to launch programs and a powerful programming environment. Any program that you interactively launch from a shell, you can also launch from a *script* — you create scripts to automate commands that you would normally manually type at the command line. Shells provide many of the functions you find in programming languages. You can put those functions into a file and you can execute that file like a program. This capability is so powerful that Microsoft has made a goal to make at least 90 percent of its GUI-based applications and utilities scriptable.

bash is the dominant shell in use today within the Linux world. Ubuntu uses bash as its default shell.

bash is a derivative of the *Bourne shell* and gets its acronym from that heritage — born again shell.

You open a shell using a Terminal Emulator in Ubuntu. A *Terminal Emulator* provides a window in which you type commands to a shell and receive output from the shell. Use the following steps to open a Terminal Emulator:

1. **Click the Applications menu option at the top-left side of the screen.**

2. **Choose Accessories⇨Terminal.**

   A window containing the bash shell opens, like the one shown in Figure 5-2.

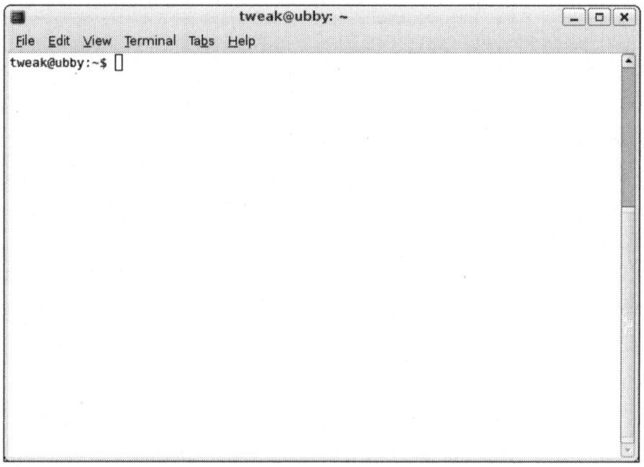

```
                     tweak@ubby: ~              _ □ ×
 File  Edit  View  Terminal  Tabs  Help
 tweak@ubby:~$ []
```

Figure 5-2:
Tweak
nervously
opens the
bash shell
on his
computer,
ubby.

The shell is configured to create a prompt of the following:

✔ **Your username.**

✔ **The computer name:** The username and computer name are separated by an *at* (@) character.

✔ **The directory you're working from:** The computer name and directory are separated by a colon (:) character. (Your home directory is represented by the tilda (~) character.

The prompt is terminated with a dollar ($) character.

Anything you type at the prompt is interpreted as a command. Any results from executing the command are displayed on subsequent lines. For instance, type ls to get a directory listing, and you'll see any files that exist within your current working directory.

The bash shell and the MS-DOS window are similar in function. Both are interactive user interfaces from which you can execute commands. Here's the key technical difference:

✔ The bash shell (and Linux shells in general) only *interprets* your input. The shell feeds your input to the Linux kernel, which then executes the program and its arguments.

✔ MS-DOS contains the commands and does all the work itself.

Linux security

Linux was born into security. Unlike other operating systems that had to be dragged kicking and screaming into that world — and doing back-flips to get there — Linux inherited the UNIX operating system model where user and system address space. This model separates each user account from all others.

In the UNIX/Linux world, processes exist in either *kernel space* or *user space:*

✔ **Kernel space processes** can do anything. They can access and control all aspects of the computer.

✔ **User space processes** are limited by the kernel in what they can do and access.

By keeping user space separate from kernel space, Linux greatly limits the ability of viruses and malware from affecting your computer; other operating systems are still working hard to obtain the same level of security that Linux has always had.

Linux user accounts

Linux user accounts separate people's files and work from one another, ensuring a reasonable level of privacy to all people who use a computer.

Chapter 4 shows how to create a user account while installing Ubuntu.

Individual user accounts have two kinds of identifiers:

✔ **UID:** A unique identifier for a particular user account.

✔ **GID:** Group identifiers allow multiple users to share information.

All files created by a user inherit a unique UID and GID by default. Other users can't read or write to the files without changing access. However, you can add UID (or UIDs) to a group to allow the user or users specified by the UID (or UIDs) access to files and directories owned by the GID.

Log in, log out

As a user, you need to know how to enter and exit Ubuntu.

To start working from a user account, you must first log in to it. Logging in to a computer requires you to authenticate to the computer by entering your

✔ **User account name (*username*, for short)**

✔ **Password**

Logging in to Ubuntu is straightforward:

1. **Type your username at the log in prompt.**

2. **Type your password when prompted.**

   The Ubuntu desktop, shown in Figure 5-3, opens.

At this point, you can start and use any program.

sudo

The *sudo* (pronounced *SUE-do*) utility allows users to perform tasks as the *superuser*, who can read any file and perform almost any action. The Linux superuser is equivalent to the Microsoft Administrator.

Actions performed as the superuser (also called `root`) are also referred to as *system-level tasks.*

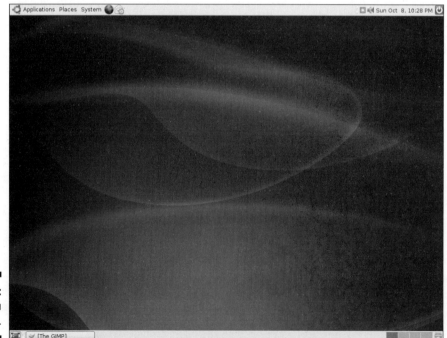

Figure 5-3:
The Ubuntu
desktop.

UID values

Linux processes with a UID of 0 are all powerful. UID 0 processes can read any file and perform almost any action. User accounts are given nonzero UIDs to limit invasion of other users' privacy and limit the damage users can intentionally or unintentionally wreak.

Ubuntu user accounts have UIDs of 1,000 or above by default.

The `root` user (also known as the *superuser*) has a UID of 0. `root` is all-powerful and should be limited to experienced system administrators.

Unlike most Linux distributions, Ubuntu doesn't configure a superuser; it exists but doesn't have a password, and can't be directly logged in to. Users are given access to root-level privileges on a case-by-case basis, so to speak.

You can find out what your UID is by typing the `id` command in a Terminal Emulator window. (Click the GNOME menu bar and select Applications⇨Accessories⇨Terminal to open a Terminal Emulator window.)

A user can perform a system-level task only if sudo is configured appropriately. For example, if sudo is configured to allow you to add a user account, you'd type the following command to create the new user account named `tweak`:

```
sudo useradd tweak
```

sudo prompts you for your password and then performs the task for you.

Using sudo has several advantages:

- ✔ You can configure access to system-level tasks in a very precise way.
- ✔ It enforces good administrative hygiene by forcing you to think a little about every system-level task you perform.
- ✔ It records what every user does, which makes it easy to assign blame!

The traditional way of performing system-level tasks is to log in as `root` (superuser) and go to town. However, this makes it easy to make mistakes that can have disastrous effects — such as erasing files you don't want to erase. For instance, typing `rm -rf /` as `root` erases your entire disk. It's much more difficult to perform such a task when you have to use sudo — typing `sudo rm -rf /` makes you think more about what you're doing because you first have to type `sudo` before typing `rm -rf /`. By encouraging the use of sudo, and discouraging operating as `root`, Ubuntu reduces the possibility of making mistakes.

Starting and Stopping Ubuntu

Starting and stopping a computer is a simple process. However, there are good ways to do so and bad ways, too. This section describes the correct startup and shutdown methods.

Booting

Booting a computer refers to the process of starting it by turning on the power. *Rebooting* means to restart the computer by telling the operating system to first gracefully stop, and then restart itself.

Generally, you shouldn't reboot a computer by turning the power off and then on.

Choosing from the options that stop your computer

There comes a time when all good things must come to an end — even if for a short time. When you stop using your computer, Ubuntu provides several options to save power and protect your data. To access these options, choose System⇨Quit from the GNOME menu bar. Or you can simply click the red Quit button in the upper-right corner of the screen.

Let Ubuntu do it

These are not good ideas, but you could just push and hold the power button until the power is cut off. Or you could just pull the power cord to turn a computer off. The reason you *don't* want to use those ways to turn your computer off is that suddenly shutting off power stops everything that's going on in your computer instantaneously:

✔ Applications and processes stop in mid-read or mid-write and possibly lose information.

✔ The file system also is stopped in mid-read or mid-write and loses its internal organization. (Sometimes you can fix this while rebooting, but sometimes you can't.)

Either way, the Quit dialog opens, with these options:

- ✔ **Shut Down:** Gracefully ends all activity and turns the power off. *Good night, Irene.*

  Your graphical desktop disappears, and Ubuntu lists the systems that it's shutting down. After Ubuntu finishes shutting down its systems, you're prompted to press the Enter key to finish the process. Press the Enter key, and your computer shuts down and turns itself off.

- ✔ **Restart:** Gracefully ends all activity and then restarts your computer processor and memory and loads Ubuntu. You can use the computer with a clean slate.

  Your computer shuts itself down — stopping all programs, applications, and services, and *unmounting* (making the file partitions unavailable to Ubuntu) all devices — and then starts itself up.

- ✔ **Log Out:** Closes your desktop and all programs running from it.

  After logging out, Ubuntu continues to run, but you have to log in again to start using it.

- ✔ **Lock Screen:** Prevents anyone who doesn't have your password from unlocking the screen.

- ✔ **Switch User:** You log in as another user using this option but continue to run the applications you were running as the original user. You can log in — switch back — to the previous user login and pick up where you left off.

- ✔ **Suspend:** Remembers your computer's current state, but uses almost no power. Your screen goes blank and you hear your hard drive and fans turn off. The power button on your computer box and monitor flash periodically so you know you're in suspend mode. Pressing a key or moving the mouse wakes the computer in a few seconds.

  You can save time and money by making use of the Suspend feature. Suspending puts your computer into a state that requires very little energy; the side benefit is that it's also very quiet.

  If your computer loses power while it's suspended, it's just like when you lose power while you're working. The computer reboots, and you lose any work that wasn't saved. If you don't want to risk losing your work while suspended, use the Hibernate option instead.

- ✔ **Hibernate:** Remembers your computer's current state and gracefully shuts down. Your computer doesn't use *any* power. This option works whether you're running from a live Ubuntu disc or from Ubuntu installed on your hard drive.

When the computer *hibernates,* it first saves its *state* (the contents of its memory and the CPU) to its hard drive. Then, unlike suspension, it completely shuts itself off. The CPU doesn't continue to operate in any fashion, nor does the monitor or computer power switch flash periodically; they can't — the computer is off.

Hibernation will survive a power outage.

To wake the slumbering beast, you must press the power button. The computer initially looks like it's doing a normal startup: You see the BIOS access instructions display, and then Ubuntu shows its startup sequence.

However, rather than continue through the entire startup process, Ubuntu sees the hibernation state file on the hard drive and reloads it. This process short-circuits and speeds the rest of the boot sequence.

You can program your computer to suspend itself automatically.

To automatically suspend your computer whenever it's unused for a period of time, follow these steps:

1. **Click the GNOME Main Menu and choose System⇨Preferences⇨Power Management.**

   The Power Management Preferences dialog opens, with the Put Computer to Sleep when It Is Inactive For slider set to the default, Never.

2. **Click the slider and move it to the time after which the computer will go to sleep.**

   The time can be between one minute and one hour.

3. **Click OK.**

It's easy to wake up Ubuntu when it's suspended. Follow these steps:

1. **Press a key or move the mouse.**

   You'll hear your computer start to wake up. It should take only 10 to 15 seconds to be back up and running.

   Many laptops wake up when you open them.

2. **Enter your password when prompted.**

   You're prompted for the password of the user account last in use when the computer was suspended. After you correctly enter the password, you see everything as it was before suspension.

Part II

Networking and the Internet

The 5th Wave   By Rich Tennant

"We take network security here very seriously."

In this part . . .

Part II concentrates on most readers' number one concern: getting a network connection and accessing the Internet. Chapter 6 describes connecting to a private network via Ethernet, Chapter 7 moves on to using wireless networks. Chapter 8 moves on to using high-speed broadband Internet connections. Chapter 9 reverts to using old-school dialup modems, and Chapter 10 provides the essential network security ingredient, the firewall.

Chapter 6

Zen and the Art of Ubuntu Networking

· ·

In This Chapter

▶ Connecting to a wired network

▶ Configuring your network connection

· ·

*Y*ou're already connected to a network if you're connected to a network. Huh? What kind of Zen network am I talking about? No, Ubuntu isn't a Zen master, but it's good at looking for and making network connections. Ubuntu is smart enough to figure out how to do all the sundry housekeeping jobs that getting connected requires.

If you booted live Ubuntu in Chapter 2 or installed it in Chapter 4, Ubuntu looked for a network. Assuming your computer was connected to a network switch (or hub), Ubuntu made the connection. At that point, you could use the network.

However, Ubuntu makes it easy to change or make a connection (in case you didn't originally have a network connection). This chapter describes using the network configuration utility for a wired network.

You can skip this chapter if you don't plug directly into a home or office network with an Ethernet cable. You probably need one of the following chapters instead for your network and Internet services:

   ✔ Chapter 7 walks you through connecting an Ubuntu computer to a *wireless* network (with or without networked Internet service).

   ✔ Chapter 8 tells you about connecting your Ubuntu computer directly to a *broadband* DSL or cable Internet modem without going through a network.

   ✔ Chapter 9 shows you how you can use your Ubuntu computer with a *dialup* Internet modem without going through a network.

Connecting to a Wired Network

Networking has advanced considerably in recent years. Back in the day, you had to work really hard to get connected. Economics dictated that using a local area network (LAN) was generally limited to medium or large businesses and organizations. Broadband Internet access was even more inaccessible. Mere mortals like me had to live with connecting to the Internet using old, slow dialup modems from a single computer.

Life was indeed hard. I personally had to take three buses and then walk through two feet of snow, uphill both ways, to get to the university to use their network. But technology marches on, and today we all can enjoy the power and utility of fast Internet and faster LANs.

Networking on a LAN is fundamentally the same as networking on the Internet. Whether you're communicating over a LAN or the Internet, your computer uses the same TCP/IP protocols. *The Transmission Control Protocol/Internet Protocol* (TCP/IP) dictates how computers and networks communicate. TCP/IP makes LANs and the Internet possible by providing the rules that every computer and network uses to communicate.

You need the following elements to connect to a wired network:

- ✔ **A computer with an Ethernet connection:** Since 2000, most PCs and laptops come equipped with a built-in Ethernet; you can purchase Ethernet add-on cards to plug into your computer for around $20. Ethernet adapters also come in USB formats and PCMCIA cards for laptops.

- ✔ **An Ethernet switch:** All cable and DSL modems include at least one Ethernet connection; many provide four or more connections. You can also purchase inexpensive Ethernet switches with four or more Ethernet connections in any electronics store.

- ✔ **A category 5 (Cat5) Ethernet cable:** Cable and DSL modems most often include a Cat5 cable. You can purchase Cat5 cables in any electronics store. You use the cable to connect your computer to the Ethernet switch.

Connect your Ubuntu computer to the Ethernet switch with a Cat5 cable, and you're ready to configure and use your LAN and the Internet.

Using the Network Configuration Tool

As expected, Ubuntu provides an easy-to-use network configuration utility. You can configure your Ubuntu computer to connect to a LAN by using the following instructions:

1. **From the GNOME menu bar, choose System⇨Administration⇨ Networking.**

   The Enter Your Password to Perform Administrative Tasks dialog opens (unless you've entered your password in the previous five minutes).

2. **Type your password in the text box and click OK.**

   The Network Settings dialog, shown in Figure 6-1, opens.

   Enter the password you chose during the Ubuntu installation process described in Chapter 4.

Figure 6-1: Looking at your network-related devices.

Most computers come equipped with an integrated Ethernet network device; many computers, especially laptops, also come with a built-in modem. The Network Settings dialog shows all the network-related devices on your computer.

3. **Click the Wired connection and click the Properties button.**

   The Interface Properties dialog opens, showing your current, if any, configuration.

At this point, you can choose between static and dynamic network configuration. The rest of the chapter describes how to use these connections.

Choosing network connections

The Internet uses *IP addresses* to identify the location of both the sender and receiver. You must assign an IP address to your Ubuntu computer before it can connect to and use your LAN and the Internet.

There are two ways you can assign an IP address to your Ubuntu computer: *dynamically* or *statically.*

You can use either method in this chapter, but consider these guidelines:

✔ Use dynamic IP addresses (DHCP) if you don't want to provide *network services* (share files and folders, provide Web pages, and so on).

DHCP reduces the configuration work required to use a network. Most cable and DSL modems and Ethernet switches dynamically assign an IP address to any computer (or printer or networking device) that connects to it by using the dynamic host configuration protocol (DHCP). DHCP allows a computer to connect to a network containing a DHCP server and automatically have an IP address assigned to it.

✔ Avoid using static IP addresses unless you're setting up a *server.*

Static IP addresses don't change and are useful when setting up a computer that provides services to a network. You generally need to know the IP address of a server so you can contact it and use the service or services it provides.

Configuring a dynamic connection

You can use Ubuntu's network configuration utility to set up dynamic networking using DHCP. DHCP provides the easiest method to configure and use a LAN or Internet connection.

You shouldn't have to configure a cable or DSL modem (or Ethernet switch) to use DHCP. Most such devices default to DHCP unless you configure them otherwise. That means you usually only need to plug your Ubuntu computer into the cable modem, DSL modem, or Ethernet switch to obtain an IP address that enables you to use the network.

Dynamic host configuration protocol

DHCP *dynamically* (automatically, on demand) assigns IP addresses to computers and any networked devices (such as printers) on your LAN. You'll find that in general, your dynamic IP addresses rarely change. That's because DHCP generally sets a time-to-live (TTL) option of a day or two on assigned IPs. Your IP will be reassigned only if you leave your computer off for more than the TTL and another computer asks for an address; even then, the DHCP server might not reassign your IP address, but hand out the one in sequence.

The following instructions tell your Ethernet interface on your Ubuntu computer to use DHCP:

1. **From the GNOME menu bar, choose System⇨Administration⇨ Networking.**

   Or if you still have the Interface Properties dialog open from earlier in the chapter, skip ahead to Step 4.

   The Enter Your Password to Perform Administrative Tasks dialog opens (unless you've entered your password in the previous five minutes).

2. **Type your password in the text box and click OK.**

   The Network Settings dialog, shown in Figure 6-1, opens.

3. **Click the Properties button in the Network Settings dialog.**

   The Interface Properties dialog, shown in Figure 6-2, opens. The Enable This Connection check box should be selected and the Configuration drop-down menu should be set to DHCP.

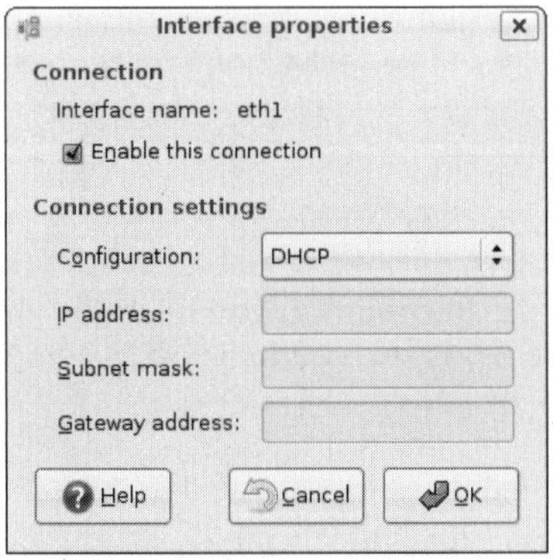

Figure 6-2:
The
Interface
Properties
dialog.

Interface properties	✕
Connection	
Interface name: eth1	
☑ E_n_able this connection	
Connection settings	
C_o_nfiguration: [DHCP ▲▼]	
IP address: [ ]	
S_u_bnet mask: [ ]	
G_a_teway address: [ ]	
⊘ _H_elp ↩_C_ancel ✓_O_K	

4. **Click OK.**

   The Interface Properties dialog closes and control returns to the Network Settings utility.

5. **Select the check box immediately to the left of the Wired connection option.**

   Your current network connection closes.

6. **Click the check box again.**

   Your new network connection, including all the changes you made in the previous steps, opens.

7. **Click OK.**

That's all there is to it! The Network Settings window closes and your Ubuntu computer is connected to your LAN or to your broadband modem. Your Ubuntu computer will now automatically get an IP address assigned to it from your broadband gateway or Ethernet switch.

If you're using DHCP (dynamic IP addresses), you can skip the rest of this chapter, which shows how to configure your Ubuntu computer to use static IP addresses.

Chapter 10 shows how to configure a *firewall*.

Configuring a static connection

Static IP addresses, as the name implies, don't change after they're set. You choose your IP address rather than letting your network switch or broadband modem make the selection.

Your static network connection configuration is not saved permanently if you're using live Ubuntu. (See Chapter 2 for instructions on using live Ubuntu.) Your configuration settings will be lost when you reboot your computer. Network configurations are saved if you're using a permanent Ubuntu installation. (See Chapter 4.)

Finding network information

If you're using a static IP address, the information you need for your Ubuntu computer's network connection depends on whether you're using someone else's network (such as at a school or a business) or your own.

Someone else's network

If you're connecting to *someone else's network* with a static IP address, ask your friendly system administrator for this information:

- **IP address for your Ubuntu computer:** _____
- **Subnetwork mask:** _____
  The subnetwork mask value usually is 255.255.255.0, except for some very large organizations.
- **Internet gateway:** _____
- **Domain name:** _____
- **DNS search domain:** _____
- **Primary DNS server:** _____
- **Secondary DNS server:** _____

When you have all the information you need to connect to someone else's network with a static IP address, skip to the "Configuring Ubuntu" section in this chapter.

Your own network

If you're connecting to your own network with a static IP address, some information is optional and other information is required.

You must have this information to set up Ubuntu on your own network:

- ✔ **An IP address for your Ubuntu computer:** _____
- ✔ **The subnetwork mask:** _____

    Your broadband router (modem) generally determines what IP address range you'll use. I've found broadband modems usually use either 192.168.0.1 or 192.168.1.1, but in one case the device used 10.0.0.1. Consult your device's manual to find out what default private IP addresses the device uses. Most devices automatically provide a private IP address space on the Ethernet ports you connect your LAN computers to. You can change the addresses if your Internet service provider (ISP) uses a nonstandard configuration, but otherwise you should use the default.

- ✔ **Internet Gateway address:** _____

    The gateway address usually is 192.168.0.1 or 192.168.1.1 for a consumer broadband cable or DSL modem. Check your DSL modem's manual to find out.

- ✔ **DNS server IP addresses:** _____

    You can find a DNS server or two by contacting your ISP. DNS servers convert Internet address names (such as www.theonion.com) to the actual IP addresses (such as 65.61.134.200).

- ✔ **Search domain (optional):** _____

    Specifying a search domain eliminates the need to specify an entire — fully qualified — address when writing Internet names with that domain. For instance, say your Ubuntu computer is connected to a network whose domain is thisismynetwork43.com, and the Web server is named www.thisismynetwork43.com. By specifying the search domain thisismynetwork43.com, you only have to write www instead of www.thisismynetwork.com when connecting to the Web server with a browser.

If you're running your own home network, you can select your own values for these elements:

| A hostname (your computer): _____

A default hostname is created when you install Ubuntu.

| Your domain name (your network): _____

Configuring Ubuntu

When you have all the information to connect to a network with a static IP address, you're ready to set up Ubuntu. The rest of this chapter guides you through the steps.

IP address

This section describes configuring your IP address, subnetwork mask, and gateway address. Follow these steps:

1. **From the Configuration drop-down menu in the Interface Properties window (refer to Figure 6-2), choose Static IP Address.**

   The IP Address and other text boxes activate.

2. **Type your IP address in the IP Address text box.**

3. **If necessary, change your subnetwork mask value.**

   You should never have to change your subnetwork mask unless you're connecting to a very large organization's LAN (in which case, the system administrator will tell you what value to use).

   255.255.255.0 (the usual subnetwork mask value) is automatically entered in the Subnet Mask text box.

4. **Type the IP address of your Internet connection in the Gateway Address text box.**

   The value usually is 192.168.0.1 or 192.168.1.1 when using a consumer broadband cable or DSL modem.

   Figure 6-3 shows a sample completed Interface Properties dialog.

5. **Click the OK button.**

After you configure your Internet gateway, you need to tell Ubuntu where to search for host and domain names. The following section, "Host and domain names," describes that configuration process.

Figure 6-3:
An example
Interface
Properties
dialog.

Host and domain names

By default, your Ubuntu computer automatically is named after your user account name when you install Ubuntu. You can change your computer name (the *hostname*) and also give your network a name (the *domain name*) by using the options found by clicking the General tab of the Network Settings dialog:

✔ When connecting to a home network using private IP addresses, you can use any hostname for your computer and any domain name for your Ubuntu computer.

✔ When connecting to a network you don't own, you should use the host and domain names given to you by the network administrator or system administrator.

If you want to change your Ubuntu computer's hostname and/or domain name, follow these steps:

1. **From the GNOME menu bar, choose System⇨Administration⇨ Networking.**

   The Enter Your Password to Perform Administrative Tasks dialog opens (unless you've entered your password in the previous five minutes).

2. **Type your password in the text box and click OK.**

   The Network Settings dialog, shown in Figure 6-4, opens.

3. **Click the General tab in the Network Settings window.**

4. **If you need a specific name for your computer, type it in the Hostname text box.**

5. **If you need a specific domain name for your LAN, type it in the Domain Name text box.**

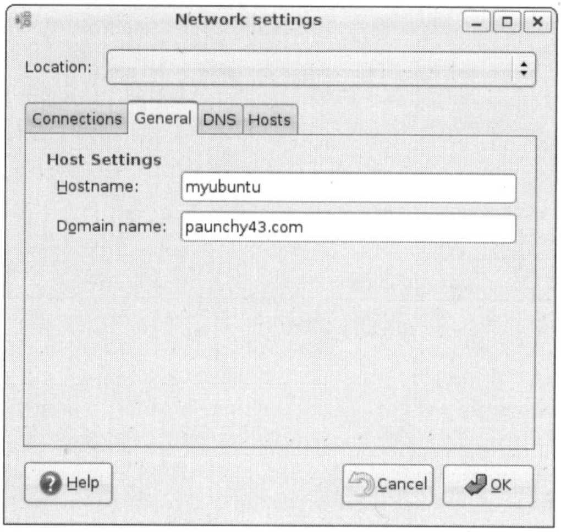

Figure 6-4:
Setting your
hostname
and domain
name.

DNS

You don't need to *know* anything about the DNS protocol to use DNS, but the sidebar "Domain name service (DNS)" tells the story. You only need to specify one or two DNS servers when using static IP addresses.

The following instructions are for configuring your Ubuntu computer to use one or two DNS servers:

1. **Click the DNS Servers Add button.**

2. **Type a DNS server IP address in the text box.**

3. **If you want to add search domains, repeat these steps for each domain:**

   a. *Click the Search Domains Add button.*

   b. *Type a domain name in the text box.*

Domain name service (DNS)

On LANs and the Internet, computers find each other by using numeric IP addresses. However, most humans can't easily use numeric IP addresses. So the Internet uses the domain name service (DNS) to convert numeric IP addresses to names.

For instance, if you want some light-hearted "news," you can enter `www.theonion.com`. Your computer checks the DNS server, finds the actual numeric IP address for the theOnion.com Web site (65.61.134.200), and uses that numeric IP address.

Figure 6-5 shows an example Network Settings dialog filled in with two DNS servers and a search domain.

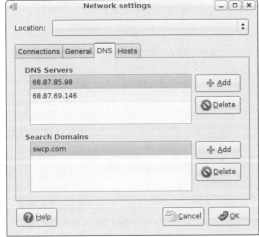

Figure 6-5:
DNS
servers and
a search
domain.

Search domains reduce the amount of typing you need to do when looking for DNS names. If you set a search domain to `wiley.com`, you only need to type in `www` when looking for `www.wiley.com`. You have to type both the host-name and domain name (called the *fully qualified domain name,* or *FQDN*) if you don't specify a search domain.

Finishing up: Activating the new settings

When you've finished making all the configuration changes to use a static IP address, you need to activate them. Follow these steps:

1. **Click the Connections tab.**

   You see the original window shown in Figure 6-1.

2. **Click the Deactivate button.**

   Your network connection is closed.

3. **Click the Activate button.**

   The Activating the Interface dialog opens while the changes are being made. Your network connection is restarted using all the changes you made.

4. **Click the OK button.**

   The Network Settings window closes.

You can use this utility to make additional changes as desired.

You should set up a firewall to protect your Ubuntu computer after you've configured its networking. Chapter 10 describes how to build a firewall that will protect you from the bad guys on the Internet.

Private IP addresses and your LAN

Most consumer-level network switches and broadband cable and DSL modems use the private network address spaces when working with your LAN. IP addresses like 192.168.0.1 through 192.168.0.255, 192.168.1.1 through 192.168.1.255, and 10.0.0.0 through 10.0.0.255 can't be routed on the Internet and are referred to as *private*. Private IP addresses are an Internet design feature defined in RFC1918 (Request for Comments).

Private IP addresses are used for small home networks and small business networks because

✔ They can't be routed.

✔ They can't interfere with the Internet.

✔ They don't require authorization from anyone.

You can use private IP addresses for your LAN if you have a broadband modem or Ethernet switch that provides Network Address Translation (NAT). Almost all cable and DSL modems provide NAT, which makes nonroute-able IP addresses a perfect fit for home networks and small business networks.

Chapter 7

Cut the Cord: Using Wireless Networking

*H*ow did people ever live without wireless networking? Before wireless fidelity networking — WiFi (pronounced *WHY-fye*), for short — we were tethered to our Ethernet cables — or worse, to telephone cords and dialup modems. In retrospect, it was like living without electricity or telephones — or for younger readers, without cellphones and text messaging.

Fortunately, the smart people from the IEEE (Institute of Electrical and Electronics Engineers) realized what wireless networking could achieve using radio frequency (RF) transmissions. The IEEE had previously designed the specifications used to create wired networking and decided to extend those protocols into the wireless realm. After the wireless protocols were designed, manufacturers used them to create the WiFi products we use today.

This chapter describes how to connect your Ubuntu computer — laptop or desktop — to an existing wireless network. I tell you how you can make three different types of connections using a Linux-compatible wireless network interface (also called a *network device* or a *network interface adapter* — *NIC*). You can do it without encryption and with either WEP (wired equivalent privacy) or WPA/WPA2 (WiFi Protected Access) encryption. I also tell you how you can adapt existing proprietary Windows wireless network interface drivers for use by Ubuntu when no Linux open source driver exists for your WiFi device.

Preparing for Wireless Networking

I assume that you connect to a pre-existing wireless network. Many businesses and organizations provide publicly accessible wireless networks on their premises.

You can also create a wireless network for yourself by purchasing an access point (AP) to connect to your private network. Many consumer-level APs cost less than $100 and are available in any electronics store. Follow the manufacturer's instructions to configure your own private wireless network.

Quick start: Getting connected fast

Before describing any details about what wireless networking is and how it works, I can help you get connected to one. The process is easy if Ubuntu provides a driver for your wireless network interface — in that case, you just connect to a wireless network. When it's connected, you can explore wireless networking at your leisure.

1. **Plug your wireless network interface into your computer if you're using an external PCMCIA or USB device.**

    You must turn on some built-in wireless network interfaces; for instance, some laptop computers have a power switch for the device. In that case, turn on your computer's interface.

    PCMCIA is short for Personal Computer . . . *take a breath* . . . Memory Card International Association (although some sources define it as Peripheral Component MicroChannel Interconnect Architecture). USB is the acronym for universal serial bus.

2. **If necessary, boot your Ubuntu computer.**

3. **Log in to your user account.**

4. **From the GNOME menu bar, choose System⇨Administration ⇨ Networking.**

    If you haven't recently performed an administrative task, the Enter Your Password to Perform Administrative Tasks dialog opens.

5. **Type your password if prompted.**

    The Network Settings dialog opens, showing all your network interfaces. Figure 7-1 shows a typical window with three network interfaces: a wireless interface, a wired (Ethernet) interface, and a modem.

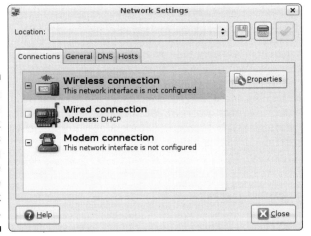

Figure 7-1:
The
Network
Settings
dialog
showing the
available
network
interfaces.

The Network Settings dialog is the front end to the Network Administration Tool utility, which is the default Ubuntu network configuration utility.

The dialog shows a wireless interface if Ubuntu has a compatible driver for the interface. In that case, locate the instructions in one of the following sections that describe how to connect to the type of wireless network you want to use. The following list describes the subsection, found in the "Connecting to Access Points" section, that you should go to depending on the type of wireless network you're connecting to:

✔ **Unencrypted APs:** When connecting to a wireless network that does not use encryption.

✔ **WEP-encrypted APs:** When connecting to a wireless network using the WEP encryption.

✔ **WPA-encrypted APs:** When connecting to a wireless network using either WPA or WPA2 encryption.

If you don't see any wireless interfaces, this chapter shows how to obtain or configure a driver in the "Obtaining a wireless network interface" section.

Wireless networking basics

Wireless networks use common radio signals used to create wireless networks and generally have a range of between 50 and 100 meters (about 150 to 300 feet). The signal range can be reduced by

✔ Weather

✔ Physical barriers (such as doors, walls, and windows)

The radio frequencies used by wireless networks are regulated by the Federal Communications Commission (FCC) in the United States and equivalent governmental agencies in other countries. The FCC designates certain parts of the electromagnetic spectrum — from low-frequency radio waves to light, X-rays, and beyond — for various purposes. For instance, the FCC licenses AM and FM frequencies to radio stations, and likewise for television stations. However, the FCC designates some frequencies for nonlicensed use. Cellphones, portable phones, garage door openers, microwaves, wireless networks, and many other devices all use nonlicensed frequencies. Wireless network devices use the 2.4 GHz (gigahertz, or billion cycles per second) frequency.

Security standards

Three different levels of security are available if you use a wireless network: high, low, and none.

High-security options

If you transmit sensitive information or conduct business over a wireless network, you should use one of these high-security options. High-security options include the WPA and WPA2 encryption standards.

WPA2 encryption

WPA2 encryption provides the best wireless network protection. It's compatible with

- Most 802.11g wireless network interfaces and APs

  Upgrading your wireless networking equipment to 802.11g usually is worth the expense.

- Some 802.11b cards that can be upgraded by installing firmware updates

WPA encryption

WPA encryption is much more secure than WEP (the original WiFi encryption), but not as secure as WPA2.

If your wireless network interface or AP currently provides WPA, you can probably upgrade it to WPA2 (the highest security level). Check the device manufacturer's Web site for firmware upgrades that add WPA2 capability.

WPA is designed to work with

- All 802-11g wireless network interfaces
- All access points, except first-generation ones

VPN (virtual private network) encryption

VPNs (virtual private networks) can safely encrypt information transmitted over unencrypted wireless networks.

Appendix B shows how to create an encrypted VPN on an unencrypted wireless network using the open source security tool OpenSSH.

Low security

WEP encryption was the first encryption method used on wireless networks. It's a little better than nothing at all. It might prevent unauthorized users from easily seeing your information, but it might be beaten by a hacker armed with the right tools and plenty of Jolt Cola and cheezpuffs.

Don't trust WEP encryption if you need to keep hackers out. WEP can be cracked using common software tools.

No security

Without any encryption, anyone in relatively close proximity can easily capture (sniff) and read your WiFi-transmitted information.

You might not need security when using a public WiFi network to view a sports page or the news. But don't transmit sensitive information or conduct business without using either wireless encryption or an encrypted VPN.

Wireless standards

When you have a wireless network, you need to connect to it. Ubuntu supports many wireless network interfaces (also called *wireless network adapters* or *WiFi network adapters*).

Table 7-1 compares current and future wireless standards, but three standards are common for wireless network interfaces:

- **802.11b** networks are the slowest standard.
- **802.11g** networks are up to five times as fast as 802.11b.
- **802.11i** networks are based on the 802.11g standard but use improved encryption, called WPA2.

Most new wireless network interfaces work with both 802.11b and 802.11g networks.

Table 7-1		Wireless Network Standards	
Standard	*Introduction Year*	*Speed (Maximum)*	*Range (Maximum)*
802.11a	1999	54Mbs	30 meters (100 feet)
802.11b	1999	11Mbs	100 meters (330 feet)
802.11g	2003	54Mbs	30 meters (100 feet)
802.11i	2004	54Mbs	30 meters (110 feet)
802.11n	2007 (or later)	540Mbs	50 meters (165 feet)

You might see references to these two infrequently used network standards:

- **802.11a** interfaces were considerably more expensive than 802.11b. 802.11a never achieved commercial success and is seldom used.

- **802.11n** will be the next generation of wireless networking. The 802.11n standard has been adopted in draft form but hasn't yet become official. At the time of publication, a few wireless network interface devices based on the draft form of 802.11n are on the market; these are called Pre-N. Few Linux drivers exist at this time.

Network scenarios

You'll find yourself in one of two situations when trying to connect your Ubuntu computer to a WiFi network:

- **Have at least one wireless network interface.**

  You already own

    • *A laptop with a built-in wireless network device*

  and/or

    • *A PCMCIA or USB device*

  In that case, the section "Using an existing wireless network interface" shows what you need to do.

- **Need to purchase a wireless network interface.**

  The section "Obtaining a wireless network interface" shows what you need to know when purchasing a device.

Using an existing wireless network interface

When you already have a wireless network interface, you need to discover whether the device works with Ubuntu. There are two ways that your device might work:

✔ Ubuntu provides Linux drivers for many wireless devices.

✔ Ubuntu provides a utility that allows you to use a Microsoft Windows device driver when no native Linux one exists.

Linux device drivers allow the device to work with the Linux kernel. Technically, Linux device drivers are actually Linux kernel modules. Kernel modules dynamically plug into the running Linux kernel and provide the connection to the device.

Here's one way to check if a wireless network interface works with Ubuntu:

1. **Plug the PCMCIA or USB wireless network interface into your computer.**

   If you're using a laptop with an embedded wireless network device, make sure it's turned on. Install a PCI wireless network interface on your desktop computer if using such a device.

2. **From the GNOME menu bar, choose System⇨Administration⇨ Networking.**

   If you haven't recently performed an administrative task, the Enter Your Password to Perform Administrative Tasks dialog opens.

3. **Type your password if prompted.**

   The Network Settings dialog opens, showing all of your network interfaces.

4. **Look for a wireless interface option.**

If the Network Settings dialog shows a wireless network interface, wireless networking is supported, and you can start configuring the device. Proceed to one of the following sections that matches your wireless network's capabilities:

✔ **"Unencrypted AP":** Use only unencrypted wireless networks if no other option exists. Public APs often provide unencrypted service.

Be careful when using unencrypted public networks. You should assume that all your communications are being monitored. Try to use a virtual private network (VPN) if at all possible to encrypt your network traffic. (Appendix B shows how to use OpenSSH to create your own VPN.) Your computer is more vulnerable to attack when using such networks because it's easier for hackers to use the network to exploit any vulnerabilities in your computer.

- ✓ **"WEP-encrypted AP":** WEP encryption is better than no encryption but can be broken with a moderate amount of effort. If possible, you should upgrade to WPA2, or at least WPA, rather than continue to use WEP.

- ✓ **"WPA-encrypted AP":** WPA offers adequate encryption, which falls between WEP and WPA2. You should definitely use WPA in place of WEP, but use WPA2 if your equipment supports that protocol.

- ✓ **"WPA2-encrypted AP":** WPA2 offers the best wireless network encryption. You can sleep well at night if you use properly configured WPA2.

Obtaining a wireless network interface

If you need to purchase or borrow a wireless network interface, there are nearly 200 commercially available devices to choose from. Ubuntu provides a convenient and detailed table at `https://help.ubuntu.com/community/ WifiDocs/WirelessCardsSupported`. This table provides information about the manufacturer and model plus whether and how well each device works with Ubuntu Linux. You can use this information to find a Linux-capable, wireless network interface before purchasing one.

Some manufacturers place a Linux sticker on their products. Look for the decal before purchasing a wireless device.

Connecting to Access Points

The process of connecting to an access point depends on the type of encryption it uses. The following sections show how to connect to

- ✓ Unencrypted APs

  This book shows how to securely encrypt *messages* over unencrypted *networks*.

- ✓ WEP-encrypted APs

- ✓ WPA-encrypted APs

Unencrypted APs

Connecting to an unencrypted AP is the easiest way to use your Ubuntu computer on a wireless network.

Public WiFi hot spots usually aren't encrypted.

Displaying your network information

You can use the lshw utility to view your Ubuntu computer's network interfaces. Type the command `lshw -C network` and you see all information about your interfaces. For instance, the following listing shows my computer's interfaces:

```
*-network:0
     description: Wireless
interface
     product: BCM4306
802.11b/g Wireless LAN
Controller
     vendor: Broadcom
Corporation
     physical id: 9
     bus info: pci@00:09.0
     logical name: wlan0
     version: 02
     serial:
00:90:4b:48:4a:25
     width: 32 bits
     clock: 33MHz
     capabilities:
bus_master cap_list
ethernet physical wireless
     configuration:
broadcast=yes
driver=ndiswrapper
driverversion=1.22
firmware=Broadcom,03/19/20
03, 3.10.53.0
ip=192.168.2.101 link=yes
multicast=yes
wireless=IEEE 802.11b
     resources:
iomemory:d0004000-d0005fff
irq:10
*-network:1
     description: Ethernet
interface
     product: DP83815
(MacPhyter) Ethernet
Controller
```

```
     vendor: National
Semiconductor Corporation
     physical id: 12
     bus info: pci@00:12.0
     logical name: eth0
     version: 00
     serial:
00:0d:9d:82:22:3c
     size: 10MB/s
     capacity: 100MB/s
     width: 32 bits
     clock: 33MHz
     capabilities:
bus_master cap_list
ethernet physical tp mii
fibre 10bt 10bt-fd 100bt
100bt-fd autonegociation
     configuration:
autonegociation=on
broadcast=yes
driver=natsemi
driverversion=1.07+LK1.0.1
7 duplex=half link=no
multicast=yes port=twisted
pair speed=10MB/s
     resources:
ioport:8c00-8cff
iomemory:d000a000-d000afff
irq:11
```

This output shows detailed information about your network interfaces. Note that if lshw shows the wireless network interface to be disabled, you haven't loaded the necessary driver. In that case, you might be able to use a Windows driver to run the device. The "Using a Windows Device Driver" section later in this chapter describes how to use a Windows device driver to enable the wireless device under Ubuntu.

If Ubuntu supports your WiFi network adapter, making the connection is easy. You just need to know the name (ESSID) of the network. Follow these steps:

1. **Turn on your computer's WiFi network interface.**

   • *If you're using an external PCMCIA or USB WiFi network interface, plug it into your computer.*

   • *If your desktop PC doesn't have a WiFi interface, install one in your desktop PC.*

2. **If necessary, log in to your Ubuntu user account.**

3. **From the GNOME menu bar, choose System⇨Administration⇨ Networking.**

   If you haven't recently performed an administrative task, the Enter Your Password to Perform Administrative Tasks dialog opens.

4. **Type your password if prompted.**

   The Network Settings dialog opens. Refer to Figure 7-1, which shows a typical configuration including a wireless network interface.

5. **Select the Wireless Connection option and click the Properties button.**

   The Settings for Interface dialog opens. Figure 7-2 shows the dialog.

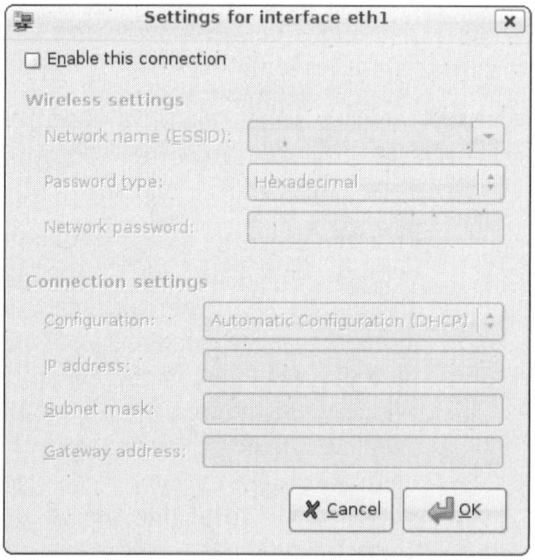

Figure 7-2:
The Settings
for Interface
dialog.

6. **Type the name of the AP you want to connect to in the Network Name (ESSID) text box.**

   The AP name isn't case sensitive.

   When you're connecting to an unencrypted network, leave the Network Password text box blank.

Secure Sockets Layer (SSL) encryption

Using an unencrypted connection is not necessarily as unsecure as it sounds. Using Secure Sockets Layer (SSL) encryption protects your communication even on unencrypted wireless networks.

✔ Most Web sites that conduct business or collect sensitive information use Secure Sockets Layer (SSL) encryption.

✔ You can configure your e-mail client to use SSL to encrypt incoming and outgoing messages.

You can tell if you're connected to an SSL-enabled Web site by the closed lock symbol at the bottom-left or bottom-right corner of your browser. SSL Web addresses always are preceded by the `https` prefix, not the non-encrypted `http` prefix.

If you don't care about anyone being theoretically able to view your Web browsing habits, you should feel comfortable about connecting to unencrypted wireless networks. Make sure you're using an SSL connection when conducting business or reading/sending sensitive information. I recommend always using SSL to send and receive e-mail whether using an unencrypted or encrypted connection.

If you're running your own unencrypted wireless network AP, you have to consider uninvited guests mooching your network resources. Anyone in your immediate vicinity, say 100 to 200 feet (or further with advanced wireless equipment) can connect to your access point and use your Internet connection; they can also sniff and possibly attack your private network. If you want to run an unencrypted wireless network, consider using the OpenSSH-based VPN described in Appendix B to protect both your information and resources.

Appendix B shows how to use and build an unencrypted wireless network and use OpenSSH to create a virtual private network (VPN) to authenticate and encrypt all Web and e-mail traffic on that network.

Figure 7-3 shows an example dialog with the ESSID set to `plinky`.

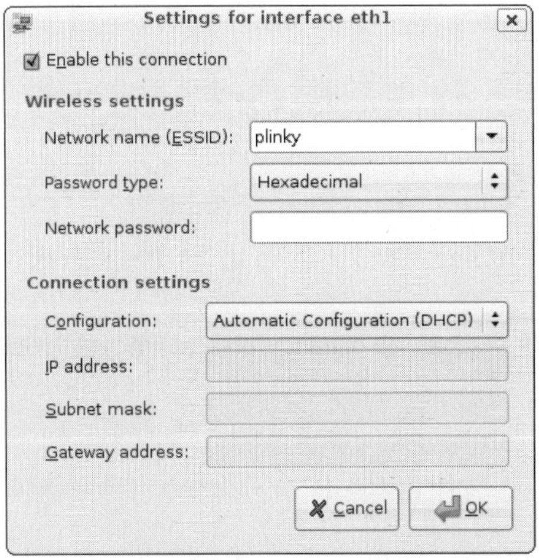

Figure 7-3: Example of the Settings for Interface dialog.

Settings for interface eth1

☑ Enable this connection

Wireless settings

Network name (ESSID): plinky

Password type: Hexadecimal

Network password:

Connection settings

Configuration: Automatic Configuration (DHCP)

IP address:

Subnet mask:

Gateway address:

✘ Cancel   ◀ OK

7. **Click the OK button.**

   Control returns to the Network Settings dialog.

8. **Select the Wireless Interface check box.**

   The Activating Network Interface dialog opens while Ubuntu connects to the AP — the WiFi network interface connects to the AP, and the AP gives your computer its IP address and other essential network parameters. The dialog closes when the connection is made, and your Ubuntu computer is connected to the wireless network.

Anyone in the vicinity with a wireless-capable computer with the right — easily obtainable — software can read your communications if you don't use encryption.

WEP-encrypted APs

Using WEP (wired equivalent privacy) to encrypt your WiFi communication is almost as easy as using an unencrypted connection.

Unfortunately, cracking WEP-based encryption is relatively easy, too. WEP gives you enough protection unless someone specifically wants entry to your network.

If the information that you will transmit over the wireless network is too valuable to put at risk, don't use WEP.

Configuring Ubuntu to connect to a WEP-encrypted network is easy. You just need to know the name (ESSID) of the network and the WEP password. Follow these steps:

1. **Make sure that your wireless device is ready to use before connecting to a wireless network.**

   You might need to either turn on your computer's internal WiFi network interface or plug an external PCMCIA or USB WiFi network interface into your computer.

2. **If necessary, log in to your Ubuntu user account.**

3. **From the GNOME menu bar, choose System➪Administration➪ Networking.**

   If you haven't recently performed an administrative task, the Enter Your Password to Perform Administrative Tasks dialog opens.

4. **Type your password if prompted.**

   The Network Settings dialog opens. Refer to Figure 7-1, which shows a typical configuration including a wireless network interface.

5. **Select the Wireless Connection option and click the Properties button.**

   The Settings for Interface dialog opens.

6. **Type the name of the AP you want to connect to in the Network Name (ESSID) text box.**

   Refer to Figure 7-3 for a sample ESSID (wireless network name) entry.

7. **From the Password Type drop-down menu, choose the Plain (ASCII) option if that's what your AP uses.**

   If you enter a plain-text password, that password is ultimately converted to binary. However, plain text is much easier to remember than hexadecimal.

   Hexadecimal is an easier way to represent a binary number. Rather than work directly with 1s and 0s, hexadecimal (*hex,* for short) converts four binary bits into an alphanumeric character. For instance, the number 1 (in decimal) is 0001 in binary and 1 in hex. The number 2 is 0010 in binary and 2 in hex, skipping to 9 is 1001 and 9 in hex. However, the number 10 is 1010 in binary but A in hex. The maximum value in hex is F, which is 15 in decimal and 1111 in binary.

8. **Type your WEP encryption key (either in hexadecimal or plain text format) in the Network Password text box.**

9. **Click the OK button.**

   Control returns to the Network Settings dialog.

10. **Select the Wireless Interface check box.**

    The Activating Network Interface dialog opens while Ubuntu connects to the AP — the WiFi network interface connects to the AP, and the AP gives your computer its IP address and other essential network parameters. The dialog closes after the connection is made.

WPA-encrypted APs

The IEEE designed the 802.11i wireless security standard, which is commonly called WPA2, to solve WEP's shortcomings. The Wi-Fi Alliance represents wireless device manufacturers' adopted parts of the 802.11i standard during its development to create an interim version they called WPA. WPA encryption is better than WEP, and WPA2 improves upon WPA.

WPA doesn't completely protect your wireless network but it's more secure than WEP. WPA2, however, gives you rock-solid encryption. Today, WPA is still more commonly available than WPA2. Use WPA2, if at all possible, and WPA if not.

Configuring WPA2 or WPA is more difficult than using either an unencrypted or WEP-protected connection. Neither WPA2 nor WPA is as widely supported by Linux as WEP. I show you how to use WPA if your WiFi network interface can support it.

Using WPA2/WPA requires a two-step configuration process. You need to do the following to use WPA2:

1. Install the NetworkManager package.

2. Configure your WiFi device for WPA2 or WPA encryption using the NetworkManager.

The following two sections describe how to perform each step.

Installing the NetworkManager

You can use the Synaptic Package Manager to install NetworkManager from an Ubuntu Internet-based software repository. You need to connect to the Internet to access the package. Unfortunately, your Ubuntu disc doesn't contain the package. Follow these steps:

1. **Use Chapter 6, 8, or 9 to connect your Ubuntu computer to the Internet — if you don't already have a connection.**

   The NetworkManager package isn't very large. You can easily use a dialup Internet connection to install the package.

2. **If necessary, log in to your Ubuntu user account.**

3. **From the GNOME menu bar, choose System⇨Administration⇨ Synaptic Package Manager.**

   If you haven't recently performed an administrative task, the Enter Your Password to Perform Administrative Tasks dialog opens.

4. **Type your password in the Password text box and press the Enter key.**

   The Synaptic Package Manager opens.

5. **Click the Search button.**

   The Find dialog opens.

6. **Type `network=manager` in the Search text box and click the Search button.**

   The Search dialog exits, and you see the network-manager and two related packages displayed in the Synaptic Package Manager window.

7. **Select the Network-Manager-Gnome check box and choose the Mark for Installation option from the drop-down menu that opens.**

   The Mark Additional Required Changes dialog opens. The dialog tells you that the network-manager-gnome package and several other packages will be installed along with the network-manager-gnome package.

8. **Click the Mark button.**

   Control returns to the Synaptic Package Manager window, which shows the network-manager and network-manager-gnome packages marked for installation.

9. **Click the Apply button.**

   The Apply dialog opens, telling you that you're about to install packages.

10. **Click the Apply button.**

    The Applying Changes dialog opens, showing the progress of the package download and installation process. The Close button activates when the installation process finishes.

11. **Click the Close button.**

    Control returns to the Synaptic Package Manager window.

12. **Click the File menu and choose Quit.**

 You can manually install the NetworkManager using the `apt-get` command. Open a GNOME Terminal window and type the command `sudo apt-get install network-manager-gnome`. Enter your password if prompted and `apt-get` downloads and then installs the network-manager-gnome and network-manager packages.

The NetworkManager is installed but not quite yet ready to use.

Disabling network interfaces to enable NetworkManager

The NetworkManager can't manage preconfigured wireless network interfaces. In order to use NetworkManager to control your network interfaces, you must first disable them.

Disabling a device is simple using the Ubuntu network configuration utility:

1. **From the GNOME menu bar, choose System⇨Administration⇨ Networking.**

   The Network Settings dialog opens. Refer to Figure 7-1 to see the dialog.

2. **Click to select a network interface.**

   In this case, you should select the wireless network interface that you want to use the NetworkManager to configure. The network interface is highlighted when you click it.

3. **Click the Properties button.**

   The Settings for Interface dialog opens. Refer to Figure 7-2 to see a sample dialog.

4. **Deselect the Enable this Connection radio button.**

   Click the button only if it's already selected (enabled). You want to disable the interface in order to use the NetworkManager to control the interface. Clicking a disabled interface will enable it, which is what we don't want to do.

5. **Click the OK button.**

   Control returns to the Network Settings window.

6. **Repeat Steps 2 through 5 to select and disable every network interface that you wish to configure with the NetworkManager.**

You could also manually disable devices by editing the `/etc/network/ interfaces` file:

1. **Make a backup copy of the file — for instance, `cp /etc/network/ interfaces /etc/network/interfaces.bak`.**

2. **Delete every line except the two relating to the loopback (lo) device.**

The NetworkManager can control and configure every device that you disable. This includes wired Ethernet and dialup modem devices.

Configuring your wireless network interface using NetworkManager

In this section, I tell you how you can configure your wireless network interface to use WPA or WPA2 encryption.

Not all wireless network interfaces can use WPA or WPA2. Older 802-11b-based devices generally can't use WPA or WPA2; the exceptions are ones whose manufacturers provide firmware updates — check your manufacturer's Web site for information about obtaining and installing an upgrade. Newer 802-11g devices can use WPA but not necessarily WPA2. Once again, check your manufacturer's Web site for your device's capabilities.

When you've installed the NetworkManager and disabled any devices you want to control with it, you're ready to go. The configuration process starts with you logging out and then back in to your user account.

By default, Ubuntu displays the Network Monitor icon on the upper GNOME panel. The Network Monitor icon looks similar to the NetworkManager icon. I get easily confused — really easily — so I like to remove the Network Settings icon to ease the strain on my brain. Right-click the Network Settings icon and select the Remove from Panel option, and that bit of confusion ends.

1. **From the GNOME menu bar, choose System⇨Quit.**

2. **Click the Log Out option in the dialog that opens.**

Ubuntu logs you out of your user account. You're automatically logged back in after 10 seconds if you're working from a live Ubuntu disc. Otherwise, when working from a permanent Ubuntu installation, you must type your username and password to log back in to your user account.

When you've logged back in to your user account, the NetworkManager recognizes your wireless devices — and any others that you disabled in the section "Disabling network interfaces to enable NetworkManager." The NetworkManager icon appears toward the left side of the upper GNOME panel, as shown in Figure 7-4; note that the red exclamation symbol indicates that no network interfaces have been configured.

Figure 7-4:
The Network Manager icon in the GNOME panel.

Click the NetworkManager icon and a dialog opens, showing the state of your network interfaces. Figure 7-5 shows an example of a laptop computer with three network interfaces — a wired Ethernet interface, which is inactive, and two wireless networks: blinky and plinky. (In this case, the Broadcom wireless interface is built into the laptop, but Linux doesn't provide a WPA-capable driver. Therefore, I'm using an external PCMCIA Proxim interface, based on the supported Atheros chipset, which is WPA capable. In this example, I use the Proxim network interface to connect to the plinky wireless network.)

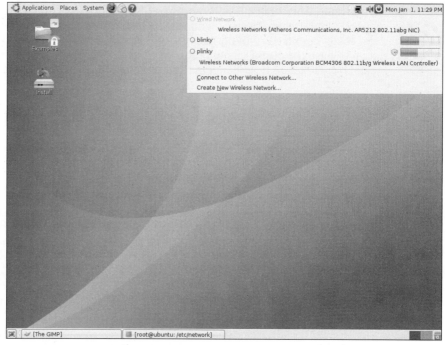

Figure 7-5:
Network
Manager
showing
three
network
interfaces.

Follow these steps to configure the Ubuntu computer to connect to a wireless network:

1. **Click the NetworkManager icon.**

   A dialog similar to the one shown in Figure 7-5 opens, showing the available network interfaces and the available wireless networks.

2. **Select the Connect to Other Wireless Network option.**

   The Connect to Other Wireless Network dialog opens. Figure 7-6 shows an example dialog showing an Atheros wireless network interface.

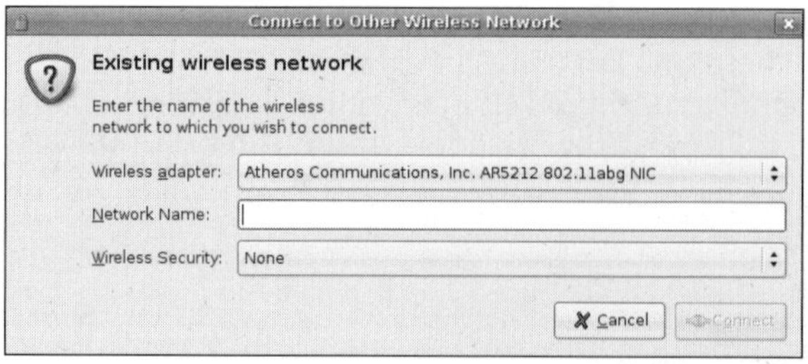

Figure 7-6:
The Connect
to Other
Wireless
Network
dialog.

3. **If you want to use a different wireless adapter than the one shown in the Wireless Adapter drop-down menu, click the menu and choose the network interface you want to use to make your connection.**

   Figure 7-6 shows the Atheros-based wireless network interface that I happen to be using. You'll see the network interface(s) installed on your computer.

4. **Type the name of the wireless network you want to connect to in the Network Name text box.**

   The network name is the ESSID of the AP you want to connect to.

5. **From the Wireless Security drop-down menu, select WPA2 Personal — or if that's unavailable, select WPA Personal.**

   You might have to select WPA2 Enterprise or WPA Enterprise if you're connecting to the wireless network of a large- or medium-sized organization. Organizations that allow more than a handful of people to connect to their wireless network almost always use a centrally managed WPA2 or WPA encryption key distribution system. Using individual encryption keys, like we do, is unwieldy and ultimately unmanageable. You need to obtain the necessary information from the organization's help desk or system administrative staff if you're connecting to such a wireless network.

6. **Type the network name you're connecting to in the Network Name text box.**

   NetworkManager uses the wpa_supplicant utility when configuring wireless network encryption. The wpa_supplicant might sound like technology borrowed from *Blade Runner,* but it's really just a Linux program used to configure a wireless network interface to use WPA2 or WPA. Before NetworkManager was invented, configuring a wireless network interface to use WPA2 or WPA was a manual, two-step process. First, you configured the network interface to connect to an AP. Second, you used wpa_supplicant to configure the network to use WPA2 or WPA encryption. You can still perform the manual configuration, but using NetworkManager is much easier.

7. **If you want to see the password as you type it, select the Show Password radio button.**

   Selecting to display the password (pass phrase) option displays the characters of the pass phrase as you enter them in Step 8. If you don't select this option, the characters are displayed as dots as you type. Being able to see the actual characters helps avoid mistakes because pass phrases should be at least 20 characters in length.

8. **Type the WPA2 or WPA pass phrase in the Password text box.**

9. **Click the Connect button.**

   The NetworkManager icon gyrates as it connects to your wireless network. When connected to the wireless network, the Create Default Keyring dialog, shown in Figure 7-7, opens.

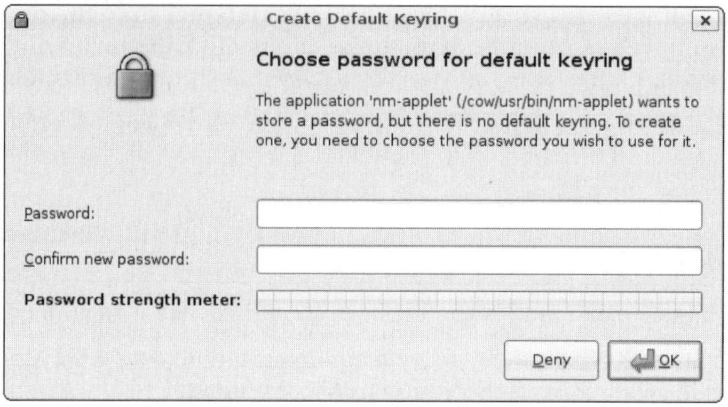

Create Default Keyring ✕

Choose password for default keyring

The application 'nm-applet' (/cow/usr/bin/nm-applet) wants to store a password, but there is no default keyring. To create one, you need to choose the password you wish to use for it.

Password:

Confirm new password:

Password strength meter:

Deny   ◀ OK

Figure 7-7:
The Create Default Keyring dialog.

Ubuntu wants to encrypt and store the pass phrase you used to make the wireless connection for later use. Storing the pass phrase makes using it in the future much easier. You won't have to retype in the necessarily long — remember, 20 characters or more — pass phrase.

1. **Select a reasonable password and type it in the Password text box.**

2. **Retype the password in the Confirm New Password text box.**

   The Password Strength Meter shows how hard the password will be to crack. Try to use a password of at least 75 percent difficulty.

3. **Click the OK button.**

   Your WPA2 or WPA encryption key (pass phrase) is saved in the GNOME key ring. You're prompted to enter your GNOME key ring password you just entered whenever you want to configure the wireless network in the future.

If the NetworkManager doesn't make the connection, its icon continues displaying the red exclamation symbol. In that case, you should check that the encryption type and pass phrase of the AP you're trying to connect to are correct. You might, for instance, be trying to use WPA2 when the AP or, more likely, your wireless network interface supports only WPA. I recommend selecting WPA if WPA2 fails.

Congratulations! You're connected to a wireless network using either the reasonably secure WPA encryption or the very secure WPA2 encryption. You can use your wireless network, secure in the knowledge that it is very, very difficult for anyone to sniff your wireless network communications.

Using a Windows Device Driver

The Network Driver Interface Specification (NDIS) standard was co-developed by the Microsoft and the 3Com corporations to develop network interface drivers. Windows network interface adapters — also called *network interface cards* — all use NDIS-based drivers.

Unfortunately, not all network interface manufacturers provide Linux drivers for their products. Nor do all manufacturers provide the specifications that would allow the open source community to build compatible Linux drivers.

I'd like to take this opportunity to thank the manufacturers who provide Linux drivers or the specifications to construct Linux drivers!

Fortunately, when you can't find a Linux driver for your wireless network interface, you might be able use the proprietary Windows driver. The `ndiswrapper` utility wraps the Windows driver so it can be used on your Ubuntu computer. That's cool!

The rest of this chapter shows how to locate your Windows wireless network interface and then copy it to and load it on your Ubuntu file partition. When loaded, you can configure your interface using the instructions described elsewhere in this chapter.

If your wireless interface requires `ndiswrapper` and you're planning to *remove* Windows from your Ubuntu computer, you need to make a copy of the Windows driver *before* you remove Windows.

Discovering your Windows wireless network interface driver

You need to find the wireless network interface driver that your Windows computer uses before Ubuntu can use it. The best way to find the driver is to see what your Windows computer says about it. In this section, you can boot to your Windows operating system, locate the device driver, and copy it to an easy-to-remember location.

1. **Boot or reboot your Ubuntu computer into the Windows operating system.**

   The following instructions assume you've either installed Ubuntu on a computer that also contains Windows in a dual-boot configuration, or you're running a live instance of Ubuntu.

2. **Log in to an account with administrative privileges or the Administrator account itself.**

3. **Click the Start button and select the Control Panel.**

   The Control Panel window opens.

4. **Double-click the System icon.**

   The System window opens.

5. **Click the Hardware tab.**

6. **Click the Device Manager button.**

   The Device Manager window opens.

7. **Click the plus (+) symbol next to the Network Adapters option.**

   A submenu opens, displaying all the network devices on your computer.

8. **Right-click the wireless networking interface and select the Properties option.**

   A Properties dialog opens, showing the properties and other information about your wireless network interface.

9. **Click the Driver tab.**

10. **Click the Driver Details button.**

    The Driver Details dialog opens, showing the location of the device driver file.

    The file most likely resides in the `C:\WINDOWS\system32\DRIVERS` folder. For instance, my Windows computer uses a built-in Broadcom wireless network interface that uses the BCMWL5.SYS driver, which is found in the `C:\WINDOWS\system32\DRIVERS` folder.

11. **Write down the location of the driver.**

Now that you've identified your computer's wireless network interface and its driver, you can use it with Ubuntu.

Copying the Windows driver files to Ubuntu

The Ubuntu `ndiswrapper` utility needs access to the driver file and its corresponding information file — such as files with the `.inf` suffix.

You might be able to find your wireless driver and information files on

- ✔ A CD-ROM that came with your computer or your network card
- ✔ The network card manufacturer's Web site
- ✔ Your existing installation of Windows

The following instructions describe how to copy those files from your Windows hard drive partition to your Ubuntu partition.

1. **Reboot your computer to Ubuntu.**

2. **From the GNOME menu bar, choose Applications⇨Accessories⇨ Terminal.**

   A GNOME Terminal window opens.

3. **Mount your Windows C: drive.**

   The mount command depends on your computer's setup. For example:

   - *If your computer uses the first partition as the C: drive, type the following command:*

     ```
     sudo mount -t ntfs /dev/hda1 /mnt
     ```

   - *If your computer uses the first partition as a recovery partition and the second partition as the C: drive, type the following command:*

     ```
     sudo mount -t ntfs /dev/hda2 /mnt
     ```

4. **Type your password if prompted.**

5. **Type the command to copy the Windows wireless network interface driver to your Ubuntu computer, like this:**

   ```
   sudo cp /mnt/windows/system32/drivers/driver.sys /
       etc/ndiswrapper
   ```

   Substitute your driver's filename for *driver.sys*. For instance, to copy my Broadcom driver, I type the following command:

   ```
   sudo cp /mnt/windows/system32/drivers/bcmwl5.sys /
       etc/ndiswrapper
   ```

6. **Type the following command and press the Enter key:**

   ```
   sudo cp `find /mnt -iname driver.inf` /etc/ndiswrapper
   ```

   If, for instance, your driver filename is m2500, type this command:

   ```
   sudo cp `find /mnt -iname bcmwl5.inf` /etc/ndiswrapper
   ```

   This command locates the driver file on the Windows partition and copies it to the /etc/ndiswrapper directory.

7. **Type the following command to unmount the Windows partition:**

```
sudo umount /mnt
```

Next, you need to install the `ndiswrapper` utility on your Ubuntu computer before using the Windows driver. The following section shows you how.

Installing the ndiswrapper utility

The following instructions install the `ndiswrapper` packages directly from your Ubuntu disc:

1. **Insert your Ubuntu disc in your computer's DVD or CD-ROM drive.**

   Ubuntu automatically mounts your CD-ROM or DVD disc.

2. **If necessary, log in to your Ubuntu user account.**

3. **From the GNOME menu bar, choose Applications⇨Accessories⇨ Terminal.**

   A GNOME Terminal window opens.

4. **Type the command to install the ndiswrapper-utils and ndiswrapper-common packages:**

   • *On a permanent Ubuntu computer, type this command:*

   ```
   sudo dpkg -i /media/cdrom0/pool/main/n/
       ndiswrapper*
   ```

   • *On a live Ubuntu computer, type this command:*

   ```
   sudo dpkg -i /cdrom/pool/main/n/ndiswrapper*
   ```

   The `ndiswrapper` utility is installed and ready to use.

Loading the Windows driver

Use the `ndiswrapper` utility to load the Windows wireless network interface driver into your Ubuntu computer's kernel. When installed, you can configure and start using your wireless computer. Follow these steps:

1. **From the GNOME menu bar, choose Applications⇨Accessories ⇨ Terminal.**

   A GNOME Terminal window opens.

2. **Type the following command to install the Windows driver file:**

```
sudo ndiswrapper -i /etc/ndiswrapper/driver.inf
```

For instance, to load the driver for a Broadcom wireless network interface, type this:

```
sudo ndiswrapper -i /etc/ndiswrapper/bcmw15.inf
```

The ndiswrapper utility uses the Windows information — any file ending in .inf — to load the actual driver file.

3. **Type your password if prompted.**

4. **Type the following command to configure Ubuntu to load the file whenever it's rebooted:**

```
sudo ndiswrapper -m
```

If you execute this command, your Windows driver will automatically load every time you reboot.

You can see all the Windows drivers loaded on your Ubuntu computer by either

- *Typing the command* ndiswrapper -1.

  The utility lists all the drivers it has loaded.

- *Reading information about loaded drivers in the* /var/log/ syslog *file.*

5. **Load the ndiswrapper kernel module by typing the following command:**

```
sudo modprobe ndiswrapper
```

You can verify that the ndiswrapper module is loaded by typing the following command:

```
lsmod | grep ndiswrapper
```

When ndiswrapper is loaded, Ubuntu makes the wlan0 network interface available for use. You can see the interface by typing iwconfig wlan0.

You configure your wireless network interface using either of these Ubuntu utilities described in this chapter:

- Network Administration Tool (the default Ubuntu configuration utility)
- NetworkManager

Chapter 8

Broadening Your Horizons with Broadband

*B*roadband networking brings Internet performance that previously was the exclusive province of large businesses, government, and universities. Broadband provides people like us the ability to download information and surf the Internet at high speed for affordable prices. There's no dialing and waiting, either, like there is for a dialup Internet connection, because you're always online with broadband.

This chapter helps you select between the two dominant broadband technologies — cable and DSL — and use them with Ubuntu. I tell you how you can make a reasonable choice about what system will work best for you.

Choosing between DSL and Cable

If you're choosing broadband Internet service, the first hurdle is availability. Consider these factors:

✔ Some telephone lines aren't equipped for DSL service.

DSL service degrades quickly as the distance to the DSL provider's central office (CO) increases. DSL doesn't work much farther than eight miles from the central office.

✔ Some cable TV companies don't offer Internet service at all homes (or any homes).

Waiting for WiMax

It's likely that in the near future, you'll be able to use WiMax microwave Internet service in place of cable and DSL modems. WiMax will make it possible for Internet service providers (ISPs) to sell you broadband Internet connections. The system will create zones, or cells, of access similar to that of cellphones.

WiMax (short for Worldwide Interoperability for Microwave Access) is the certification given to equipment that adheres to the IEEE 802.16 standards suite.

✔ The 802.16 standards describe how a new generation of wireless devices will work.

✔ The 802.16e standard will be used by vendors to provide the "last mile" connections to their customers.

This will help expand access to Internet broadband throughout the world; it will also help reduce the price of current broadband technology by expanding competition.

If you have only one broadband option, the decision is simple. But if you have a choice, the decision, basically, is a trade between cost and download speed.

✔ **Cost:** DSL generally is cheaper.

In my experience, the difference is about $10–$15. You might be able to compare DSL providers and find a lower price. (This chapter explains the ins and outs of DSL shopping. See the "Selecting your DSL provider" section.)

DSL modems can interfere with your telephones and other electronic devices. You must put a telephone line filter between all telephones and the jacks they connect to. DSL modems use high-frequency connections, while telephones use low-frequency ones. The filters electronically separate the two types of devices. The filters provided with DSL modems usually work, but in some cases, especially homes with older wiring, you can get interference.

✔ **Speed:** Cable generally provides faster download speeds.

Cable networks are optimized for downloading data. They sacrifice *upload* (data going out from your computer to the Internet) speed because most Internet activities download more data than they upload. Cable uploads are generally slower than DSL uploads.

Cable Internet service costs more if you don't subscribe to cable television service.

Most DSL and cable Internet providers don't require long-term commitments to subscribe to their service. Because most providers let you rent their equipment — cable or DSL modem — you can try one with the knowledge that you can inexpensively switch if you aren't satisfied. (You might have to pay one-time charges, such as shipping.)

The rest of this chapter describes how to use either DSL or cable modems.

Using Cable Modems

Using a cable modem is a straightforward process. You only need to subscribe, connect, and configure.

Subscribing and getting your cable modem

You need to subscribe with your cable Internet service provider (ISP) to gain access to their service. You can lease a cable modem from the service provider or you can purchase a cable modem from electronics stores in many places.

Your ISP will ship your cable modem if you subscribe via telephone or the Internet. You can bring the modem home with you if you subscribe to the cable ISP service and purchase the device at a store.

Your cable Internet service provider must configure its network for your cable modem before you can start using it. Enabling your cable modem is a straightforward process. Many ISPs register your modem at the time of purchase. For instance, if you purchase a modem as part of a package at a retailer, the CATV will register and activate it at that point.

If your cable modem isn't registered, all you should have to do is contact your ISP and give them the machine address (MAC) displayed on the back of the modem.

I've had cable Internet service for a number of years now. When I first subscribed, I did so over the phone and was sent the cable modem, which I rented. Later, when that modem died, I was pleased that I could purchase one from a consumer electronics store. I brought the modem home and registered its MAC address over the phone and regained my connection. More recently, I subscribed my parents to a cable ISP and purchased their cable modem, which I registered at the store. Their cable modem worked right out of the box when I installed it in their home.

The registration process is necessary because the CATV ISP must have your cable modem's MAC address to allow it to work on its network. Other than giving the company the MAC address, that's all the configuration you have to do.

The big picture

Most of the work of using cable Internet service involves going to a store or making a phone call to obtain your cable modem. The overall process is described below.

1. **Subscribe with your cable Internet provider and obtain a cable modem.**

   You can make the subscription over the phone — a little ironic? — or via the Internet, or in many consumer electronic stores. (See Chapter 9 for instructions on using dialup modems.)

2. **Connect your cable modem.**

You'll need to wait for Jim Carrey the Cable Guy to come by if you don't already have CATV (cable television) service at your home. He'll be there between 8 a.m. and 5 p.m. someday.

After you have your cable, you just have to connect the modem to the cable.

3. **Connect your computer or LAN to the cable modem.**

   You can connect your computer directly to the cable modem or through a LAN.

Connecting your computer and cable modem

After you obtain your cable modem, the process of connecting and configuration is straightforward. You should have the following equipment:

- ✔ **Cable modem:** Current cable modems use the DOCSIS (Data Over Cable Service Interface Specification) protocol.
- ✔ **CATV splitter:** This device connects to the incoming CATV cable and splits the output in two.
- ✔ **Extra cables:** Most cable modems come with an extra CATV cable.
- ✔ **Instruction manual:** This comes with the cable modem package.

First, you need to connect the cable modem to your cable service.

1. **Disconnect (unscrew) the cable from the wall jack.**

   The cable will most likely be connected to a television, cable box, or VCR.

2. **Connect a spare cable to the cable wall jack.**

3. **Connect the splitter's input connector to the cable you just installed.**

   You can purchase an inexpensive cable splitter from any electronics store. You can even find them in many drug stores and convenience stores.

4. **Connect a spare cable to one of the splitter's output connectors.**

5. **Connect the other end to the cable modem's input port.**

6. **Reconnect your original cable to the splitter's other output port.**

After you make all the physical connections, you need to make sure your Ubuntu computer is configured to work with the cable modem. The following section describes the simple process.

Configuring your Ubuntu computer to work with your cable modem

Cable modems use DHCP — dynamic host control protocol — and Ubuntu also uses DHCP by default. You can skip this section unless your Ubuntu computer is configured to use a static IP address.

Ubuntu, of course, makes the process simple and easy.

1. **From the GNOME menu bar, choose System➪Administration➪ Networking.**

   The Enter Your Password to Perform Administrative Tasks dialog opens.

2. **Type your password and click OK.**

   The Networking Settings dialog opens.

3. **Click the Ethernet connection and click the Properties button.**

   The Interface Properties dialog opens.

4. **Click and select DHCP from the Configuration drop-down menu, only if your Ethernet connection currently is set to use a static IP address.**

   Chapter 6 explains the differences in static and dynamic IP addresses.

   Your Ubuntu computer starts to use a dynamic IP address.

5. **Click OK.**

Cable modems are designed to use the dynamic host configuration protocol (DHCP). Setting your Ubuntu computer (if it isn't already so configured) to use DHCP enables your computer to get its IP address and other important network settings directly from the cable modem. You should now be set to use your new cable Internet connection. Surf's up!

Using DSL Modems

Much of the technology behind plain old telephone service (POTS) is more than a century old. The technology is based on the human voice and limits the speeds that dialup modems (also referred to as *data/fax modems*) can achieve. However, it's possible to use POTS wiring to obtain faster and better Internet connections than is possible with plain old dialup modems.

The big picture

To get a DSL-based Internet connection, you need to subscribe with your local telephone company, and obtain and then configure a DSL modem. The process works as follows:

1. **Subscribe to DSL service and obtain a DSL modem.**

   DSL is limited by the distance you live from the telephone company's central office (CO). Therefore, DSL might not be available if you live too far away.

   After you subscribe to DSL service, your telephone company will send you a DSL modem. DSL modems are also available in some consumer electronics stores, but check with your provider first.

2. **Connect your DSL modem to your computer and telephone jack.**

3. **Configure your computer to work with the DSL modem.**

   You simply have to tell your computer to use DHCP and your DSL modem will configure its network connection.

4. **Configure your DSL modem to connect and authenticate with your DSL provider.**

   You must configure your modem to connect and authenticate with your DSL provider.

Telephone companies make use of their POTS infrastructure by providing DSL connections. DSL uses the same old wires as telephones do but at a different frequency. DSL also bypasses the voice-oriented technology that we all use to make phone calls. DSL piggybacks on the existing equipment to provide much better Internet service than is available via dialup modems.

The following sections describe the process in detail.

Selecting your DSL provider

You're pretty much limited by geography when selecting a DSL provider. In the United States, national telephone companies like AT&T and Verizon do offer DSL service in some areas. However, your highest probability of obtaining service is through your local company. Other countries will have their own vagaries.

Contact your local telephone company and find out what they offer. You can also visit sites such as www.consumer.att.com and www.verizon.com to find out if they provide local service.

DSL lags behind cable Internet in terms of retail outlet availability, but it's catching up. I had DSL years ago but could purchase or lease equipment only from my telephone company; on the other hand, I could purchase cable modems at local stores — a big advantage. Now, you can find some stores that offer DSL subscription packages. Subscribe at the store and you can purchase a DSL modem. Unfortunately, it takes longer to activate DSL service than it does for Internet cable. For instance, I wanted to get my parents DSL but would have had to wait for over a week for it to activate.

After you subscribe, you need to activate the DSL modem. Activation occurs automatically if you purchase a package at a retail outlet or directly from the telephone company. However, if you purchase a DSL modem separately, you'll have to call the DSL service provider and register the device.

Your DSL provider will give you a username and password that authenticates your DSL modem to their service.

Connecting to your DSL modem

You get the following equipment when you purchase or lease a DSL modem:

- ✔ **DSL modem:** This is the device that converts your computer network traffic into a signal that can be carried over telephone (POTS) cables.

- ✔ **Extra telephone cable: Connects your DSL modem to your telephone wall jack.**

- ✔ **Telephone filters:** These devices let your DSL modem and telephones use the same wiring. The DSL modem uses much higher frequencies than your telephones do. The filters prevent the DSL modem from interfering with the phones.

- ✔ **A network cable:** Use the cable to connect the DSL modem to your computer.

Installing the DSL modem is as simple as the following instructions outline:

1. **Locate the room and telephone jack you want to use for your DSL modem.**

   The jack must be close enough to your computer for the network cable to reach. You can purchase longer cables, but be careful about spanning too long of a distance. You don't want to trip!

2. **Unplug the existing telephone cable and plug the DSL modem's designated filter into the jack.**

3. **Plug the DSL modem into the filter using another telephone cable.**

4. **Plug the power supply into the DSL modem.**

That's all there is to it. Now you're ready to connect your Ubuntu computer to the DSL modem.

Configuring your Ubuntu computer to work with the DSL modem

After you have your cable modem and computer connected, you can configure your Ubuntu computer to work with the modem. Ubuntu, of course, makes the process simple and easy.

1. **Choose System⇨Administration⇨Networking from the GNOME menu bar.**

   The Enter Your Password to Perform Administrative Tasks dialog opens.

2. **Type your password and click OK.**

   The Networking Settings dialog opens.

3. **Click the Ethernet connection and click the Properties button.**

   The Interface properties dialog opens.

4. **From the Configuration drop-down menu, choose DHCP.**

   Your Ubuntu computer is set to use the a dynamic IP address.

   This action is necessary only if your Ethernet connection is set to use a static IP address.

5. **Click OK.**

   The dialog closes.

Configuring the DSL modem to connect and authenticate with your DSL provider

You need to configure a DSL modem to connect and authenticate with the DSL service provider. The process is similar to that of a dialup modem, except you assign the configuration information directly to the DSL modem — you configure your computer to dial up and authenticate with an ISP.

The configuration process differs greatly among DSL service providers. The overall process goes as follows:

1. **Log in to your Ubuntu computer.**

2. **Click the blue globe on the upper panel.**

   The Mozilla Firefox Web browser opens.

3. **Type the DSL configuration address in the Location text box.**

   The Location text box is the white space immediately to the left of the Home icon near the top, center portion of the Firefox window.

   Consult your DSL modem manual for the configuration address to use. The address will generally be of the form `http://127.0.0.1/` followed by another location.

4. **Type your DSL service username and password in the appropriate text boxes.**

5. **Select the appropriate action to save your settings.**

Your DSL modem connects and authenticates itself to the DSL service provider. Your computer is now connected to the Internet.

Chapter 9

Internet Old School: Using Dialup Modems

Modems are old school. Back in the day — oh, way back at the turn of the century — they were the only game in town for most people. The only broadband Internet connections you could get were through large organizations such as universities. Otherwise, you had to live with the slow connections modems provided.

Modems enabled a lot of people to get onto the Internet. As large numbers of us got online, economies of scale drove the introduction of consumer-level broadband connections. Today, it's hard to think of a world without those fast, always-on connections. But not everyone has access to such luxuries, and modems still serve as an inexpensive, widely available connection method.

Ubuntu provides all the tools necessary for using modems. This chapter describes how to make your modem connection. We play to the classic hits here. It's old school, baby!

Your dialup modem configuration is not saved permanently when running live Ubuntu. (See Chapter 2.) Your configuration settings will be lost when you reboot your computer. Your dialup settings are saved, however, if you're running a permanent Ubuntu installation. (See Chapter 4.)

Selecting a dialup ISP

Internet service providers (ISPs) come in all shapes and sizes. You don't have to make any long-term commitments to an ISP. You can quickly change companies if you don't like the one you subscribe to.

You can subscribe to a couple of types of ISPs:

✔ **Large, corporate-type ISPs:** Larger ISPs often offer very low-cost or free service. Large ISPs can offer lower costs, but not much lower than small operations — the difference is about $5 to $15.

National ISPs provide service over a larger area than small ISPs. This might be important if you travel a lot.

✔ **Small, mom-and-pop ISPs:** Smaller ISPs tend to cost a little more but also tend to offer better service.

I get my broadband Internet service through my cable television company but maintain a subscription with my long-time (over a decade) ISP, Southwest Cyberport (SWCP). I use their lowest cost service, which costs a little more than $5 per month. This might be $5 more than a no-cost ISP, but it's well worth the cost of one quad-venti-nonfat cappuccino extra-wet, given the service SWCP provides.

Local ISPs can offer varied service, too, and they tend to be more sensitive to their customers' needs and provide better service. Local ISPs also tend to offer better personalized service because they work in the communities they serve.

I think living near your ISP makes for better reliability. Again, the local ISP knows their environment better than a company with no local ties to the community.

Choosing a Modem

Most PCs include an internal modem. Unfortunately, these modems are almost always WinModems. WinModems need special software that isn't always available in Linux.

WinModems aren't modems in the traditional sense because they use the computer's sound card to modulate and demodulate the signal on the telephone wire to make a connection to an ISP. Unlike full-function modems, all this is controlled via software contained in the Windows operating system.

The minimalist construction of WinModems makes them very inexpensive. The downside is that WinModems are generally incompatible with Linux computers. This means that you probably can't use your laptop's internal modem with Ubuntu.

Fortunately, third-party internal and external modems are inexpensive. They sell for less than $50 and up to $100. You can purchase "real" modems at electronics and computer stores.

I recommend an external modem for use with both laptops and desktop PCs. The only disadvantages of external modems are that they take more space and cost a little more.

Internal modems have several disadvantages, including these:

- ✔ You must open your desktop computer to install an internal modem.

- ✔ You can't install internal modems in a laptop.

   You can find PCMCIA (Personal Computer Memory Card International Association) modems that plug into a laptop. They're relatively inexpensive and provide an alternative to purchasing an external modem.

- ✔ You can't physically control an internal modem. (Internal modems don't have power switches.)

- ✔ Internal modems don't have light-emitting diodes (LED) to display status.

- ✔ Power surges can damage your computer! Because the internal modem is plugged directly into your computer's motherboard, a power surge from a lightning strike can find its way through the telephone wire into the internal modem — and from there, into your computer.

Configuring Your Modem

If you aren't using a WinModem, Ubuntu is good at finding and configuring your modem. You use the network administration utility, as I describe in these steps:

1. **From the GNOME menu bar, choose System⇨Administration⇨ Networking.**

   The Enter Your Password to Perform Administrative Tasks dialog opens.

2. **Type your password and click OK.**

   The Network Settings dialog, shown in Figure 9-1, opens. The dialog shows your modem if you have one attached.

3. **Click the Modem Connection option and click the Properties button.**

   Figure 9-2 shows the Interface Properties dialog that opens.

4. **Click the Enable this Connection check box.**

   This action activates the other options, such as the Phone Number text box.

Figure 9-1:
Network
Settings
dialog
showing a
modem.

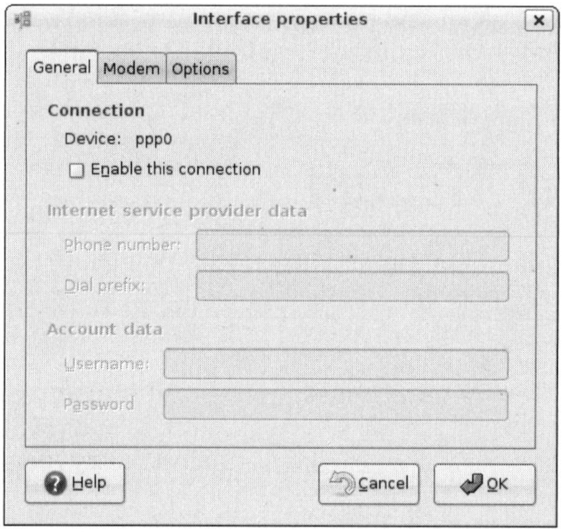

Figure 9-2:
Interface
Properties
dialog.

5. **Type your ISP's dialup telephone number in the Phone Number text box.**

   You can enter a dial-out number, if necessary, in the Dial Prefix text box.

6. **Click the Modem tab.**

   The dialog shows options for

   - Designating the serial port you want to connect to your modem.

   - Changing the volume and dial tones used for dialing out.

7. Click the Autodetect button.

If you have an internal modem — most laptops and many desktop PCs have one — it might be detected and displayed in the Mode Port text box. (WinModems are generally not detected by Ubuntu.) If your external modem is powered on and connected properly, it should be detected and displayed. Figure 9-3 shows an example where the modem has been detected.

Figure 9-3: Selecting modem options.

8. If your modem isn't detected, choose /dev/ttyS0 from the Modem Port drop-down menu.

If selecting /dev/ttyS0 doesn't work when you try connecting to your ISP in the next section, return to this step and select /dev/ttyS1. Try connecting again. If you're unsuccessful, come back and try /dev/ttyS2 and finally /dev/ttyS3.

9. From the Volume drop-down menu, choose Media or Loud.

Being able to hear your modem is useful when setting up your modem for the first time. You can always return to this menu and turn the volume down or off after you establish a connection.

10. Click the Options tab.

The default is to let your modem connection be your primary Internet connection. Leave this setting in place if you have no other Internet — broadband — connection. Figure 9-4 shows the dialog with your modem controlling the Internet connection.

Figure 9-4:
Your modem
set as your
primary
Internet
connection.

Your modem connection will also set your ISP to control domain name service (DNS) by default. *DNS* is the system that converts human-readable Internet names — for instance, www.wiley.com — into computer-readable numeric IP addresses.

11. **Click OK.**

You return to the Network Settings window. You should hear the familiar sounds of old school Internet. Beep, beep, buzz, screech, buzz, and you're connected to your ISP and the Internet.

If you don't get connected, you might need to return to Step 8 and try another serial device.

Firing Up Your Modem

After you configure your modem, you can connect to your ISP. It's simple using the Network Settings utility. Follow these steps:

1. **If necessary, open the Network Settings dialog.**

2. **Click the Modem connection option and click the Activate button.**

   Surf's up. Browse, e-mail, transfer files.

3. **When you're finished surfing, click the Deactivate button.**

   Your connection closes, and you're no longer connected to the Internet.

Chapter 10

Protecting Yourself with a Firewall

*Y*our newly installed Ubuntu desktop computer is quite network safe. Ubuntu, out of the box, doesn't run any unnecessary, network-aware services; *network-aware services* are *processes* (running programs or applications) that respond to network connections.

Network services that don't exist can't be hacked. This is a good thing.

However, Ubuntu supplies a firewall configuration utility because life changes. As you use your computer, you'll probably want to change and modify it. Changing and modifying might introduce new network services, and those services need to be protected with a firewall. *Firewalls* limit access to and from networks and are generally used to prevent unwanted incoming connections, especially ones from the Internet.

Protecting Your Computer with Firewalls

In the past, firewalls were absolutely necessary because Linux distributions installed and activated many network-aware services by default. They installed the proverbial kitchen sink. Most people didn't need the services — or the sink — but someone always did. Vendors turned services on in order to make as many as possible of their customers happy.

Well, as the adage says, you can please some of the people all of the time, but . . . well, you get my drift. Turning on services was very bad from a security standpoint. Some services were poorly configured, some were buggy, and hackers went to town.

Ubuntu practices good security hygiene. It installs only a relatively small amount of software — enough to make your Ubuntu computer very useful but without installing the kitchen sink. So there aren't any network-aware services running under the default installation described in Chapter 4.

So why run a firewall? It isn't absolutely necessary, but good security requires multiple layers of defense. There's no silver bullet when it comes to computer security. You might not have a network-based vulnerability now, but that might not be true in the future.

I show you how to install a lot of software throughout this book. Some software is network-aware, and software always contains exploitable vulnerabilities. Therefore, be proactive and install a firewall now. It's easy to install and configure.

Quest for Firestarter: Installing a Firewall Configuration Tool

In its quest to give you the tools you need, Ubuntu includes the Firestarter utility on its distribution disc (the companion CD). The utility makes it easy to create firewall rules that best fit your needs. This section describes how to install Firestarter.

Your firewall configuration is not saved permanently if you're using live Ubuntu. (See Chapter 2.) You configuration settings will be lost when you reboot your computer. Your firewall settings are saved, however, if you're running a permanent Ubuntu installation. (See Chapter 4.)

The instructions in this section assume your Ubuntu computer is connected to the Internet. Chapters 6 through 9 describe how to use various technologies to obtain your connection. You download Firestarter using Ubuntu's Add/Remove Applications utility. Please refer to the sidebar "Living off the land" and the companion Ubuntu disc if you don't have an Internet connection.

The following instructions guide you through the straightforward Firestarter installation process:

1. **From the GNOME menu bar, choose Applications⇨Add/Remove.**

   This action starts the Add/Remove Applications dialog.

2. **Type `fire` in the Search text box located in the upper-right corner of the dialog window.**

   The utility locates and displays the Firestarter package, as shown in Figure 10-1.

Living off the land

You can still install Firestarter if you don't have an Internet connection — or haven't yet connected your Ubuntu computer to the Internet. (Your Internet connection can be through an existing local area network [LAN] or dialup or broadband modem. Please see Chapters 6, 7, 8, and 9 for instructions about using such connections.)

1. Insert your Ubuntu CD-ROM or DVD.

The File Browser dialog opens, showing the contents of the disc.

2. Click the Close Window control.

The Close Window control is the X in the extreme, upper-right corner of the window. Alternatively, click the File menu and choose the Close option.

Use the instructions in the "Quest for Firestarter: Installing a Firewall Configuration Tool" section.

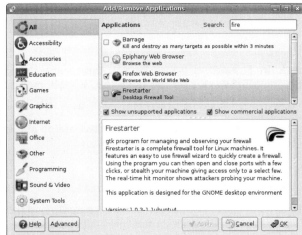

Figure 10-1: The Add/Remove utility located the Firestarter package.

3. Select the check box next to the Firestarter package.

4. Click the Apply button.

The Apply the Following Changes? query dialog opens.

5. Click the Apply button.

The Administration Rights Are Required to Install and Remove Applications dialog opens.

6. Type your password and click OK.

The package utility takes some time to determine what, if any, additional software packages you need. After it finishes checking, the New

Applications dialog opens and prompts you to double-click to start Firestarter.

You've successfully installed Firestarter. Now you can use Firestarter to prevent fire.

Ubuntu uses the Netfilter/iptables firewall system. *Netfilter* refers to the kernel-level program that allows or denies network transmissions. *iptables* is the user-level program that controls Netfilter. The overall system is generally referred to as *iptables.* Firestarter configures rules that are fed to iptables to set up your firewall.

Using the Firestarter Configuration Wizard

After Firestarter is installed (see the installation instructions in the preceding section), the New Applications dialog opens and gives you the opportunity to start the utility. Follow these steps:

1. **Double-click the Firestarter option or you can choose the System⇨ Administration⇨Firestarter option from the GNOME menu bar.**

   The Firewall Wizard: Welcome to Firestarter dialog opens.

2. **Click the Close button in the New Applications dialog and click OK in the Add/Remove Applications window.**

   Neatness can make life a little bit easier.

3. **Click the Forward button in the Firewall Wizard.**

   The wizard detects all network devices and displays one of them in the Detected Device(s) drop-down menu. Figure 10-2 shows a sample window.

Figure 10-2:
The Firewall
Wizard
Network
Device
Setup
dialog.

4. **If your network device isn't shown, click the Detected-Device(s) drop-down menu and select it.**

   The dominant network device is Ethernet.

5. **Select the Start the Firewall on Dial-Out check box if you're using a dialup modem to make your Internet connection.**

6. **Select the IP Address Is Assigned via DHCP check box.**

   Leave the check box deselected if you manually assigned a static IP address to your Ubuntu computer in Chapter 6.

   Figure 10-3 shows your firewall configured for DHCP but not for dial-out modem.

Figure 10-3:
Firewall configured for DHCP but not dial-out modem.

At this point, your firewall is configured to prevent incoming connections. Your firewall will let you use your computer to initiate only outgoing connections (such as Web browsing and e-mail), but nothing else.

7. **Click the Forward button.**

   The Internet Connection Sharing Setup dialog opens. At this point, Firestarter can make your computer act as a *router,* meaning that other computers can connect to the Internet (or LAN) through your Ubuntu computer and actually appear as the same IP address as that computer. You shouldn't need to use this function when using your computer as a workstation.

8. **Click the Forward button again.**

   The Ready to Start Your Firewall dialog, shown in Figure 10-4, opens.

9. **Click Save.**

   Your firewall configuration is saved, and the firewall starts; Ubuntu is also configured to automatically start your firewall whenever it reboots. The Firestarter control dialog also opens, as shown in Figure 10-5. It's described in the following section, "Fine-Tuning Your Firewall."

Figure 10-4:
Saving your
configu-
ration and
starting your
firewall.

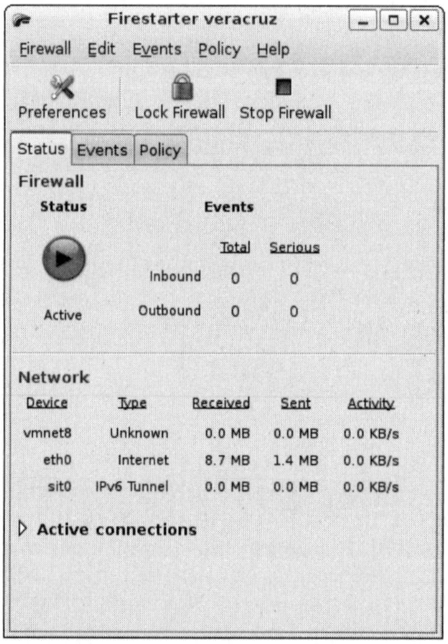

Figure 10-5:
Firestarter's
control
dialog.

Fine-Tuning Your Firewall

In the preceding section, you configure your firewall to allow any outgoing connection you might want to make. It's also set up to prevent incoming new connections from anywhere. This policy is great if you never intend to access your computer from someplace else. If that's your desire, you can skip this section.

However, if you'd like to access your Ubuntu computer from another computer on your LAN or the Internet, you can easily configure your firewall to do so. The following section describes in general how you can

✔ Configure your firewall to allow applications to make incoming connections.

✔ Limit the originating IP address that an incoming connection can be made from.

Configuring Firestarter to allow incoming connections

Try adding a rule to allow SSH (Secure Shell) connections. Follow these steps:

1. **From the GNOME menu bar, choose System⇨Administration⇨ Firestarter.**

   The Firestarter utility, shown in Figure 10-5, opens.

2. **Click the Policy tab in the Firestarter control dialog.**

3. **Click anywhere in the Allow Service subwindow.**

   The Allow Service subwindow is immediately below the Allow Connections subwindow.

4. **Click the Add Rule button.**

   The Add New Inbound Rule dialog opens.

5. **From the Name drop-down menu, choose the application to allow in.**

6. **If you want to control where incoming connections can be made from, do the following:**

   a. *Click the IP, Host, or Network radio button.*

   If you don't select this option, incoming connections can be made from any computer.

   b. *Type the IP address or IP address range in the IP, Host, or Network text box.*

7. **(Optional) Type any comment you think helpful in the Comment text box.**

   Adding comments helps you recall in the future why you entered a rule. A comment like `I want to allow incoming SSH connections so I can connect to my home computer from work` will help you recall what purpose a rule serves.

8. **Click the Add button.**

   The Add New Inbound Rule dialog closes.

9. **Click the Apply Policy button and the new rule is displayed.**

   You can continue adding and deleting incoming policies as you wish.

10. **Choose Quit from the Firewall menu to exit the Firestarter control dialog.**

    That's it. Your computer accepts incoming connections for the specified application from any computer; alternatively, the connection can be made from specific IP addresses or networks. Pretty cool.

You can give full access through the firewall to individual computers or networks. Clicking the Allow Connections from Host subwindow and selecting Add Rule opens a dialog similar to the Add New Inbound Rule dialog described above. Using this option allows you to enter the IP address of a single machine or the IP address of an entire network. Any connection from that machine or machines will then be allowed through the firewall.

Allowing incoming SSH connections

I use *Secure Shell (SSH)* — which encrypts interactive connections — to securely communicate with my home computer. It's an amazing tool and useful in many, many ways; using SSH is described in Appendix B.

For instance, I use SSH to connect to my home Ubuntu computer when I'm traveling. SSH allows me to securely interact with my home computer and also transfer files to and from it. However, you need to modify the default Ubuntu firewall before it will allow incoming SSH connections. Here's how you can do just that:

1. **Open the Firestarter control dialog by choosing System⇨Administration⇨Firestarter from the GNOME menu bar.**

   The Enter Your Password to Perform Administration Tasks dialog opens (if you haven't performed an administrative task in the past 5 minutes).

   Ubuntu uses the sudo system to perform all system-level (superuser) tasks. When using sudo to perform a task, it asks you for your password and remembers if you successfully entered it in the past 5 minutes. After 5 minutes, sudo asks you for your password the next time you perform a system task.

2. **Type your password and click OK.**

3. **Click the Policy tab.**

4. **Click anywhere in the Allow Service subwindow.**

5. **Click the Add Rule button.**

6. **From the Name drop-down menu, choose SSH.**

   SSH operates on port 22 by default, as shown in Figure 10-6.

7. **Click the Add button.**

8. **Click the Apply Policy button and the SSH rule is displayed.**

   Figure 10-6 shows the result.

   You can continue adding and deleting incoming policies as you wish.

9. **Choose the Quit option from the Firewall menu to exit the Firestarter control dialog.**

The firewall is configured to allow a little bit of information to escape from your Ubuntu computer. You can ping your Ubuntu computer from another computer or device on your private LAN (if connected to one). A *ping* basically allows the other computer to know that your computer is active on the network.

Figure 10-6:
SSH
connections
are allowed
from
anywhere.

Testing Your Firewall

If you've implemented the preceding instructions in this chapter, you have a very effective firewall in place. It blocks all new incoming connections unless you specifically tell it not to. Any misconfigured or buggy network-aware services that you currently run or run in the future won't "see" probes or attacks, thus, they won't be vulnerable.

Your firewall is configured to block new incoming connections. However, it allows incoming connections that result from outgoing ones. For instance, if you browse a Web site, you make an outgoing connection to the Web server. The Web site responds to your browsing and sends network traffic back to your computer. Your firewall is smart enough to recognize network traffic resulting from outgoing connections that you make and let the return traffic back in.

You can assure yourself that the firewall is indeed blocking unwanted network traffic. Open Firestarter and click the Events tab. If your computer is connected to the Internet, you'll see information similar to that shown in Figure 10-7.

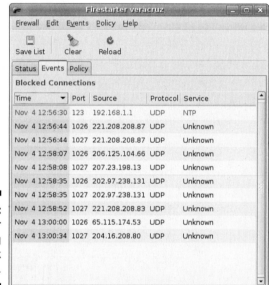

Figure 10-7:
Firestarter showing network events.

This figure shows one network time protocol packet (NTP) from my cable modem (192.168.1.1) and several packets from unknown addresses. (*NTP* is used to synchronize your Ubuntu computer's time with atomic clocks made available via the Internet.) I haven't configured Firestarter to allow those types of connections or probes; therefore, my firewall's blocking them. If I had a vulnerable service operating on one of those ports, it wouldn't be accessible to an attack.

Part III
Working with Ubuntu Workstation

The 5th Wave   By Rich Tennant

"This is your GNOME desktop?"

In this part . . .

This part shows how to use Ubuntu as your everyday workstation. The primary focus is using productivity tools such as OpenOffice.org (a Microsoft Office-compatible office suite), Mozilla Firefox Web browser, plus multimedia, graphics, and other applications.

Chapters 11 and 12 introduce the GNOME graphical desktop environment and how to use it; Chapter 13 helps you set up your computer for printing. Chapter 14 covers using the ground-breaking Mozilla Firefox Web browser. In Chapter 15, I tell you about the Evolution e-mail client. Chapter 16 is close to my heart, as it describes using the Microsoft Word-compatible OpenOffice.org Writer.

Chapter 11

Introducing GNOME

What do gnomes have to do with Ubuntu? Do they come by late at night and help you maintain your computer? Maybe someplace in the world, but not here. In this case, I'm not talking about little system administrators or even lawn gnomes, I'm talking about GNOME, the Linux desktop.

GNOME stands for GNU Network Object Model Environment, and GNU (some people pronounce it *guh-NEW*) stands for GNU's not UNIX. Ubuntu uses numerous GNU applications, libraries, and utilities. You don't need to know about all of that to be able to use Ubuntu. For now, I'll let you get on with checking out your new operating system. But if you'd like to look into how the concept of free software came to be, www.gnu.org is a great place to start. Confusing acronyms aside, it's an interesting story.

Forget the long acronym and just think of GNOME as a great desktop and desktop environment. *Desktop environments* pull together all the various elements that make it possible to use your computer in a convenient and productive manner.

This chapter describes GNOME and how to use it.

Getting to Know the GNOME Desktop

Microsoft Windows doesn't have a catchy name for its desktop, but as you might have noticed, things are a little different in the Linux world. GNOME (as well as other elements of Linux) is an *open source* project. *Open source projects* produce software that everyone can freely use, and anyone can modify — just so long as whoever does the modification doesn't restrict others from doing the same. It's supported and developed by the GNOME project — www.gnome.org. GNOME creates a desktop environment that is both easy to use and pleasant to look at. The default Ubuntu GNOME desktop uses a neutral but pleasing background, as shown in Figure 11-1. (This figure shows an example of live Ubuntu.)

The following sections describe each primary part of GNOME.

Looking at the default desktop

The *desktop* is the background you see before you start opening applications — plus the menu bars and icons. Everything that you do or see in GNOME, you do from the desktop. The GNOME panels, icons, and applications all work from the desktop. The desktop is the basis for everything you do on your Ubuntu computer.

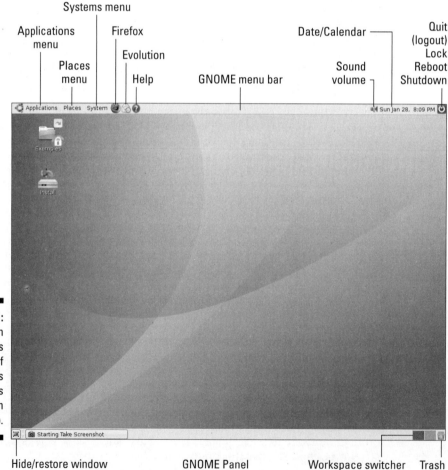

Systems menu

Applications menu

Firefox

Date/Calendar

Quit (logout)
Lock
Reboot
Shutdown

Places menu

Evolution

Help

GNOME menu bar

Sound volume

Figure 11-1:
You can access many of Ubuntu's features right from the desktop.

Hide/restore window   GNOME Panel   Workspace switcher   Trash

TECHNICAL STUFF

The big picture

Miguel de Icaza started the GNOME project in 1997. He was motivated to create a graphical desktop environment over concerns about the licensing of other desktop software. The intervening ten years has seen GNOME become one of the most popular graphical environments in the world.

The GNOME environment consists of the following primary parts:

✔ **Desktop:** The GNOME desktop is analogous to the top of your desk.

✔ **Panels:** These are menu bars. Panels can be laid out horizontally or vertically. Ubuntu gives you two panels, one along the bottom and the other along the top of the desktop.

✔ **Icons:** Graphical objects placed on the desktop that provide access to specific resources. You click (or double-click) an icon, and a window opens. You can use the resource that the window is connected to.

✔ **Nautilus file manager:** Nautilus helps you use and manage files and folders. It can also browse network file shares (which I discuss in more detail later in the chapter). Chapter 12 describes how to use Nautilus.

✔ **Applications:** You use your computer to get work done, surf the Internet, communicate with others, and sometimes just have fun. You can engage in these activities by using the appropriate applications. GNOME provides a lot of applications, outlined in Chapter 12, for you to use.

You're given a default desktop when you use live Ubuntu or install Ubuntu on your computer. The desktop is shown in Figure 11-1 and provides the following objects:

✔ **Ubuntu background:** This is the image you see onscreen after you log into your user account. You can change the background using images provided as part of the Ubuntu installation. From the GNOME menu bar, choose System⇨Preferences⇨Desktop Background. The Desktop Background Preferences dialog opens, from which you can select another image.

✔ **Two panels:** *Panels* are *menu bars* and are equivalent to the familiar Windows menu bar.

  • The top panel contains applications and system administration menus. It also includes icons for the Mozilla Firefox browser, the Evolution messaging and calendar system, available software package updates, and the clock.

  • The bottom panel includes a Trash icon, a workspace switcher (more about that later in this chapter), and an icon to minimize all open windows.

✔ **Disk icon:** Displays all available disks.

All of these objects are described in more detail later in this chapter.

X marks the spot

While GNOME provides Ubuntu with its desktop environment, the X Window System (also referred to as simply X) gives GNOME its graphics. In other words, GNOME runs on top of X.

X consists of three parts:

✔ **X Server:** The interface for your computer's graphics video card, keyboard, mouse, and monitor. GNOME asks X to perform basic graphical tasks, and X does the grunt work while GNOME does the higher-level work.

✔ **X Clients:** Applications such as Mozilla Firefox and Evolution are X Clients. X Clients communicate with the X Server. You interface with X Client, which itself interfaces with the X Server.

✔ **X Libraries:** The X Server and X Clients use X Libraries to perform their tasks. Using a suite of common libraries eliminates the need to rewrite code to perform similar tasks.

X provides the graphical underpinnings for GNOME.

Taking a closer look at the GNOME panels

The GNOME panels (menu bars) house menus, icons, and displays. The panels group commonly used features in order to make them easier to access.

By default, Ubuntu's implementation of GNOME includes two panels.

Top panel

The top panel includes the GNOME menu bar, which provides access to the following menus:

✔ **Applications:** From this menu, you can open applications such as the OpenOffice.org word processor, the Evolution e-mail and calendaring program, and the GNOME Terminal Emulator.

✔ **Places:** Travel within your Ubuntu world via this menu. The Places menu gives quick access to your home directory and desktop folders, documents, and network places.

✔ **System:** You can open system administration applications and utilities such as the Network Settings utility, the user account utility, and the printer configuration tool.

The top panel also includes the following icons:

✔ **Firefox:** Click this icon to open the Internet browser Mozilla Firefox, which I describe in more detail in Chapter 14.

✔ **Evolution:** Use this icon to open the Evolution messaging, contact list, and calendaring system. (See Chapter 15.)

✔ **Volume control:** Click this icon to adjust your computer's audio volume via a simple slider volume dialog.

✔ **Clock/calendar:** This icon displays the current time and date. Click it to open a simple calendar dialog.

✔ **Log off:** Clicking this icon opens a logout dialog. You can log out, switch users, shutdown, reboot, and suspend your Ubuntu computer using these options.

Bottom panel

The panel at the bottom of your desktop provides these options:

✔ **Hide/Display:** Sometimes your desktop gets cluttered with too many windows. Clicking this icon *minimizes* (hides) all windows. The minimized windows show up as icons on the bottom panel. Clicking it again reopens those windows.

✔ **Workspace switcher:** GNOME lives in a virtual reality. The desktop can span many *virtual windows*.

To visualize this, imagine that you have a huge monitor, let's say 4 feet by 4 feet. Put four pieces of paper over the monitor's screen so that it's completely covered. Now, pull off one section of paper and one quarter of the screen is visible. If you want to view another section of the screen, you have to put back the piece of paper that's currently not attached before pulling off anther section. Doing this divides the desktop into four sections and helps reduce clutter. GNOME's virtual windows effectively perform the same task.

Each window is represented as a small pane on the workspace switcher. Click any pane, and you're transported to the designated virtual window. This capability makes it easy to reduce clutter by using different virtual windows to group different tasks.

✔ **Trash folder:** This is where you put files you'd like to delete. You can click and drag files to the Trash or right-click a file and select the Move to Trash option.

Trashed objects aren't actually deleted until you empty the Trash folder. You can empty the trash can — permanently delete the files you sent to the trash — by choosing File➪Empty Trash from within any Nautilus window. When the Empty All of the Items from the Trash? dialog opens, click the Empty Trash button.

GNOME panels are highly configurable. I describe how to modify them later in this chapter.

Introducing GNOME icons

Icons are shortcuts to files, folders, and applications. They're very simple to use and create. Clicking or double-clicking an icon opens whatever resource it represents. For instance, if you have a CD inserted in your computer, Ubuntu shows an icon, as shown in Figure 11-2. Double-clicking the CD icon opens a window showing the contents of the CD.

Figure 11-2: Icon showing a CD-ROM.

Managing files and folders with Nautilus

Nautilus is a file manager that helps you use and manipulate files, folders, and network shares. It's a powerful, yet easy-to-use, system.

Clicking the icon of a device or folder on your desktop opens Nautilus, which displays the contents of the device or folder. For instance, if you insert your Ubuntu CD in your computer, an icon like that shown in Figure 11-2 opens. You can double-click the icon and a Nautilus window opens, displaying the CD's contents, as shown in Figure 11-3.

Figure 11-3: The Nautilus file manager, showing the Ubuntu CD contents.

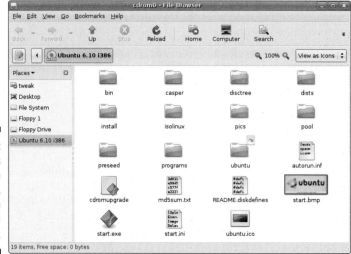

Nautilus provides the following functions:

- ✔ **Display disk drives**
- ✔ **Display folder contents**
- ✔ **Open network file shares**
- ✔ **Create folders**
- ✔ **Create documents**
- ✔ **Search for files**
- ✔ **Run applications**

Nautilus is easy to use. Double-click (or right-click and select Open) any desktop icon, and Nautilus opens a window displaying the contents of the resource. For instance, opening a folder icon opens a window displaying the contents of the folder.

Chapter 12 describes the Nautilus file manager in more detail.

Navigating the GNOME Desktop

Using the GNOME desktop is as simple as pointing and clicking your mouse. Select and click an icon, and you can tell GNOME what to do and where to go with the icon.

Take a quick look through the various navigation methods.

Using panel menus

Menus are designed to group common applications, utilities, and locations so you can more easily use your computer.

Chapter 12 describes many of the applications you find in these menus.

The Applications menu

The Applications menu (refer to Figure 11-1) provides the following submenus:

- ✔ **Accessories:** This menu groups miscellaneous utilities and applications. For instance, you access the dictionary and calculator from here.
- ✔ **Games:** GNOME provides some simple games, such as Blackjack, via this menu.

✔ **Graphics:** This is where you can find programs that display and manipulate graphics. For instance, I used the GIMP (GNU Image Manipulation Program) graphical imaging and editing tool to make all the screen shots in this book. The GIMP and other graphical-oriented applications can be found in this menu.

✔ **Internet:** All these applications have the common thread of being Internet aware. From here, you can access such applications as

- Mozilla Firefox browser (Chapter 14)

- Evolution mail and calendaring program (Chapter 15)

- Gaim Internet Messenger (Chapter 18)

✔ **Office:** Access the OpenOffice.org suite of word processing, spreadsheet, slideshow, and other functions from here.

Chapter 16 describes what OpenOffice.org is and how to use it.

✔ **Sound & Video:** Ubuntu provides many multimedia applications, such as CD rippers and burners, plus music players and more. This menu provides access to them.

✔ **Add & Remove:** Ubuntu provides this utility for installing and removing software.

The Places menu

The Places menu helps you go to GNOME places. It gives access to the following locations:

✔ **Home Folder:** Selecting the Home Folder menu opens the Nautilus file manager, which shows the contents of your home directory (folder). The Home Folder is where you should save your personal files and folders — it's similar to Microsoft XP's My Documents and Microsoft Vista's Documents folders.

✔ **Desktop:** This option opens the file manager in your Desktop folder; Desktop is a subdirectory of your home directory. Files and folders that you save here are automatically displayed on your GNOME desktop. Saving files here is a convenient way to display icons that you want to be easily accessible.

✔ **Computer:** Clicking Computer opens the file manager, showing a view of your computer's drives. You see an icon for your hard drive, CD-ROM drive, and any other drives connected to your computer.

✔ **CD/DVD Creator:** Opens a window that lets you write files to your writable CD-ROM or DVD drive.

Chapter 20 describes how to use this application to burn CDs and DVDs.

- ✔ **Network Servers:** You can browse any file shares available on your network. *(File shares* are folders that appear to be and act like they're located on your Ubuntu computer but are really attached to other computers and are accessible via a network.)

- ✔ **Connect to Server:** Connect to any file shares on your network.

- ✔ **Search for Files:** Look for files on your computer. Did you type a letter to Aunt Maude but don't remember where you saved it? This feature can help you find it.

- ✔ **Recent Documents:** Shows any documents that you've used recently. It provides a shortcut to reopening any of those documents.

Selecting any of these options — except Connect to Server and Search for Files — opens the Nautilus file manager (see Chapter 12) in the designated context.

The System menu

The System menu helps you manage the look and feel plus the operation of your Ubuntu computer.

- ✔ **Preferences:** Opens a submenu providing access to GNOME and Ubuntu configuration editors that help you configure things such as your desktop background, screen saver, and the sound volume.

- ✔ **Administration:** Opens a submenu displaying system administration utilities and applications such as your network configuration utility and printer setup.

- ✔ **Help:** Opens the Ubuntu help system. (For more information about getting help with Ubuntu, see Chapter 22.)

- ✔ **About GNOME:** Opens a dialog giving access to GNOME information — including what version of GNOME you're using, in case you forget.

- ✔ **About Ubuntu:** Opens a dialog giving access to Ubuntu information — including what version of Ubuntu you're using, if anyone asks.

- ✔ **Quit:** Opens the logout dialog that lets you either log out, shutdown, reboot, or suspend your computer.

  I explain the Quit options in Chapter 5.

Manipulating GNOME windows

Clicking icons and selecting menu options opens windows — *windows* with a small w, that is. You get your work done within these windows. For instance, clicking the Firefox icon on the top panel opens the Firefox window, which lets you browse the Internet.

After you open an application window, you can move it around, resize it, and so on, just as you would in that *other* operating system. Here's what you can do:

- ✔ **Minimize Window:** Click the small, horizontal bar button (looks like a minus sign) at the top-right corner of the window. The window disappears from the desktop and is represented by an icon in the bottom panel.

- ✔ **Maximize Window:** Click the square button in the top-right corner of the window, and the window enlarges to occupy the entire desktop. Click the same button again and the window shrinks to its original size.

- ✔ **Close Window:** Click the X button, and the window exits. Finished. Kaput.

    Alternatively, you can close a window by clicking the File menu in the program and selecting the Quit, Close, or Exit option.

You can move a window by clicking its top border, holding the mouse button, and then dragging the window to its new location. Release the button and the window stays there.

Resizing a window is also straightforward. Move the pointer to any of the window's corner edges until the cursor changes to an arrow within a right-angle bracket. At that point, click the mouse and drag the arrow to resize the window.

Exiting from or locking GNOME

If you work with other people, you'll want to exit (log out from) GNOME when you leave your computer; alternatively, you can lock your GNOME session without ending your session. The idea is to protect your work and computer from unauthorized use.

To log out, click the red Quit icon at the top-right side of the top panel. The Quit dialog opens, from which you can

- ✔ **Logout:** Selecting this option logs you out of your user account and ends any applications you're currently running.

- ✔ **Lock:** Locks your current GNOME session. You can unlock your session by typing your password in the Unlock dialog that's displayed as soon as you lock your session.

- ✔ **Switch Users:** Change from one user account to another. You must, of course, know the other user account password to use this option.

- ✔ **Restart:** Shutdown your Ubuntu computer and immediately, and automatically, restart the computer.

- ✔ **Shutdown:** Shuts down your Ubuntu computer, turning off the power.

    Chapter 5 describes these functions in more detail.

Altering GNOME's Appearance

GNOME is highly configurable. You can change the look and feel of the GNOME desktop, add and remove panels, manipulate icons, and change many other aspects of your graphical environment.

In this section, I describe how to perform some of the more useful configurations.

Creating and modifying folders

You can create desktop icons by right-clicking the GNOME desktop and selecting any of the following options:

- ✔ **Create Folder:** Select the New Folder option to create a folder.
- ✔ **Create Document:** Select the Empty File option. This creates an empty document.
- ✔ **Application:** Select the Create Launcher option. (A *launcher* is like a shortcut.) The Create Launcher dialog opens. Type the name and application that you want the new icon to control; you can also click the Icon button to select from generic GNOME icon images.

When you release the right mouse button, the icon appears on the desktop as an untitled folder. Type the name that you want to label the file, folder, or action with and press the Enter key.

To rename an icon, right-click it and select the Rename option in the menu that opens. Type the new name at the prompt.

If you want to copy an icon from the desktop to a panel, click the icon and drag it to the panel. Release the mouse, and you'll see the icon on both the desktop and the panel.

The opposite is also true. Open a menu on a panel and find the application or place you want to create a desktop icon for. Click the object and drag it to the desktop. Release the mouse button, and the icon is created for you.

To delete an icon, you can click it and drag it to the Trash folder, or follow these steps:

1. **Right-click the icon.**

   A menu opens.

2. **Select the Move to Trash option.**

   The icon, but not the object (file, folder, or application) it represents, disappears from the desktop and is moved to the Trash folder. The object isn't deleted until you right-click the Trash folder and select the Empty Trash option.

3. **Double-click the Trash folder near the upper-right corner of the desktop.**

   The Trash - File Browser dialog opens.

4. **Click the File menu and select the Empty Trash option.**

   The Empty all of the Items from Trash? dialog opens.

5. **Click Empty Trash.**

   Control returns to the Trash - File Browser window.

6. **Close the window by clicking the File menu and choosing the Close option.**

Changing themes and backgrounds

GNOME uses themes to control its look and feel. Customizing your GNOME theme is fun and easy. Here's how:

1. **From the GNOME menu bar, choose System⇨Preferences⇨Theme.**

   The Theme Preferences dialog, shown in Figure 11-4, opens. The default theme is Ubuntu's Human theme.

Figure 11-4:
Choose how you want the GNOME desktop to look.

2. **Click the theme icon to select the theme.**

   Each theme icon displays a preview of what the theme looks like.

3. **Click Close.**

   Your GNOME session changes to a new theme. You can change themes as much and as often as you want.

Creating desktop shortcuts

GNOME panels are very useful. They simplify your access to GNOME and other applications and utilities. If you don't know where to find a program that you want to use, your best bet is to click the Applications or System menu and select the submenu that seems closest to your need. For instance, if you want to listen to or create an audio CD but don't know the name of the application, just click Applications and select Sound & Video. You'll find the Serpentine Audio CD Creator there.

However, rather than constantly searching for an application or place that you use often, you can create an icon on the panel for easy access.

1. **Right-click any blank section of a panel.**

   A menu opens.

2. **Select the Add to Panel option.**

   The Add to Panel dialog, as shown in Figure 11-5, opens.

Figure 11-5: Create a shortcut with the Add to Panel dialog.

3. **Click to select any of the standard GNOME applications or utilities.**

   The applications and utilities are organized logically by type.

4. **(Optional) Select the Application Launcher to select non-GNOME applications such as Firefox, Evolution, and so on.**

5. **Click the Close button.**

An icon representing the application or utility you select appears on the panel. You can move the panel icon around as you want by clicking and dragging it.

You can lock an icon in place by right-clicking it and selecting the Lock option. The icon can't be moved from its current location when locked. Right-click the icon and select Unlock to unlock it.

Create new panels by right-clicking an existing panel and selecting the New Panel option. Given that Ubuntu already includes top and bottom panels, using this option creates vertical panels on the left and right sides of the desktop.

Chapter 12

GNOME's Going Places

....

In This Chapter

▶ Navigating and managing your file system with Nautilus

▶ Discovering the applications that come with GNOME

....

*N*autilus is the Swiss Army knife of the GNOME world. Nautilus is a file manager that helps you to graphically use and manage files, folders, and other resources found on your computer. Nautilus is developed as part of the GNOME project.

Linux *directories* are the same as Windows *folders.* I refer to Linux directories as folders when using graphical systems like file managers.

This chapter describes how to use Nautilus to navigate your Ubuntu computer. You can use this file manager to find and use files, create folders, and even browse network files.

Introducing the Nautilus File Manager

Nautilus is an open source file manager that Ubuntu supplies to help you maneuver around your computer. Nautilus is equivalent to Windows Explorer and provides all the facilities that you need to work with files, folders, and network file shares.

You can start Nautilus by either

- ✓ **Double-clicking any desktop icon.**
- ✓ **Clicking the Places menu and choosing any of the options (other than Search for Files).**

Each option opens Nautilus within a specific context. The Nautilus contexts associated with each menu option are

- ✔ **Home Folder:** Opens with a view of your home directory. Figure 12-1 shows an example.

- ✔ **Desktop:** Displays your desktop directory in your home directory.

- ✔ **Computer:** Shows your computer disk drives. Figure 12-2 shows a typical computer setup.

- ✔ **CD/DVD Creator:** Opens a file manager window that you can drag files into and create a CD or DVD.

- ✔ **Network Servers:** Browses network file shares. (*Network file shares* are folders that appear to be on your Ubuntu computer, but are really located on another machine and are accessible via a network.) See Figure 12-3.

- ✔ **Connect to Server:** Connect to a specific file share.

- ✔ **Recent Documents:** Provides shortcuts to documents and files you've recently accessed.

GNOME menu bar   Location Bar   Main Toolbar

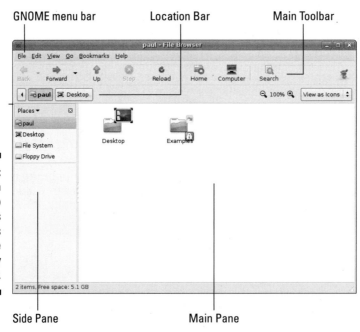

Figure 12-1: You can navigate to your files and folders in the home directory view.

Side Pane   Main Pane

Selecting the Search for Files option opens the — you guessed it — Search for Files dialog. Follow these steps:

1. **Type any filename or partial filename in the Name Contains text box.**

   By default, Ubuntu looks for the file in your home directory.

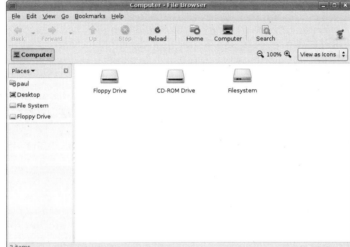

Figure 12-2: Select any of your computer's storage devices in the Computer folder view.

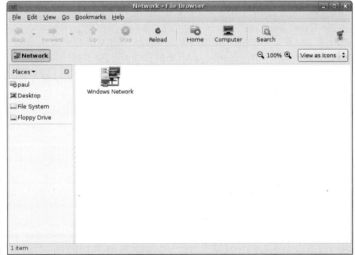

Figure 12-3: Find the accessible network storage devices in the network file shares.

2. **If you want to search a specific folder, click the Look in Folder drop-down menu and select the location.**

   All subfolders contained within the folder — that you start your search from — are also searched. So, for example, if you start the search from your home directory and the file or folder you're looking for is in your Desktop folder, the file or folder will be found.

3. **Click the Find button.**

   For instance, type passwd in the Name Contains text box, select File System from the Look in Folder drop-down menu, and click the Find button. Ubuntu displays all the matches in the Search Results subwindow.

Finding out what you can do in Nautilus

Nautilus contains familiar file system navigation options in the menu bar:

- ✔ **File:** Open new Nautilus windows and close existing ones; create folders and empty documents.

- ✔ **Edit:** Cut, copy, and paste. Use the mouse cursor to cut or copy a file or files into a temporary buffer. You then navigate to another folder to which you paste the file or files. These options let you easily copy or move files from one folder to another.

- ✔ **View:** Activate or deactivate the Main Toolbar, Side Pane, Location Bar, or Status bar.

- ✔ **Main Toolbar:** Contains buttons that provide shortcuts to the most commonly used Nautilus functions, such as moving Up, Forward, and Back, going to your home folder, and starting the Search for Files function.

- ✔ **Side Pane:** A submenu, located on the left side of the Nautilus window, that shows shortcuts to commonly accessed places on your Ubuntu computer. Clicking any one of these shortcuts displays the specified folder, such as

  - Your home directory (folder)

  - Your desktop folder

  - The Ubuntu file system

  - Any available disk drives

- ✔ **Location Bar:** Located immediately below the Main Toolbar, displaying your current location. Click the leftmost button and the current location changes from an icon to the Location text box; you can type any directory name in the Location text box to change your location to that directory. You can also click the buttons that look like magnifier glasses to zoom in and out, respectively. Finally, from the drop-down menu on the far right of the Location Bar, you can change the way files and folders are displayed, from icons to a list.

✔ **Go:** Provides an option to move up to the parent of the current directory view. (For more information on directories, see Chapter 5.)

You also get shortcuts to all standard Nautilus views (such as Home Folder, Desktop, and Network Servers).

✔ **Bookmarks:** Create, edit, and delete bookmarks. Nautilus bookmarks work just like Web browser bookmarks — they create shortcuts to files and folders on your Ubuntu computer instead of the shortcuts to Web sites that Web browser bookmarks create.

✔ **Help:** Opens a help system. Click Help and choose Contents to open a dialog that lets you search for various help topics. Selecting Get Help Online opens the Firefox browser to Ubuntu's Web site that lets you search for more help topics.

You find the Nautilus toolbar underneath the menu bar, and it provides buttons that perform frequently used operations such as moving up and down one directory.

The rest of the window is divided into three panes (subwindows):

✔ **Places pane:** Shows the directory Nautilus is connected to.

✔ **Side pane:** Shows shortcuts to your home and desktop directories, the computer's file system, and removable disks (for example, a CD-ROM drive).

✔ **Main pane:** Displays all files and folders. (I can barely resist making silly puns.)

Working with files and folders

Nautilus makes it easy to create new folders and files. Simply right-click a blank portion of the Main pane and a menu opens. The first two options are Create Folders and Create Documents.

Creating new folders

There are two ways to create new folders in GNOME:

✔ **Right-click a blank portion of the Main pane and select Create Folders.**

A new folder opens in Nautilus, with the name Untitled Folder. You then type the name of the folder and press Enter. Your new folder is created with that name.

✔ **Choose File⇨Create Folder.**

An Untitled Folder dialog opens. The default name — Untitled Folder — is displayed in a text box immediately below the folder icon. Type the folder's name in the text box and the folder takes that name.

Creating new files

To create a new file, right-click an empty portion of the Main pane and select Create Document⇨Empty File. An icon, initially labeled New File, opens; you can type in any name you want and press the Enter key.

Double-click the new document file and the Ubuntu default editor, gedit, opens, displaying a blank document. gedit is a good utility for creating simple documents.

Managing existing files and folders

You can go back at any time and change the name of a folder or file. Right-click an icon and select Rename from the menu. Likewise, you can delete the folder or file by right-clicking the icon and selecting Move to Trash.

Follow these steps to copy and move folders and files:

1. **Right-click the icon and select either**

   • *Cut:* Removes the icon from the window.

   • *Copy:* Leaves the icon in the window.

2. **Open the folder in which you want to place the file or folder.**

3. **Right-click any unused portion of the Main pane and select Paste.**

   The file or folder is moved to that folder if you selected the Cut option, or copied there if you used the Copy option.

Files and folders are displayed as icons in Nautilus. You can change to a list of files by choosing View⇨View as List from the Nautilus menu bar.

Starting applications

Nautilus can do more than merely list files and folders. There are a couple of ways you can use Nautilus to start graphical applications:

✔ **Double-click a graphical application icon.**

✔ **Right-click a graphical application icon and select either of these:**

   • *Open*

   • *Open with other Application*

For instance, these steps show how to use Nautilus to open an application that displays a clock:

1. **Open a Nautilus window.**

2. **Click the Go menu, and select the Location option.**

3. **Type `/usr/bin/X11` in the Location text box, and press the Enter key.**

   Type the preceding command *exactly* as shown, including the capital X in X11. Unlike Windows, Linux directory (and file) names are *case sensitive.* You must use exactly the same capitalization as the directory or filename. Most Linux directories use lowercase; however, the X11 directory is a rare example of a directory name that uses an uppercase character.

   Nautilus opens a view to the `/usr/bin/X11` directory, where various graphical applications are stored.

4. **Double-click the Xclock icon.**

   The Xclock application, shown in Figure 12-4, opens. The Xclock application displays a simple analog clock on your desktop.

Figure 12-4:
Xclock
displays an
analog clock
on your
desktop.

You can open files using an application. For instance, clicking on a document file that has a suffix like `.doc` or `.sxw` opens with the OpenOffice.org Writer word processor.

In general, Nautilus is configured to recognize file types that have open source applications capable of opening, playing, or displaying their contents. You can also tell Nautilus to use any application to handle a file that it doesn't recognize. Right-click a file icon and select the Open with Other Application option. A dialog opens, from which you can select another application.

Finding and using network shares

Nautilus is also *network aware,* which means that you can browse for and use network file shares just like you do local ones. Nautilus networking works on both your private network (LAN) and on the Internet.

Nautilus understands the following network file sharing protocols:

- ✔ **FTP:** The File Transfer Protocol (FTP) is as old as the Internet. FTP is used to transfer files between computers. It's simple and easy to use.

- ✔ **SFTP:** This is a secure version of FTP. File transfers are encrypted when SFTP is used.

- ✔ **Windows SMB:** Windows file shares use the SMB (Server Message Block) protocol. Nautilus can browse, read, and write to Windows file shares.

- ✔ **WebDAV:** The Web-based Distributed Authoring and Versioning (WebDAV) protocol lets you read and write to Web servers that use this protocol.

Browse a network resource as follows:

1. **Open a Nautilus window.**

2. **Choose Go⇨Location.**

   The Location text box (similar in look and function to the Firefox Location text box) opens in the Nautilus window.

3. **Type the URL of the network resource in the text box and press the Enter key.**

URLs (uniform resource locator) can be Web, FTP, or Windows file share addresses.

- ✔ **Web:** Looks like `http://some.web.address`

- ✔ **FTP:** Looks like `ftp://some.web.address`

- ✔ **SMB:** Looks like `smb://some.web.address`

If your Ubuntu computer is connected to the Internet, you can view Ubuntu's FTP site by clicking the Nautilus Go menu and selecting the Location option. You type `ftp://ftp.ubuntu.com/ubuntu` in the Location text box. Select the anonymous login option, and you can browse Ubuntu's FTP repository, which includes

- ✔ All the software found on the companion Ubuntu CD

- ✔ Lots of extras, such as the XMMS music player

Nautilus provides a simple but effective search tool. Click the Search button on the Nautilus toolbar and type your search term in the Search text box. Press the Enter key, and Nautilus displays all the files and folders that meet your criteria.

Introducing GNOME Applications

Knowing what applications GNOME provides is quite useful. Having that information can save you time looking for programs that are — or aren't — installed. This section outlines the applications that GNOME installs by default.

Click the Applications menu on the top panel and you see the following menu options. Selecting each option opens a submenu containing applications organized by category. The following sections list the applications found in each category.

Accessories

This submenu contains applications that don't fit into any specific class.

These GNOME menus tend to change from version to version. The following list was extracted from Ubuntu 6.10, which uses GNOME 2.16.1. If you aren't using the Ubuntu and GNOME versions from the *Ubuntu Linux For Dummies* CD, you might see some differences.

- **Archive Manager:** View and extract files from Linux tar files. Linux uses tar to archive files in much the same way Windows uses Zip. The Archive Manager utility lets you look inside tar archives before deciding what you want to do with them.

- **Calculator:** A simple calculator program. I use this program all the time to perform simple calculation tasks.

- **Character Map:** This utility lets you use symbols from all the world's languages in your word processing documents. You open the Character Map utility, select the language from the Script menu on the left of the dialog, and click on a character and drag it to your document. For instance, if you're writing a homework assignment and need to represent the Greek letter Alpha, you select the Greek option from the Script menu, double-click the Alpha character in the Character Table, click the Copy button in the lower-right corner of the dialog, and then select Edit⇨Paste in your homework assignment document. Q.E.D.!

- **Dictionary:** Opens a simple dictionary window. You type a word in the Look Up text box and the application returns a definition.

- **Take Screenshot:** This application makes a copy of the current screen. You can then save the image as a file.

✔ **Terminal:** The Terminal Emulator. You type interactive shell commands in a Terminal Emulator.

See Chapter 5 for a description of how to use this program.

✔ **Text Editor:** Opens a simple text editor. It's actually quite powerful, giving you many of the features found in full-featured word processors like OpenOffice.org Writer.

Games

All work and no play make Ubuntu a dull distribution. Ubuntu includes some simple games, such as Solitaire and Blackjack, that are worth a look on a rainy Saturday afternoon. However, I won't describe them here. I'll let you try them out and discover your favorites.

Graphics

Edit graphical images and view them with the tools found here.

✔ **The GIMP Image Editor:** This is a powerful, image-capture and -editing system. You can capture screen images and then edit them; you can also edit the images that you import from other sources, such as photographs.

✔ **gThumb Image Viewer:** Preview images. gThumb provides a quick and easy way to preview images.

Previewing images is faster than opening each one individually.

✔ **XSane Image Scanner:** Scan and import photographs and other images from a scan device.

Internet

All major Internet categories are covered by applications found in this menu.

✔ **Ekiga Softphone:** Call other Linux computers. You can also call other telephones using the Ekiga service.

Chapter 17 describes how to use Ekiga.

✔ **Evolution Mail:** Use the fabulous Evolution messaging program.

Chapter 15 describes how to use the Evolution e-mail system in some detail.

✔ **Firefox Web Browser:** See how the Web should be surfed with Mozilla Firefox. Firefox includes many features that other browsers are trying to catch up to, such as encrypted password storage, tabbed browsing, and automatic removal of cookies and other potentially sensitive information.

Chapter 14 describes how to use and configure Firefox.

✔ **Gaim Internet Messenger:** This is an instant messaging program. Communicate in real-time with friends and acquaintances.

✔ **Terminal Server Client:** Connect and interact with Microsoft Windows computers.

Chapter 19 describes how to use the Terminal Server Client.

Office

Ubuntu provides all the tools you need to use your computer for reading, writing, and 'rithmatic. OpenOffice.org is an open source suite of programs that provides a word processing, spreadsheet, and slideshow program, along with other tools.

✔ **Evolution:** Evolution provides a great e-mail application, plus calendaring, contacts, and more.

See Chapter 15 for more information about this system.

✔ **OpenOffice.org Database:** Open existing databases and create new ones using this application.

✔ **OpenOffice.org Presentation:** Create slide presentations that are compatible with Microsoft PowerPoint.

✔ **OpenOffice.org Spreadsheet:** OpenOffice.org Calc creates spreadsheets that can be compatible with Microsoft Excel. See Chapter 16 for more information.

✔ **OpenOffice.org Word Processor:** OpenOffice.org Writer is a full-featured word processor compatible with Microsoft Word.

Sound & Video

Ubuntu goes Hollywood, letting you play and record music and more.

✔ **Rhythmbox Music Player:** Play open source audio files and Internet radio streams.

> ✔ **Serpentine Audio CD Creator:** Create audio CDs from digital audio files and play any standard-format audio CD (such as store-bought CDs).
>
> ✔ **Sound Juicer CD Extractor:** Extract (rip) audio CDs.
>
> ✔ **Sound Recorder:** Record audio on your computer.

All these subjects are described in Chapter 20.

Add/Remove

Selecting this option opens the Add/Remove application, from which you can install software packages from CDs, DVDs, or the Internet.

Chapter 23 describes how to add and/or remove software to/from your Ubuntu computer.

Preferences

This menu provides access to the utilities that help you change the look and feel of your Ubuntu computer. Change settings such as your desktop background and your screen saver from this menu.

Administration

This menu provides access to utilities that help you manage your Ubuntu computer. For instance, you can modify your network settings by selecting System⇨Administration⇨Networking.

Chapter 13

Printing with GNOME

● ●

In This Chapter

▶ Connecting your printer to your Ubuntu computer

▶ Connecting remote network printers

● ●

*U*buntu and GNOME provide a printer configuration utility that's easy to use. This chapter describes how to configure your Ubuntu computer to use a printer.

I tell you about using both

✔ **Local printers** that plug directly into your Ubuntu computer

✔ **Network printers** that are connected through your LAN

Connecting Printers

The steps for connecting a printer in Ubuntu depend on whether you're using a local printer that's directly connected through a dedicated cable or a networked printer that's accessed through your network connection.

Setting up local printers

Locally connected printers connect directly to your Ubuntu computer using a dedicated cable. After you connect the cable, you set up the printer through Ubuntu.

Cables

Two types of cables (parallel and USB) are used to connect a computer to a printer. Ubuntu is compatible with either type, if your computer and printer have the necessary connectors.

Parallel

These bulky cables have been used for decades. They're called *parallel* because within the outer cable housing, they contain over two dozen wires. Each wire provides a data signal to the printer. Parallel cables are limited in length to not much more than 10 to 13 feet (3 or 4 meters) because the electrical signals interfere with each other and degrade quickly with distance.

USB

Universal Serial Bus (USB) cables are slim, fast, and used for many different applications. Printers started switching from parallel to USB cables around the turn of the century. (I love saying that.) They've quickly become the industry standard.

Setup

Connecting your computer to a local printer is a simple process. Follow these steps:

1. **Plug your parallel or USB cable into your Ubuntu computer and printer.**

2. **From the GNOME menu bar, choose System⇨Administration⇨Printing.**

   The Printers dialog opens.

3. **Double-click New Printer.**

   The Add a Printer dialog (Figure 13-1) opens. The printer configuration utility shows your printer if it recognizes it.

   If your printer is detected, click the Forward button and skip to Step 5.

4. **If your printer isn't detected, follow these steps to help Ubuntu find the printer:**

   a. *Click the Use Another Printer by Specifying a Port radio button.*

   b. *From the Printer Port drop-down menu, select the printer port that you connected your printer to in Step 1.*

   Select the USB option if using a USB cable. Otherwise, select the appropriate parallel port when using a parallel cable.

c. Click the Forward button.

The Add a Printer (Step 2 of 3: Printer Driver) dialog opens and displays the manufacturer, model, and driver for your printer.

5. **Select a manufacturer, model, and the recommended printer driver, if necessary.**

6. **Click the Forward button.**

The Add a Printer (Step 3 of 3: Printer Information) dialog opens, displaying a default printer name.

This dialog lets you

- Customize the printer name that appears on your system.

- Add a description and location.

7. **After you've edited the printer information to your satisfaction, click the Apply button.**

Control returns to the Printers dialog, where your new printer icon is displayed.

You can print to your new printer now from any GNOME application.

After you install your printers, you should select a default printer for Ubuntu (even if you only have one printer). The last section of this chapter shows you how.

Setting up network printers

Network printer setup requires some essential information about your printer (and a working network connection, of course).

After you install your printers, you should select a *default printer* for Ubuntu. The end of this chapter shows you how to select a default and use the printer.

Network printer setup usually requires a little information about the specific printer you're accessing. The information you need depends on how your network operates. Modern network printers usually display this information. Consult your printer manual and either print the network information or, if available, display it on the printer console. The following instructions in this chapter list the information you need to find for your printer.

The steps to set up your network printer with the GNOME printer utility depend upon its *network protocol: LPD, CUPS, SMB,* or *HP JetDirect.*

Samba printers use the SMB protocol.

The following sections provide setup instructions for each of these protocols.

LPD

The Line Printer Daemon protocol is as old as dirt. LPD is used by UNIX and Linux computers and works quite well.

LPD is rapidly being replaced by CUPS.

Information

Before you begin configuring an LPD printer, obtain the information you need about it:

- ✔ The printer's *queue name* (essentially, the printer name)
- ✔ The printer's *hostname* (like myprinter.mydomain) or *numeric IP address* (like 192.168.1.10)
- ✔ The printer manufacturer and model

Configuration

Follow these steps to configure a printer using the LPD interface:

1. **Choose System⇨Administration⇨Printing from the GNOME menu bar.**

   The Printers dialog opens.

2. **Double-click New Printer.**

   The Add a Printer dialog opens.

3. **Click the Network Printer radio button.**

   The Add a Printer (Step 1 of 3: Printer Connection) dialog opens. Figure 13-2 shows the window.

Figure 13-2:
Adding a network printer.

4. **From the Network Printer drop-down menu, select Unix Printer (LPD).**

   The Properties dialog opens.

5. **Type the hostname or numeric IP address in the Host text box.**

6. **Type the name of the *printer queue*.**

   The queue name is effectively the printer name.

7. **Click the Forward button.**

   The Add a Printer (Step 2 of 3: Printer Driver) dialog opens and displays the manufacturer, model, and driver for your printer.

8. **Select the printer manufacturer, model, and the recommended printer driver.**

   Consult your printer manufacturer's Web site for support if your printer isn't listed here. Many manufacturers let you download Linux printer drivers from their Web sites. If that's the case, follow their instructions.

9. **Click the Forward button.**

   The Add a Printer (Step 3 of 3: Printer Information) dialog opens.

   This dialog lets you

   • Customize the printer name that appears on your system.

   • Add a description and location.

10. **After you've edited the printer information to your satisfaction, click the Apply button.**

    You're finished! Control returns to the Printers dialog, where your new printer icon is displayed.

CUPS

The Common UNIX Printer System (CUPS) is widely used by Linux and UNIX computers to communicate with printers.

Information

Before you begin configuring a CUPS printer, obtain the information you need about it:

✔ The *Universal Resource Identifier* (URI)

   URIs take the following form: ipp://*hostname/printername*. The *hostname* can be either a hostname or a numeric IP address.

   For instance, if your printer's network hostname is myprinter.mydomain and you want to name the printer Gutenberg, the URI is `ipp://my printer.mydomain/Gutenberg`.

✔ The printer manufacturer and model

Configuration

Follow these steps to configure a printer using the CUPS protocol:

1. **Choose System⇨Administration⇨Printing.**

   The Printer dialog opens.

2. **Double-click New Printer.**

   The Add a Printer dialog opens.

3. **Click the Network Printer radio button.**

   The Add a Printer (Step 1 of 3: Printer Connection) dialog opens.

4. **From the Network Printer drop-down menu, choose CUPS Printer (IPP).**

   The Properties dialog opens.

5. **Type the printer's Universal Resource Identifier (URI) address in the URI text box.**

6. **Click the Forward button.**

   The Add a Printer (Step 2 of 3: Printer Driver) dialog opens and displays the manufacturer, model, and driver for your printer.

7. **Select the printer manufacturer, model, and the recommended printer driver.**

   Consult your printer manufacturer's Web site for support if your printer isn't listed here. Many manufacturers let you download Linux printer drivers from their Web sites. If that's the case, follow their instructions.

8. **Click the Forward button.**

   The Add a Printer (Step 3 of 3: Printer Information) dialog opens.

   This dialog lets you

   • Customize the printer name that appears on your system.

   • Add a description and location.

9. **After you've edited the printer information to your satisfaction, click the Apply button.**

   You're finished! Control returns to the Printers dialog, where your new printer icon is displayed.

SMB (Windows and Samba)

Windows network file sharing uses the Service Message Block (SMB) protocol to transmit information. If a printer uses Microsoft-style printing, you can use SMB to print to it from your Ubuntu computer.

Linux provides access to SMB file and printer shares through *Samba*. Samba is a suite of programs that allows Linux to use the SMB protocols and communicate with SMB file and printer shares; Samba also allows Linux to provide SMB-based services.

Information

Before you begin configuring an SMB printer, obtain the information you need about it:

- ✔ SMB network printers combine the hostname and printer name into a *share name*. (It's a Microsoft thing.)

  A printer share name takes the form *//hostname/printername,* where *hostname* and *printer* are provided by the printer's system administrator.

- ✔ *Authentication* information, if required (a *username* and *password*). If needed, you must acquire that information from the printer's system administrator.

  Most consumer-level printers don't require authentication.

- ✔ The printer manufacturer and model.

Configuration

Follow these steps to configure a Windows (or Samba) share-based printer with SMB:

1. **From the GNOME menu bar, choose System⟿Administration⟿ Printing.**

   The Printers dialog opens.

2. **Double-click New Printer.**

   The Add a Printer dialog opens.

3. **Click the Network Printer radio button.**

   The Add a Printer (Step 1 of 3: Printer Connection) dialog opens.

4. **From the Network Printer drop-down menu, choose Windows Printer (SMB).**

   The Properties dialog opens.

5. **Type the printer's share name in the Host text box.**

6. **Type the printer's name in the Printer text box.**

7. **Type your username and password in the appropriate text boxes, if required.**

8. **Click the Forward button.**

   The Add a Printer (Step 2 of 3: Printer Driver) dialog opens and displays the manufacturer, model, and driver for your printer.

9. **Select the printer manufacturer, model, and the recommended printer driver.**

   Consult your printer manufacturer's Web site for support if your printer isn't listed here. Many manufacturers let you download Linux printer drivers from their Web sites. If that's the case, follow their instructions.

10. **Click the Forward button.**

    The Add a Printer (Step 3 of 3: Printer Information) dialog opens.

    This dialog lets you

    - Customize the printer name that appears on your system.

    - Add a description and location.

11. **After you've edited the printer information to your satisfaction, click the Apply button.**

    You're finished! Control returns to the Printers dialog, where your new printer icon is displayed.

HP JetDirect

The JetDirect protocol is used by Hewlett Packard (HP) printers. HP computers are plentiful, so JetDirect is widely used.

Information

Before you begin configuring an HP JetDirect printer, obtain the information you need about it:

✔ The printer's *hostname* (like myprinter.mydomain) or *numeric IP address* (like 192.168.1.10)

✔ The printer manufacturer and model

Configuration

Follow these steps to configure an HP JetDirect printer:

1. **From the GNOME menu bar, choose System⇨Administration⇨ Printing.**

    The Printers dialog opens.

2. **Double-click New Printer.**

    The Add a Printer dialog opens.

3. **Click the Network Printer radio button.**

    The Add a Printer (Step 1 of 3: Printer Connection) dialog opens.

4. **From the Network Printer drop-down menu, select HP JetDirect.**

    The Properties dialog opens.

5. **Type the printer's network hostname in the Host text box.**

    The default JetDirect network port is 9100 and should not be changed.

6. **Click the Forward button.**

    The Add a Printer (Step 2 of 3: Printer Driver) dialog opens and displays the manufacturer, model, and driver for your printer.

7. **Select the printer manufacturer, model, and the recommended printer driver.**

    You need to consult your printer manufacturer's Web site for support if your printer isn't listed here. Many manufacturers let you download Linux printer drivers from their Web sites. If that's the case, follow their instructions.

8. **Click the Forward button.**

    The Add a Printer (Step 3 of 3: Printer Information) dialog opens.

    This dialog lets you

    -   Customize the printer name that appears on your system.
    -   Add a description and location.

9. **After you've edited the printer information to your satisfaction, click the Apply button.**

    You're finished! Control returns to the Printers dialog, where your new printer icon is displayed.

Using Your Printer

After you configure GNOME for your local or network printer, you can print from any application. Most applications recognize printers you configure with GNOME, and you can choose File⇨Print to print to the printer.

It's useful to select a default printer (even if you have only one printer). Otherwise, you'll have to specify what printer you want to use each time you print. To set a default printer, follow these steps:

1. **Right-click your printer icon in the Printers dialog.**

   A menu opens, showing the following options:

   - **Jobs:** Show the documents — jobs — that are waiting to be printed (pending) and those that are currently printing.
   - **Pause:** Temporarily stop a job from printing.
   - **Resume:** Restart a waiting job.
   - **Make Default:** Select the printer as your default printer.
   - **Remove:** Stop and remove a print job from the queue.
   - **Properties:** Display the printer's configuration information.

2. **Select the Make Default option.**

   This makes the printer you selected the default printer.

To test your printer, follow these steps:

1. **Right-click the printer's icon in the Printers dialog and select Properties.**

   The Properties dialog opens.

2. **Click the Print a Test Page button.**

   An Information dialog opens.

3. **Click OK.**

   A test page prints.

Command line printing

You can print the old-fashioned way, using the Linux command line. Open a Terminal Emulator window (as shown in Chapter 5) and use one of these options:

✔ lp *filename* Uses the default printer to print the file.

For example, type lp /etc/passwd to print Ubuntu's password file.

✔ lp -d *printer filename* Identifies the specific printer you want to use.

For example, type lp -d Gutenberg /etc/passwd to print the /etc/ passwd file on the printer Gutenberg.

You can use the command line to see the status of any print job. Type this command:

lpq

Chapter 14

Firing up Firefox

● ●

In This Chapter
▶ Introducing Mozilla Firefox

▶ Discovering what you can do with Firefox

▶ Setting some preferences and installing plug-ins

● ●

*M*ozilla Firefox is the most advanced and powerful Web browser on the market today. Firefox has pioneered many technologies that other browsers are still trying to catch up with.

This chapter describes many, but not all, of Firefox's basic and advanced capabilities. It also explores how to use and configure Firefox.

If you'd like even more information on using Firefox, check out *Firefox For Dummies,* by Blake Ross (Wiley Publishing).

Introducing the Firefox Browser

The Internet was a sleepy, quite place back in the early 1990s. Nothing much was going on in that placid place. Nerds and engineers used it to communicate using a fairly novel system called *electronic mail,* and some file sharing took place. You could also communicate with like-minded individuals using things called *bulletin boards* and *news.*

Then something earth-shattering took place. Tim Berners-Lee took a concept he originated back in the 1980s and designed a thing called HyperText Markup Language (HTML). A client and server system was devised to use the protocol, and soon it was possible to view text and, most importantly, graphics from any computer that wanted to provide such a service. The World Wide Web (WWW) was born.

One of the first browsers to find commercial success was the Netscape Navigator browser. Netscape provided its browser free of charge but soon spun off an open source version called Mozilla. Mozilla grew and grew like a monster and became the monster we know as Mozilla Firefox. Firefox is the Linux browser of choice and is distributed with Ubuntu.

Mosaic was one of the original Web browsers. Netscape's internal name for its Navigator browser was Mozilla. The name *Mozilla* was — in typical technogeekology — a contraction of *Mosaic Killer. Killer* became *killa,* and you could make the two into *Mos-illa* or *Mozilla;* it didn't hurt that *Mozilla* sounded like *Godzilla.* You gotta love technology!

Using Firefox

Firefox is the most advanced browser available today. Other browsers are trying to catch up with the numerous features it offers. Some of the most usable and interesting features that Firefox offers are

- ✔ **Pop-up blocking:** Blocks those annoying, maddening, advertisement windows that pop up all the time. Yuck! You can configure Firefox to allow pop-ups on a site-by-site basis. *Hasta la vista,* pop-ups!

- ✔ **Anti-spyware:** Firefox never downloads and installs or executes programs without asking you first.

  Spyware is currently much more of a Windows problem than a Linux problem, but that will change as Linux becomes more popular.

- ✔ **Clearing data:** This simple but effective option lets you have Firefox remove and clear items such as cookies, cache files, and browsing history. (See the "Clearing private data" section later in the chapter for instructions.)

- ✔ **Tabbed browsing:** Opens a new pane within your existing window for every new Web site you visit. Other browsers need to open an entirely new browser window for every Web site visited.

- ✔ **Automatic updates:** Automatically looks for updates to itself. It downloads and installs security updates as necessary.

- ✔ **Encrypting passwords:** Firefox and other browsers offer the convenience of saving passwords for you. However, unlike other browsers, Firefox can encrypt your passwords, protecting them from hackers.

- ✔ **And much, much more:** Yes, and that's not all, you get much, much more.

Firefox is easy to use. Click the blue globe icon on the top menu bar, and Firefox opens, displaying the Ubuntu home page, as shown in Figure 14-1. From there, you can browse the Web using its many advanced features, described in this chapter.

The Ubuntu home page is actually a file on your Ubuntu computer that displays information about Ubuntu. A file is used in case you don't have an Internet connection.

Firefox consists of the following elements:

✔ **Menu bar:** Provides access to familiar options, such as File, Edit, View and other functions. Table 14-1 shows the Firefox menu bar options.

✔ **Display pane:** This is the main body of Firefox, where you view a Web page.

Figure 14-1:
Surf the
Web with
Firefox.

✔ **Toolbars:** Group common information or capabilities in an easy-to-see-and-use location. Firefox provides the following toolbars:

- *Navigation:* Use this toolbar to navigate (surf) the Internet. It includes the Location text box, which is the long, horizontal text box where you type Web addresses and then press the Enter key to view. This toolbar also includes a Web search (Google, by default) text box that you can type queries into. You'll also find shortcut icons for your home page, printing, and so on.

- *Personal Toolbar Folder:* You can save bookmarks in the Bookmarks menu folder, found near the top, center area of the Firefox window, or in the Personal Toolbar Folder.

- *Status:* Displays information such as the progress of a loading Web page at the bottom of the browser window.

Table 14-1	Firefox Menu Options
Name	*Function*
File	Opens new windows and tabs. You can also find options to open new Web pages, as well as e-mail and print them.
Edit	Copy, cut, and paste text. Undo and redo changes. Find text in Web pages and open the Firefox Preferences dialog.
View	Display or hide toolbars.
Go	Firefox stores recently viewed Web pages, which you can access from this menu.
Bookmarks	Bookmarks conveniently save Web page addresses that you like to visit.
Tools	Firefox is highly configurable. Use this menu to access configuration options.
Help	Seek help! This menu gives you the help you need in the form of locally stored and online Firefox documentation.

Configuring Firefox

This section describes how to configure some of Firefox's popular functions. I describe how to select a home page, block annoying pop-up advertisements, and encrypt saved passwords. I also show how to install popular plug-ins such as Java and Shockwave Flash.

Selecting a home page

Firefox automatically displays your home page when started. To select a home page, start by choosing Edit⇨Preferences. Figure 14-2 shows the Firefox Preferences dialog that opens. The initial home page is set in the Home Page text box to the Ubuntu introduction file.

Change Firefox's home page to any place you want using the following methods:

- **Manually:** Type the Universal Resource Locater (URL) in the Home Page text box.

  A URL is the familiar Web page address, such as `www.wiley.com`.

- **Use Current Page:** You can first browse to the location and then open the Firefox Preferences dialog. From the Preferences dialog, click the Use Current Page button, which is just below the Home Page text box, and the home page is set to the current location.

- **Use Bookmark:** Click the Use Bookmarks button, immediately to the right of the Use Current Page button. The Set Home Page dialog opens, and you can select a Web page pointed to by a bookmark to be your home page.

Updating Firefox

Application software changes all the time. Applications such as Firefox are constantly improved, bugs are fixed, and nothing stands still for long. The Firefox developers realized this and added a simple but amazingly effective tool to their system — an automatic update system.

Mozilla Firefox can update itself whenever security-related updates become available. The browser checks in with the mothership and looks for updates. Firefox downloads and installs updates as they occur. You don't have to worry about using an outdated version of Firefox.

However, Ubuntu disables Firefox's ability to update itself because Ubuntu wants to do the job. Ubuntu takes care of updating all software that it runs, and Firefox is no exception. Rather than allowing the software update job to be handled by individual applications, Ubuntu wants to be sure it performs the update process uniformly.

Clicking the Home button — looks like a home — near the top-left side of the Firefox window sends you to the designated home page. Going home has never been so easy.

Blocking pop-ups

Firefox blocks pop-ups by default. Whenever you visit a pop-up-infested Web site, Firefox blocks the annoyance and displays a menu bar, near the top of the Firefox window, telling you of its good deed.

When Firefox blocks a pop-up, it displays a Preferences button in the menu bar that also opens. Click the Preferences button if you want to allow pop-ups from the Web site. Select the Allow Pop-ups option.

You can also fine-tune the pop-up blocking configuration as follows:

1. **Choose Edit⇨Preferences from the Firefox menu bar.**

   The Firefox Preferences dialog opens.

2. **Select the Content tab.**

3. **Click the Exceptions button to the far right of the Block Pop-Up Windows check box.**

   The Allowed Sites - Popups dialog opens.

4. **Type the Web site URL in the Address of Web Site text box.**

Encrypting passwords

Many Web sites require you to authenticate yourself before allowing you access. Browsers can save passwords for you, but at the risk of storing them unprotected on your computer. Unprotected passwords can be stolen by hackers, and that isn't good.

Firefox has pioneered the practice of letting you protect your passwords by encrypting them. But Firefox doesn't encrypt passwords by default; you have to tell it to do so. Here's how:

1. **Choose Edit⇨Preferences from the Firefox menu bar.**

   The Firefox Preferences dialog (Figure 14-2) opens.

2. **Click the Security tab.**

3. **Select the Use Master Password check box.**

   The Change Master Password dialog, shown in Figure 14-3, opens.

Figure 14-3: Configure Firefox to encrypt passwords.

Change Master Password	☒

A Master Password is used to protect sensitive information like site passwords. If you create a Master Password you will be asked to enter it once per session when Firefox retrieves saved information protected by the password.

Current password: (not set)

Enter new password:

Re-enter password:

Password quality meter

Please make sure you remember the Master Password you have set. If you forget your Master Password, you will be unable to access any of the information protected by it.

Cancel   OK

4. **Type your password in the Enter New Password text box.**

5. **Retype your password in the Re-Enter Password text box.**

The Password Quality Meter shows how difficult your password is to crack (decrypt) by a hacker. Using simple words and phrases for a password registers a lower quality than using passwords with numbers and special characters. The longer, the better, too. Use the meter to find the balance between passwords that are easy to remember and passwords that are difficult to crack. The quality meter shows a horizontal bar that moves to the right as the password becomes more complex — better.

6. Click the Cancel button.

Firefox now protects all of your passwords by encrypting them. From now on, you're asked to enter the master password before Firefox lets you use your stored passwords. This feature greatly increases your security.

Clearing private data

Web browsing is a complicated process. A lot goes on behind the scenes while you're surfing 'da net. A consequence of the complexity is that browsers store information that can potentially be used against you if your computer is ever hacked.

Once again, Firefox has pioneered a simple but effective tool for protecting your data. You can configure Firefox to delete some or all of the data it stores — behind the scenes — when you exit. Follow these steps:

1. Choose Edit⇨Preferences from the Firefox menu bar.

The Firefox Preferences dialog opens.

2. Click the Privacy tab.

3. Select the Always Clear Private Data When I Close Firefox check box.

4. Click the Settings button.

The Clear Private Data dialog opens. (See Figure 14-4.)

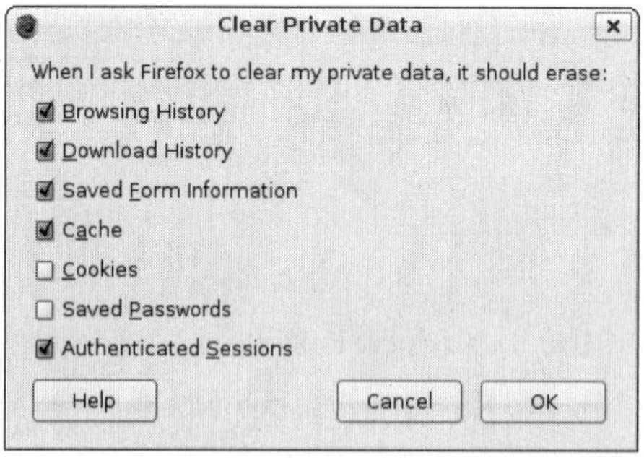

Figure 14-4:
Tell Firefox how you'd like it to clear private data.

Clear Private Data

When I ask Firefox to clear my private data, it should erase:

☑ Browsing History
☑ Download History
☑ Saved Form Information
☑ Cache
☐ Cookies
☐ Saved Passwords
☑ Authenticated Sessions

Help   Cancel   OK

5. Select the Cookies check box.

You can select any combination of options, depending on your needs and preferences. I suggest using the defaults and adding Cookies but not Saved Passwords.

6. **Click OK.**

   Control returns to the Preferences dialog.

7. **Click the Close button.**

   Your private data is erased.

Adding multimedia plug-ins

Multimedia makes the world go 'round. The Web browsing experience is greatly enhanced by audio, video, and other capabilities.

Most of the capabilities that we take for granted aren't actually part of the Web browser itself. Web browsers use *add-ons* to provide extra functions. This section shows how to add add-ons to Firefox. Follow these steps:

1. **Type addons.mozilla.org in the Firefox Location text box.**

2. **Click the Plugins link.**

   You see a listing of numerous plug-ins. The following sections describe how to install several of the popular plug-ins listed on the Web page.

You can see which Firefox plug-ins are installed by typing about:plugins in the Location text box.

Installing the Flash Player plug-in

Flash Player allows Web sites to provide animation within their content. Download and unpack the Flash Player plug-in as follows:

1. **Using the steps in the preceding section, find the Flash Player section and click Version 7 under the For Linux heading.**

   Another Web page opens, describing how to download and install Flash Player.

   You find the Version 7 button in the Flash Player section. The version number might change after this book is published, so select the latest version, if necessary.

2. **Click the Download Now button.**

   The Opening Install_Flash_Player_7_Linux.tar.gz dialog opens.

3. **Click OK.**

4. Click the Extract button.

The Extract dialog opens.

5. Click the Extract button.

Control returns to the Install_Flash_Player_7_Linux.tar.gz dialog.

6. Close the dialog.

Next, you have to copy the Flash Player plug-in files to a place where Firefox can find them.

1. Open a Terminal window by choosing System⇨Accessories⇨Terminal from the GNOME menu bar.

A Terminal Emulator window opens.

See Chapter 5 for information about using Terminal Emulators.

2. Type the following command and press the Enter key:

```
sudo cp /tmp/install_flash_player*/*so
        /usr/lib/firefox/plugins
sudo cp /tmp/install_flash_player*/*xpt
        /usr/lib/firefox/plugins
```

This copies the plug-in files to the Firefox plug-in (`/usr/lib/firefox/plugins`) directory.

Your plug-in is now ready to be used.

You can test your Flash Player plug-in by browsing the `www.adobe.com/shockwave/welcome` Web page.

Installing the Java plug-in

Java is widely used on the Internet to allow people to interact with Web sites. Download and unpack the Java plug-in as follows:

1. Using the steps in the "Adding multimedia plug-ins" section a little earlier in this chapter, find the Java section on the Web site and click Latest Version under the For Linux heading.

A Web page opens, telling you that you can download Java for free.

2. Click the Download Now button.

3. Click the Linux (Self-Extracting File) option and click the Download Now button.

The Opening jre-*current-version*-linux-i586.*Bin* Z dialog opens. The version of the Java download changes frequently, so I don't mention the specific version here to avoid confusion.

4. **Click OK.**

   The Downloads dialog opens and displays the progress of the download.

5. **Click Clean Up and then close the window.**

Now you need to execute the Java installation script. Follow these steps:

1. **Open a Terminal window by choosing SystemAccessoriesTerminal from the GNOME menu bar.**

   A Terminal Emulator window opens.

   See Chapter 5 for information about using Terminal Emulators.

2. **Type the following command and press the Enter key:**

   ```
   chmod +x jre*bin
   ```

3. **Type the following command and press the Enter key:**

   ```
   sudo jre*bin
   ```

   The Sun Microsystem Java license is displayed.

4. **Press the spacebar to read the entire license.**

5. **Type yes and press the Enter key if you agree to the license.**

   Java is installed for you.

6. **Type your user account password when prompted.**

   This copies the plug-in files to the Firefox plug-in (`/usr/lib/firefox/plugins`) directory.

Your plug-in is now ready to be used.

You can test your Java installation by browsing the `www.javatester.org/enabled.html` Web page.

Installing the RealPlayer plug-in

I'll tell you how to install one more useful plug-in. You can listen to and view *streamed* (content that you don't have to download) audio-visual content using the freely available RealPlayer plug-in. Follow these steps:

1. **Using the steps in the "Adding multimedia plug-ins" section earlier in this chapter, find the RealPlayer section on the Web site and click Version 10 under the For Linux heading.**

   You jump to the Real, Inc., download Web page.

2. **Click the Download RealPlayer button.**

   The Opening RealPlayer10GOLD.Bin dialog opens.

   The version number might be different by the time you read this.

3. **Click the OK button.**

   The Downloads dialog opens and displays the progress of the download.

4. **Click Clean Up and then close the window.**

Now you need to execute the RealPlayer installation script. Follow these steps:

1. **Open a Terminal window by choosing System⇨Accessories⇨Terminal from the GNOME menu bar.**

   A Terminal Emulator window opens.

   See Chapter 5 for information about using Terminal Emulators.

2. **Type the following command and press the Enter key:**

   ```
   chmod +x RealPlayer*bin
   ```

3. **Type the following command and press the Enter key:**

   ```
   sudo RealPlayer*bin
   ```

4. **Type your user account password when prompted.**

   The files are extracted, and you're prompted to continue.

5. **Press the Enter key to accept the RealPlayer installation defaults every time you're prompted.**

   RealPlayer installs.

You need to tell Ubuntu to use RealPlayer when it encounters multimedia encoded as RealAudio or RealVideo. Follow these steps:

1. **Open `http://service.real.com/test/` in Firefox.**

2. **Click any RealVideo or RealAudio links.**

   The Opening dialog appears.

3. **From the Open With drop-down menu, choose Other.**

   The Choose Helper Application dialog opens in your home directory. RealPlayer was just installed into your home directory, which makes it easy to select.

4. **Double-click the RealPlayer folder.**

5. **Scroll down and select the realplay file.**

6. **Click Open.**

    Control returns to the Opening dialog.

7. **Select the Do This Automatically for Files Like This One from Now On check box.**

    Selecting this option makes Firefox use RealPlayer by default for RealAudio and RealVideo files.

8. **Click OK.**

    A RealPlayer window opens and plays the audio or video clip you selected.

 RealPlayer can play many familiar formats. For instance, it can play MP3 files.

Adding Themes to Firefox

You can add a theme to the browser to beautify its look and feel. Follow these steps:

1. **Browse to addons.mozilla.org.**

2. **Click the Themes link.**

3. **Select any theme listed.**

    For instance, select Firefox Vista under the Popular Themes heading.

4. **Click the Install Now button.**

    The Confirm dialog opens.

5. **Click OK.**

    The Themes dialog opens and displays the installation process progression.

6. **Select the theme you just added.**

    The Use Theme button activates at the bottom of the dialog.

7. **Click the Use Theme button.**

8. Close the Themes dialog window.

9. Restart Firefox and it uses the new theme.

When you restart Firefox, you notice that the menu system, icons, and even the borders look different. That's the new theme you installed. You can change back to the original or any other theme you have installed by choosing Tools⇨Themes from the Firefox menu bar and using the Themes dialog to change themes.

Chapter 15

Evolution E-Mail, Calendars, and Addresses

*E*volution is the de facto GNOME and Ubuntu e-mail program. Evolution provides messaging plus calendaring and address book functions. It's a full-featured system similar to Microsoft Outlook.

This chapter describes how to use Evolution e-mail and related functions. I guide you through configuring your e-mail account, using calendars, and making contact lists.

Introducing Evolution

Evolution is an all-in-one system that provides a wealth of features that makes your computing life easier. Some Evolution features are

✔ **E-mail:** Create one or more e-mail accounts.

✔ **Junk mail filtering:** Filter junk mail using Evolution's adaptive filtering system. Evolution learns what is and isn't junk mail as you receive messages.

✔ **Searching:** Search your messages using Evolution's advanced searching system.

✔ **Message integrity:** Digitally sign and encrypt your messages.

✔ **Web sharing:** Share your calendar and contacts on the Web.

Configuring Evolution for E-Mail

You can use Evolution to access your existing e-mail accounts. Using Evolution's calendar and contact list also requires a little bit of work.

Evolution provides an easy-to-use configuration wizard that helps you do the setup work. In the steps that follow, I walk you through the setup process, but first you need to know some information about your e-mail account. Contact your ISP (Internet service provider) to find out the following information:

- ✔ Account username: _____
- ✔ E-mail address: _____
- ✔ Account password: _____
- ✔ Incoming e-mail server name: _____
- ✔ Incoming e-mail server encryption (None, SSL, TLS):
  _____
- ✔ Outgoing e-mail server name: _____
- ✔ Outgoing e-mail server encryption (None, SSL, TLS):
  _____

You will need this information to configure Evolution to send and receive e-mail to and from your ISP.

Opening the configuration wizard and setting up your e-mail account identity

Start by opening Evolution and entering your name and e-mail account username. Follow these steps:

1. **Click the Evolution icon (looks like an envelope with a clock in front of it) on the GNOME menu bar.**

   The Evolution Setup Assistant dialog opens.

   Or you can start Evolution by choosing Applications➪Internet➪Evolution from the GNOME menu bar.

2. **Click the Forward button.**

   The Evolution Setup Assistant dialog, shown in Figure 15-1, opens.

3. **Type your name and e-mail address in their respective text boxes.**

   You can also enter an alternative e-mail address and a company or organization name in the appropriate text boxes.

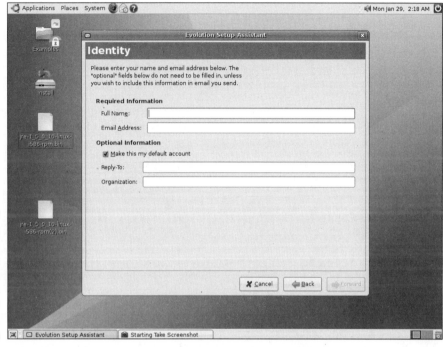

Figure 15-1:
The
Evolution
Setup
Assistant -
Identity
dialog.

After you've entered your identity, you need to configure Evolution to receive incoming e-mail. That process is described in the following section.

Setting your incoming e-mail server

After you enter your identity, you tell Evolution about the server handling your e-mail account. The server is managed by the ISP (Internet service provider) whom you have registered your e-mail account with.

Chapters 8 and 9 provide advice about finding and selecting an ISP.

Follow these steps to continue with the configuration wizard you began in the preceding section:

1. **Click the Forward button in the Evolution Setup Assistant - Identity dialog.**

   The Evolution Setup Assistant - Receiving Email dialog opens. Figure 15-2 shows a sample window.

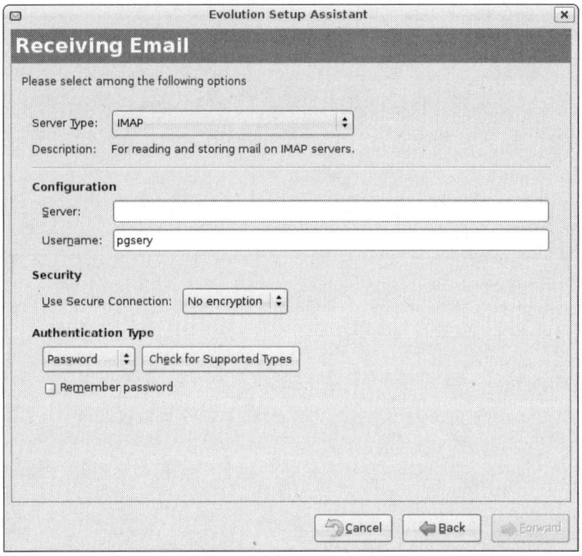

Figure 15-2:
Evolution
Setup
Assistant -
Receiving
Email
window.

2. **From the Server Type drop-down menu, choose your e-mail server's protocol.**

   You need to obtain the server's e-mail protocol from the person who runs the system. The most popular protocols are IMAP, POP, and Microsoft Exchange.

3. **Type the server's network name (or numeric IP address) in the Server text box.**

   You need to get the e-mail server's network name from your ISP.

4. **If your ISP provides SSL (Secure Sockets Layer) or TLS (Transport Layer Security), choose that encryption from the Use Secure Connection drop-down menu.**

   Use encryption if available.

5. **Click the Check for Supported Types button.**

6. **Click the Forward button in the Evolution Setup Assistant - Receiving Email dialog.**

   The Evolution Setup Assistant - Receiving Options dialog opens.

Selecting optional e-mail receiving options

You can select options such as automatically polling your e-mail account for new messages; you can specify the polling period to be one or more minutes.

Follow these steps to continue with the Evolution Setup Assistant from the preceding section:

1. **If you want Evolution to automatically check for and display new incoming messages, select the Automatically Check for New Mail Every check box.**

2. **Change the time value to the minimum of 1 minute (if you're connected to the Internet via a broadband connection) or select an interval of 10 minutes (if you use a slower, dial-up Internet connection).**

3. **Click the Forward button in the Evolution Setup Assistant - Receiving Options dialog.**

   The Evolution Setup Assistant - Sending Email dialog opens.

Setting your e-mail sending options

Now you set up Evolution to send messages to your e-mail server. Figure 15-3 shows the Evolution Setup Assistant - Sending Email window that you open in the preceding section.

Figure 15-3: Setting your e-mail sending options.

1. **From the Server Type drop-down menu, select the Sendmail option if that's what your mail server uses.**

   Most e-mail systems use the Simple Mail Transfer Protocol (SMTP).

2. **Type your server network name or numerical IP address in the Server text box.**

3. **If your server supports an encryption option, select it from the Use Secure Connection drop-down menu.**

4. **Click the Forward button in the Evolution Setup Assistant - Sending Email dialog.**

   The Evolution Setup Assistant - Account Management dialog opens.

Choosing your time zone

E-mail messages that you send contain time and date stamps. You need to tell Evolution what time zone you live in so that the time stamp is accurate. Follow these steps to set up your time zone:

1. **Click the Forward button in the Evolution Setup Assistant - Account Management dialog you open in the preceding section.**

   The Evolution Setup Assistant - Timezone dialog opens and shows a map of the world's time zones. Figure 15-4 shows the window.

Figure 15-4:
Select your
time zone.

2. **Select your city.**

   You can either choose your city from the Selection drop-down menu or follow these steps to use the map:

a. Click the diamond icon of the city closest to your location.

The map enlarges, zooming in on the area where you clicked.

b. If you didn't locate your closest city, click again in the enlarged map.

c. If you still can't locate your time zone — for instance, you live in the Twilight Time Zone — type your time zone in the Selection text box.

3. **Click the Forward button in the Evolution Setup Assistant - Timezone dialog.**

The Evolution Setup Assistant - Done dialog opens.

4. **Click Apply.**

The Enter Password For dialog opens.

Entering your e-mail account password

The final configuration steps require you to set a password for outgoing messages:

1. **In the Enter Password For dialog that you open in the preceding section, type your e-mail account password in the text box and press Enter.**

2. **If you want Evolution to remember your password (rather than typing it each time you open Evolution), select the Remember this Password radio button.**

Evolution saves your password and uses it to log in to your account in the future.

3. **Click OK.**

The Evolution - Mail window opens.

Evolution provides a default e-mail account called On This Computer that isn't connected to any external service. Your new account is located below the local one.

• Click the arrow next to your e-mail account and a list of your account folders unfolds.

• Click your inbox and you see your messages.

You can create as many e-mail accounts as you want and need. Repeat the steps described in this section to create additional ones.

Using Evolution

Evolution provides many services in addition to e-mail messaging. This section starts by describing how to use its messaging service and proceeds to explore its address book and calendaring services.

E-mail messaging with Evolution

Evolution performs basic messaging services such as sending and receiving e-mails. It also provides helpful features such as spell checking.

The following list outlines Evolution's basic messaging capabilities:

- ✔ **New:** Click the New drop-down menu and select Mail Message to create a new e-mail message. The Compose Message window opens, in which you type your recipient's address, a subject, and of course, your message.

  Click the Attach button, near the top, center of the Compose Message dialog, to include attachments in your message.

- ✔ **Receive:** Click any message displayed in your inbox or other folders to select and display the message.

Evolution provides the following buttons to provide shortcuts to its basic functions:

- ✔ **Send/Receive:** Evolution queues outgoing messages until you click this button. Clicking this button sends any outgoing messages you've composed and also forces Evolution to download any messages addressed to you from the e-mail server.

- ✔ **Reply:** Using the Reply button opens the selected message and includes the message in a new message addressed to the sender. Reply to All performs the same function and additionally copies the message to all other addressees from the original e-mail.

- ✔ **Forward:** Using the Forward button copies and forwards the selected message to an address of your choosing.

- ✔ **Print:** Prints the selected message.

- ✔ **Delete:** Deletes the selected message.

- ✔ **Junk:** Selecting a message and clicking the Junk button declares the message junk mail and moves it to the Junk folder. Evolution learns what messages are junk as you declare more junk messages. With time, Evolution filters out junk messages automatically, placing them in the Junk folder. (You should check the Junk folder to weed out any mistakes.

Click the Not Junk button when a message has erroneously been declared; this also helps Evolution to make better selections.)

✔ **Cancel:** Clicking this button cancels any operation in progress.

Keeping track of contact information

Keep contact lists will Evolution. Who it matters not. Click the Contacts button in the submenu in the lower-left corner of the Evolution window, and Evolution displays your contact list.

Click the New button on the Evolution toolbar and the Contact Editor dialog, shown in Figure 15-5, opens.

Type the person's full name, nickname, and other information in the appropriate text boxes. You can file the contact in various categories: friends, family, business, enemies. (No, just kidding. There aren't any Evolution enemies!)

You can also use received messages to populate your contact list. Here's how to shuffle the data from an incoming e-mail into your contact list:

1. **Open any message and right-click the sender's e-mail address.**

2. **Select the Add to Address Book option in the menu that opens.**

   The Contact Quick-Add dialog opens.

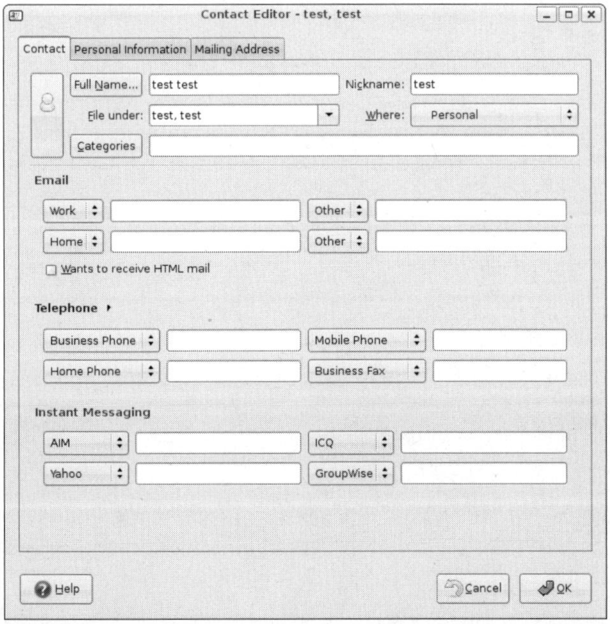

Figure 15-5:
Enter the contact information for the person you want to keep in touch with.

3. **If you want to add information like addresses and phone numbers to your contact, click the Edit Full button.**

   The Contact Editor dialog opens. (Refer to Figure 15-6.) Add any additional, but unessential, information you want to your new contact.

4. **Click OK.**

   Your new contact is added to your address book.

Calendaring with Evolution

Evolution also provides calendaring capabilities. Evolution can run a calendar for you on your Ubuntu computer. This section describes the basics to using the calendar function.

Select the calendar operation by clicking the Calendars button in the lower-left corner of the Evolution window. The Evolution - Calendars window opens. Figure 15-6 shows an example.

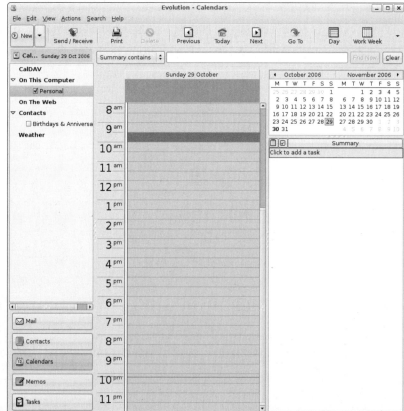

Figure 15-6:
Organize your time with the Evolution calendar.

Adding alarms

Evolution can sound an alarm (beep) before your appointment. The following steps set an alarm:

1. **Click Edit and select Preferences.**

   The Evolution Preference dialog opens.

2. **Select the Show a reminder radio button under the Alarms heading near the bottom of the dialog.**

The alarm is automatically set for 15 minutes before an appointment.

3. **If you want more or less time before the appointment, click and choose another number in the Alarm text box.**

Once you set the Show a reminder option, Evolution will alert you before every appointment.

Adding events

Editing the calendar is a straightforward process. Follow these steps:

1. **If necessary, select the month by clicking the Forward/Backward button immediately next to the month. Select the day by clicking it.**

   You can select another year, if you're super organized!

   An hour-by-hour schedule for the selected date opens in the middle of the window.

2. **Click the desired hour and type a message.**

Your event is saved in the Evolution calendar. Any date with a scheduled event is displayed in bold font in the month box. Clicking a date displays any scheduled events.

Deleting events

You can delete events from the calendar, too. Follow these steps:

1. **Click the date of the event.**

   The daily schedule opens.

2. **Right-click the event and choose Delete.**

   The Evolution Query dialog opens.

3. **Click Delete.**

   You've successfully canceled your appointment.

You should confirm any appointments you delete with the person you have the appointment with. Evolution is great, but your boss might not think you're so great if you don't confirm.

Setting up meetings using Evolution calendars

Evolution can help you schedule meetings. Let's say you want to schedule a meeting with your barber shop quartet to discuss your imminent fame on American Idol.

The guys are hard to get hold of but they all, of course, use Evolution on their Ubuntu computers. Using Evolution, you'll all be famous — or perhaps infamous — soon. Here's how:

1. **If necessary, open Evolution by selecting Applications⇨Internet⇨Evolution Mail from the GNOME menu bar.**

   The Evolution window opens.

   Using Evolution to setup meetings requires you to configure Evolution to send and receive e-mail messages. See sections Configuring Evolution for Email for configuration instructions.

2. **Click the Calendars button towards the lower, left of the window.**

   Your personal Calendar is displayed.

3. **Click on the day and time you want to setup the meeting.**

   The text box to the right of the selected hour is highlighted.

4. **Type in the name you want to call the meeting.**

5. **Right-click on the meeting and select the Forward as Icalendar from the unnamed drop-down menu that appears.**

   An outgoing message window opens.

6. **Type in the e-mail addresses of all the attendees, including yourself, separated by commas in the To: text box.**

7. **Click the Send button.**

The e-mail window closes and the message is sent to every addressee. You'll receive your own message and can see how it works by using the following instructions.

1. **Click the Mail button in the left side of the Evolution window.**

   Evolution displays your e-mail folders.

2. **Click the Send/Receive button.**

   Evolution reads all message headers from your e-mail provider and displays the new one, requesting the meeting, that you just sent.

3. **Click on the meeting message.**

   Evolution displays the message, which includes the meeting information.

4. **Click the on Open Calendar button at the bottom of the message and Evolution opens your calendar and displays the meeting details.**

5. **Click on the Mail button again to return to the Mail window.**

6. **Click the Accept button at the bottom of the message, to the right of the Open Calendar button, and a message will be sent to the sender — you in this case — affirming that you will be in attendance.**

Chapter 16

Opening Your Ubuntu Office with OpenOffice.org

....

In This Chapter

▶ Introducing OpenOffice.org

▶ Using OpenOffice.org applications

▶ Printing with OpenOffice.org

....

*O*penOffice.org is a suite of applications similar in function to Microsoft Office. OpenOffice.org's application suite provides a word processor, spreadsheet, slide presentation editor, Web page editor, and other utilities. It's a powerful and sophisticated system.

OpenOffice.org's applications are compatible with their Microsoft Office peers. OpenOffice.org Writer, for instance, can read and write documents stored in Office 97/2000/XP, Office 95, and Office 6.0 — as well as many other non-Microsoft formats. It's a powerful tool and well worth its cost. Oh yeah, OpenOffice.org is developed as an open source project, which means it costs nothing. Amazing.

Thanks to all the people in the world who put their energy and inspiration into projects like OpenOffice.org. Because of all of them, people like you me get to use sophisticated software such as Writer — which I'm writing with right now, of course. This chapter describes how to harness, configure, and use OpenOffice.org Writer — in other words, how to get the most bang for your buck.

Getting to Know OpenOffice.org

OpenOffice.org provides the following applications:

- ✔ **Writer:** Use a full-featured word processor.
- ✔ **Calc:** Use a full-featured spreadsheet.

✔ **Impress:** Create static and dynamic slide presentations.

✔ **Drawing:** Create drawings and diagrams.

✔ **Database:** Read and write to databases.

✔ **HTML editor:** Edit Web forms.

Writer the word processor

The OpenOffice.org word processor is called Writer. This section describes how to open Writer and get started using it.

Choose Applications⇨Office⇨OpenOffice.org from the GNOME menu at the top-left side of your desktop. Figure 16-1 shows the initial OpenOffice.org Writer window.

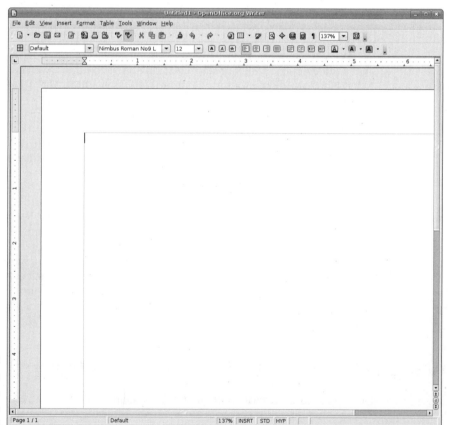

Figure 16-1: OpenOffice. org Writer.

You can immediately start writing the next great novel. "It was a dark and stormy night when Paul was startled from his writing by a knock at the door. He had made a lot of enemies in certain corners writing about Linux, so he pulled out his .45 and. . . ." Or you can start writing a letter to Mom. It doesn't matter, Writer is ready to record your thoughts.

Calc the spreadsheet

OpenOffice.org Calc is a spreadsheet application — the equivalent of Microsoft Excel. This section shows how to start Calc.

Choose Applications⇨Office⇨OpenOffice.org Spreadsheet from the GNOME menu at the top-left side of your desktop.

Figure 16-2 shows the familiar spreadsheet form.

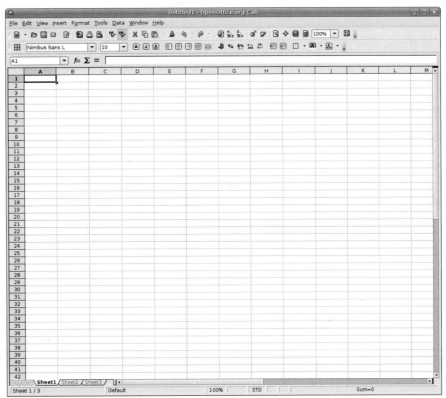

Figure 16-2:
OpenOffice.
org Calc.

Impress slide presentation editor

Impress is an Openoffice.org slideshow editor and is compatible with Microsoft PowerPoint presentation manager. Follow these steps to open and take a look at the application:

1. **Choose Applications⇨Office⇨OpenOffice.org Presentation from the GNOME menu bar.**

   Figure 16-3 shows the Presentation Wizard that opens.

2. **Use the Presentation Wizard to do any of the following:**

   • *Create a new, empty presentation.*

     You can open a new presentation window (see Figure 16-4) using the Impress defaults by clicking the Create button.

   • *Use an existing template to create a new presentation.*

   • *Open an existing presentation.*

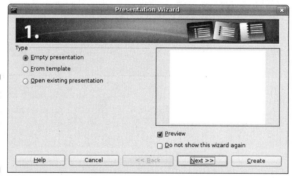

Figure 16-3:
OpenOffice.
org
Presentation
Wizard.

The following instructions open the OpenOffice.org Presentation application to create and edit slideshows:

1. **Choose Applications⇨Office⇨OpenOffice.org Presentation from the GNOME menu bar.**

   The Presentation Wizard opens.

2. **Click Next.**

   This starts the creation of an empty presentation document.

3. **Click Next.**

   This selects the default background.

4. **Select Create.**

   Impress opens a blank presentation.

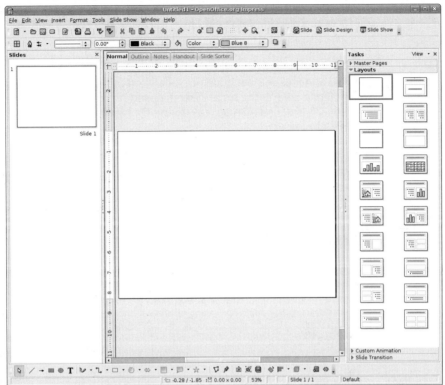

Figure 16-4:
Shows the
initial
Impress.

Popular Functions and Tools

All OpenOffice.org applications share a similar set of capabilities. The following list shows the capabilities for the Writer word processor. The menus are organized in the familiar menu layout:

- ✔ **File:** Use file-oriented processes, such as opening and saving files.

  You can also e-mail and print documents from the File menu.

- ✔ **Edit:** Provides document-editing functions such as cutting, copying, and pasting text.

- ✔ **View:** Select and modify different document layouts, toolbars, and related functions. Display or hide menus, text, and paragraphs.

- ✔ **Insert:** Insert formats, bookmarks, headers, footers, tables, and objects into the document.

- ✔ **Format:** Add and change document formatting. You can change formatting based on individual characters, paragraphs, or the entire document.

- ✔ **Table:** Insert and modify tables in a document.

✔ **Tools:** Access utilities such as the spell checker and macro editor. You can also customize menus, toolbars, key sequences, and change global options.

✔ **Window:** Open and close OpenOffice.org windows.

✔ **Help:** Access OpenOffice.org local- and Internet-based help systems. You can search the local system based on its index or its own search engine. You can also access online OpenOffice.org help via the Firefox Web browser.

OpenOffice.org features could, as they say, fill a book. It's loaded with many capabilities, too many to cover in depth here, so I examine some of its most commonly used and useful ones.

Managing files

At some point after you open a new file, you eventually need to save it. After you save a file, at some point you need to be able to open it. The circle of life is complete. In the text that follows, I tell you how to do both.

Opening files

Use the File menu on the Openoffice.org Writer menu bar to open files:

1. **Choose File⇨Open from the program's menu bar.**

   The Open dialog opens. The dialog is a file manager window.

2. **Use your mouse to select a file or maneuver to another directory (folder).**

3. **Click the Open button to select a file to open.**

   • The icons along the top of the Writer window represent the subdirectories containing the one you're currently working in.

   • The left subwindow shows your home directory, the Desktop folder in your home directory, the overall file system, and any additional directories available to you; for instance, the subwindow can show any USB thumb drives plugged into your Ubuntu computer.

   For example, Figure 16-5 shows what I see when I want to open this chapter file.

You can open OpenOffice.org files through Nautilus file manager:

1. **To open a Nautilus file manager window, from the GNOME menu bar, choose Places⇨Home Folder.**

   See Chapter 12 for more information about the Nautilus file manager.

2. **Double-click any OpenOffice.org document file.**

The appropriate OpenOffice.org application opens the file. For instance, double-clicking a file created with Writer opens the file in the word processor.

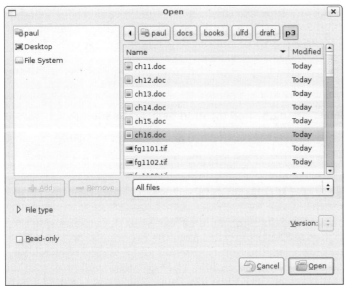

Figure 16-5:
This chapter's Open dialog.

Saving files

OpenOffice.org gives you the option of saving a file using either

✔ **Its current filename, location (folder), and file type**

You can use any of these methods:

  • *Choose File⇨Save from the program's menu bar.*

  • *Click the floppy-diskette-like icon near the upper-left side of an OpenOffice.org window.*

  • *Simultaneously press the Control and S keys (Ctrl+S).*

✔ **A different filename, location (folder), or file type**

You can change the filename, location, or type by choosing File⇨Save As from the program's menu bar. The Save dialog opens.

The dialog selects the current filename, location, and type by default, but you can change any of those items:

  • *Name:* Type a new filename in the Name text box.

> - *Save in Folder:* Click this submenu and browse for another folder (directory) to save to. Alternatively, click Browse to select another folder.
> - *File type:* Click the File Type drop-down menu and select a different file format.

OpenOffice.org provides the useful option of saving a file using the Portable Document Format (PDF). You can easily distribute documents with others by saving files with the PDF option. Here's how:

1. **Choose File⇨Export as PDF from the Openoffice.org Writer menu.**

   The Export dialog opens.

2. **Select the name and location to save the file.**

   Your document is converted and saved as a PDF file.

Setting properties

You can enter useful information about your document using the Properties utility. Choose File⇨Properties from the program's menu bar. The Properties dialog opens. Click the Description tab and add descriptive information that is saved as part of your document but not displayed as part of the text (or cells, in a spreadsheet). Close the Properties dialog by clicking the OK button. You can view a document's description by choosing File⇨Properties and clicking the Description tab.

The Properties dialog also provides document statistics, such as the number of characters, words, and lines used in the document. Click the Statistics tab to see this information.

Using macros

Sometimes you repetitively perform an editing sequence on a document. OpenOffice.org's macro system lets you record and save an editing sequence. You can run the macro in order to replay the editing sequence and save yourself some work.

Creating macros

To record a series of OpenOffice.org Writer editing steps as a macro, follow these steps:

1. **Choose Tools⇨Macros⇨Record Macros from the program's menu bar.**

   A small Record dialog opens.

OpenOffice.org file extensions

OpenOffice.org can read and write many different file formats, including its own and the Open Document Format (ODF). The ODF can be used by any application — open source or proprietary. OpenOffice.org uses the ODF by default unless you specify otherwise.

OpenOffice.org uses different file suffixes when saving files. The following list describes the suffixes that the three most popular OpenOffice.org applications use when saving ODF files:

✔ **Writer:** Saves ODF files using the `.odt` file suffix. (Writer uses the `.sxw` suffix when using its own format.)

✔ **Calc:** Uses the `.ods` file suffix. (Calc also can save files using its own format and the file suffix `.sxc`.)

✔ **Impress:** Uses the `.odp` suffix. (Impress-formatted files use the `.sxi` file suffix.)

OpenOffice.org provides a large number of formats to save documents with. You can use popular formats such as Microsoft Office or new ones such as ODF.

   2. Perform the repetitive task as you would without using the macro utility.

   Every action you perform is recorded.

   3. Click the Stop Recording button in the dialog.

   The OpenOffice.org Basic Macros dialog opens.

   4. Type the macro name in the Macro Name text box.

   5. Click the Save button.

   Your macro is saved.

For instance, let's say you want to create a simple list of numbers from 1 to 3. Your list will look as follows:

1.

2.

3.

You can create a macro to create the list as follows:

   1. Click the OpenOffice.org Writer File menu and choose New⇨Text Document.

   2. Choose Tools⇨Macros⇨Record Macros from the program's menu bar.

   The Record dialog opens.

   3. Click anywhere in the document and press the Enter key.

4. **Type the number 1 followed by a period and press the Enter key.**

5. **Type the number 2 followed by a period and press the Enter key.**

6. **Type the number 3 followed by a period and press the Enter key.**

7. **Click the Stop Recording button in the dialog.**

    The OpenOffice.org Basic Macros dialog opens.

8. **Type `testmacro` in the Macro Name text box.**

9. **Click the Save button.**

    Your macro is saved. The following steps show how to use it.

Executing macros

To use a saved macro, follow these steps:

1. **Choose Tools⇨Macros⇨Run Macros from the program's menu bar.**

    The Macro Selector dialog opens.

2. **Select your macro from the Libraries subwindow on the left side of the Macro Selector dialog.**

3. **Click the Run button.**

    Your macro executes and you minimize the chances of getting carpal tunnel syndrome.

Change tracking

OpenOffice.org Writer provides powerful change-tracking capabilities. Change tracking lets you record, and optionally display, changes that you make to a document.

This feature is useful when you want to be able to refer to older versions of your documents. Change tracking is essential when you work with other people and trade files.

Change tracking provides the following capabilities:

- ✔ **Record changes:** Start change tracking by choosing Edit⇨Changes ⇨ Record from the program's menu bar. All changes are recorded but not displayed.

- ✔ **Display changes:** You can view changes by choosing Edit⇨Changes⇨ Show from the program's menu bar:

    • *Deletions are displayed with red strikethrough font.*

    • *Inserted text shows up with red underlined font.*

✔ **Accept or reject changes:** You can make all changes permanent by choosing Edit⇨Accept or Reject. The Accept or Reject Changes dialog opens, showing all changes you've made. You can accept individual changes by clicking the Accept button, or accept all changes by clicking the Accept All button. Accepting a change integrates the change into the document.

Seeking help

OpenOffice.org gives you extensive documentation and help. Click the Help menu and you get a menu with these options:

✔ **OpenOffice.org Help:** Opens a window similar to the one shown in Figure 16-6. You can use the table of contents to view various topics; you can also search topics via the index or by specifying a search term. Click on the following tabs:

- **Contents:** View the help system's table of contents.

- **Index:** Search through the help system's index.

- **Find:** Search the help system using a search string.

- **Bookmarks:** Go to help system topics marked by bookmarks.

You can create bookmarks to topics that you use frequently. Click the Bookmarks tab to create bookmarks. After saving a bookmark, you can access it by choosing a bookmark and clicking the Display button.

✔ **What's This?:** It's a directed help system is what it is. Select this option and your cursor transmogrifies into a question mark. Place the cursor over an OpenOffice.org object and a little yellow dialog opens and displays information about the object.

✔ **Get Help Online:** Clicking this option directs your browser to the OpenOffice.org online help system. You should use this option if you don't find the answer you're looking for using the local help system.

✔ **Translate This Document:** This option directs your browser to the OpenOffice.org information about language translation options.

✔ **About OpenOffice.org:** You can see the version and copyright information about OpenOffice.org.

Printing

Configuring OpenOffice.org to print requires very little work. You can immediately print documents after you configure Ubuntu for your printer. (See Chapter 13.) Follow these steps:

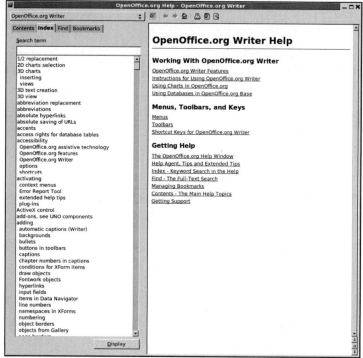

Figure 16-6:
Get
help with
using the
OpenOffice.
org appli-
cations.

1. **Choose File⇨Print from the program's menu bar.**

   The Print dialog opens.

2. **Select your printer by clicking the Name drop-down menu and choosing the device.**

   No selection is required if you have only one printer.

3. **Select any options, if desired.**

   By default, OpenOffice.org prints one copy of every page of the document. You can choose to print

   - *Selected pages*

   - *Multiple copies*

   Clicking the Properties button opens another dialog. You can select

   - *Paper size, orientation (portrait or landscape), and scale*

   - *Special options that your printer might offer, such as duplex printing (both sides of the paper) and trays of special paper*

4. **Click OK.**

   Your document prints.

Part IV
Multimedia Ubuntu

The 5th Wave   By Rich Tennant

"I'm ordering our new PC. Do you want
it left-brain or right-brain oriented?"

In this part . . .

Part IV focuses on using Ubuntu as a communication platform and multimedia center.

You can use Ubuntu as a telephone and instant messenger as described in chapters 17 and 18. Chapter 19 describes how to use Ubuntu to remotely manage Windows computers. We move on the playing music, burning music CDs and listening to Internet radio in chapter 20. Finally, chapter 21 shows how to use and manipulate graphic images.

Chapter 17

Telephonic Ubuntu

● ●

In This Chapter

▶ Setting up an Ekiga account and client

▶ Finding phone numbers and determining availability

▶ Calling a PC and chatting

▶ Establishing a PC-to-phone account

● ●

*T*he Internet connects us all. Over the last decade, we've learned to use the Internet to conduct business, gather and disseminate information via the Web, and communicate directly using e-mail and instant messaging.

The next step is to start using the Internet to communicate. Ubuntu provides just such a tool, called Ekiga. Ekiga gives you the ability to talk, text message, and conduct video conferences with other people over the Internet.

Ekiga used to be called *GnomeMeeting*.

This chapter shows how to configure and use Ekiga to talk with other Ekiga clients. You also learn how to use Ekiga to talk to people with hard-wired telephones and cellphones.

Ekiga video conferencing is beyond the scope of this book.

Configuring Ekiga

Ekiga is an Internet-based service that requires you to

✔ Sign up for an Ekiga account on the Internet.

✔ Set up the Ekiga *client* (software) on your Ubuntu computer.

Registering your Ekiga.net account

To communicate with other Ekiga users, you need to register with Ekiga network service on the Internet. The following steps *register* and *confirm* your free Ekiga account:

1. **Open Firefox and browse to the `www.gnomemeeting.org` home page.**

   Firefox displays the GnomeMeeting/Ekiga home page.

2. **Click the SIP Address (the red telephone) icon.**

   Your browser shows the `www.ekiga.net` Web page.

3. **Click the Subscribe link.**

   The next Web page, shown in Figure 17-1, asks you for registration information.

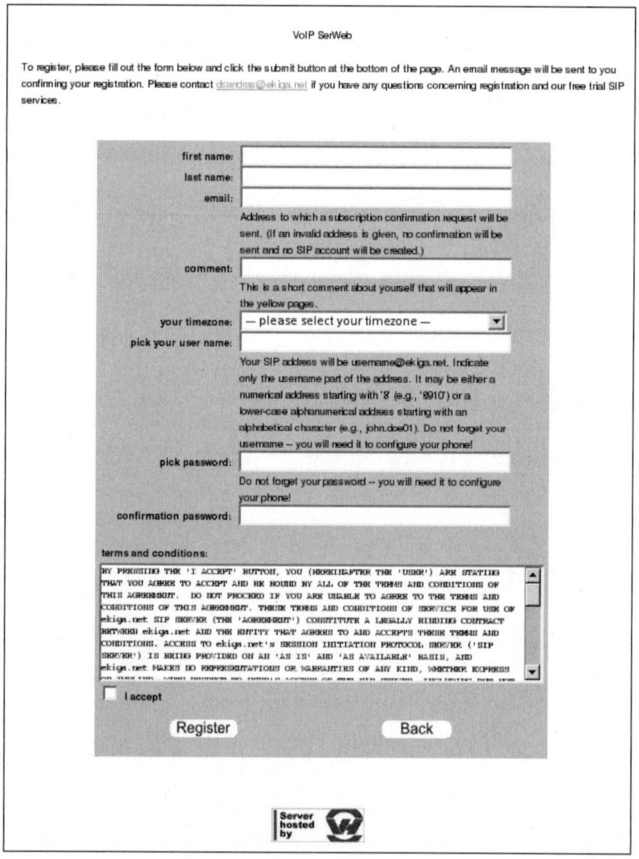

Figure 17-1:
The
Ekiga.net
registration
page.

Introducing Ekiga

Ubuntu includes Ekiga on its live DVD (or CD-ROM) and as part of its permanent installation. Ekiga is an application that communicates with other Ekiga clients on other computers. Ekiga is also part of an Internet-based system that you subscribe to and use to find, contact, and communicate with other Ekiga users.

Ekiga is an open source product that provides two-way voice and video communications over networks. (The technical terms for these capabilities are *IP telephony* and *video conferencing*.) By using industry-standard protocols, Ekiga is able to communicate with other applications like Microsoft's NetMeeting. Ekiga uses the following industry-standard protocols:

- **SIP:** SIP stands for Session Initiation Protocol. SIP lets you initiate, use, and stop two-way voice, video, and instant messaging sessions. SIP has been in use since late 2000.

- **H.323:** This protocol is older than SIP and was originally designed to transmit multimedia over private networks. H.323 now encompasses voice over IP (voice over the Internet).

Ekiga provides many capabilities to set up and enhance your Internet communications:

- **PC-to-PC:** Communicates from one computer to another using voice and video.

- **PC-to-phone:** Connects with land lines and cellphones.

- **Autoanswer:** Answers incoming calls without you being present.

- **Call forward:** Forwards calls to another Ekiga SIP address.

- **Address book:** Keeps your addresses and contacts.

- **Instant messaging:** Allows text messaging in a give-and-take format.

- **Call history:** Records who's called you and when.

This chapter shows the process of using Ekiga from beginning to end:

1. Register with Ekiga PC-to-PC service.

2. Confirm your registration.

3. Configure the Ekiga client application on your Ubuntu computer.

4. Use the Ekiga client to communicate with other Ekiga users.

The equipment you need for Ekiga depends on the kind of messages you want to use:

- Of course, you need an Ubuntu (or other Linux) computer with an Internet connection.

- Voice calls require a microphone on the computer's audio input port and speakers on the computer's audio output port. (You can buy headsets for less than $20.)

  Any Internet connection should work for voice, including dialup modems.

- *Video* requires a *webcam* (USB video camera).

  You should also have high-speed Internet service (such as DSL or cable) if you're using video.

4. **Provide the following information to complete your registration:**

- Type your *name* and *e-mail address* in the appropriate text boxes.

  This is the e-mail account you'll use to *confirm* your registration in Step 7.

- Choose your *time zone* from the drop-down menu.

- Type your *username* and *password* in the appropriate text boxes.

  You need your username and password when you log in to Ekiga.

5. **Read and accept the terms and conditions by selecting the I Accept check box.**

6. **Click the Register button.**

   Ekiga.net shows a Thank You notice and informs you that you'll receive a confirmation e-mail message.

7. **In your e-mail account, open the message from Damien Sandras at dsandras@ekiga.net.**

   This is your confirmation e-mail.

8. **Find this section in the confirmation e-mail and click the link address (your address may be slightly different):**

   ```
   To finalize your registration please check the
   following URL within 24 hours:
   http://www.ekiga.net/serweb/user/reg/confirmation.php?
   nr=5892b64af9257d7d2cbc07455f9
   ```

If Ekiga doesn't congratulate you when you click the link, copy and paste the confirmation link URL into Firefox and go to that address.

When your registration is successfully completed, your Ekiga registration browser window shows a congratulations notice, informing you that your registration has been completed.

If you want to call real telephones through Ekiga, you also need to register for a *PC-to-phone* account. This service isn't free, but it's cheaper than traditional telephone service. The end of this chapter shows you how.

Configuring the Ekiga client

Ubuntu automatically installs the *client* (software) for Ekiga. You configure the Ekiga client application on your Ubuntu system to use your system and your account information.

If you're running Ubuntu directly from a CD-ROM or DVD (*live* Ubuntu), your Ekiga configuration will not be saved permanently on your PC.

The following steps tell Ekiga your name, your Ekiga account username and password, plus information about your Internet connection and computer:

1. **Choose Applications➪Internet➪Ekiga Softphone from the GNOME menu bar.**

   The First Time Configuration Assistant dialog opens.

2. **Click the Forward button.**

   By default, the wizard displays the *first name* and *surname* (last name) you will use when connecting to other Ekiga clients.

   If you want to use a *different* name when connecting to other Ekiga clients, *change* the name in the text box. (You *must* have a surname to continue.)

3. **Click the Forward button.**

4. **Type your username and password in the appropriate text boxes.**

5. **Click the I Do Not Want to Sign Up for the Ekiga.net Free Service check box.**

   This step assumes you've already registered with Ekiga, as shown previously in this chapter.

6. **Click the Forward button.**

   The next dialog wants to know what Internet connection you're using.

7. **From the Connection Type drop-down menu, select the type of Internet connection you use.**

   The default is 56K Modem. I use an Internet cable modem, so I select the xDSL/Cable option, as shown in Figure 17-2.

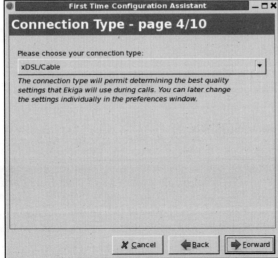

Figure 17-2:
Selecting
the xDSL/
Cable
Internet
connection
option.

Network address translation

Your Ubuntu computer, private network, and the Internet use the Internet Protocol (IP) to communicate. Networked devices and computers use IP addresses to find each other. *IP addresses* are roughly equivalent to the street addresses that we humans use to locate each other. IP addresses are represented by four sets of numbers separated by dots; for instance, 192.168.1.1 or 208.215.179.146. The specific network services are identified by *IP port numbers;* for instance, Web servers use port 80. *IP packets* contain the information that you're sending or receiving. For instance, the contents of an after page or e-mail message.

When you communicate with another machine on your private network or the Internet, your computer sends IP packets to that machine. Each IP packet consists of a source IP address (your computer), a source IP port, plus a destination IP address and port.

Most DSL and cable modems, and many LAN routers, use network address translation (NAT) when connecting to the Internet. NAT translates the originating device's IP address to the IP address of the modem or router. The IP address of outgoing packets is translated by the modem or router, and the corresponding return traffic is restored on the way back; IP ports are translated, too.

NAT makes all the networked devices on your private network appear as a single IP address to the outside world. This lets you use any unregistered IP addresses on your private network.

Using NAT prevents new, incoming connections because only the return traffic from connections originating from inside the private network are allowed.

Here's a simple example. Let's say your Ubuntu workstation is assigned the IP address of 192.168.1.100 on your private LAN, and your Internet access device (dialup modem, cable modem, DSL modem, or LAN router) uses the internal IP address of 192.168.1.1. Let's also assume that your modem or router has an external, Internet facing IP address of 10.0.0.25.

Now when you browse the Web, for instance to www.wiley.com, your Ubuntu computer sends IP packets to the modem or router. The modem or router uses NAT to change your Ubuntu computer's source IP address of 192.168.1.100 to 10.0.0.25; the destination IP address — www.wiley.com — remains unchanged. When www.wiley.com receives the packets, it processes them and sends IP packets containing the after page information back to 10.0.0.25. Your modem or router receives the packets from www.wiley.com and translates them to your Ubuntu computer at 192.168.1.100. NAT enables you to use the Internet.

8. **Click the Forward button.**

Ekiga detects whether your Internet connection uses network address translation (NAT) and opens a dialog displaying the results. Ekiga asks if you want to use the STUN (Simple Traversal of User Datagram Protocol Through Network Address Translators — yikes, that's the longest acronym yet!) option. NAT effectively acts as a firewall and prevents Ekiga from working unless you make use of STUN.

9. **Click the Yes button.**

   The Detection of Your NAT Type is Finished dialog closes, and control returns to the Ekiga configuration wizard.

10. **Click the Forward button.**

    Ekiga detects your audio system and displays the result.

11. **Click the Forward button.**

    Ekiga configures your audio input.

12. **Click the Test Settings button and speak into the microphone as directed.**

13. **Click the Forward button.**

    Ekiga displays a Please Choose Your Video Manager drop-down menu, from which you can specify the video manager to use.

    The default video manager selection (V4L) should suffice.

14. **Click the Forward button.**

    The Video Devices - Page 9/10 dialog appears.

15. **Click the Forward button.**

    The dialog displays the Configuration Complete - Page 10/10 message.

16. **Click the Apply button.**

    The Ekiga application window opens, as shown in Figure 17-3.

You can change any settings that you define in this section by choosing Edit⇨Configuration Druid from the Ekiga application window. Selecting the Configuration Druid opens the Ekiga configuration wizard.

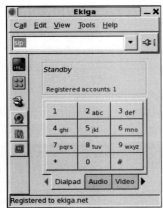

Figure 17-3:
The Ekiga application is ready to go.

After you configure Ekiga, you should test it. Follow these steps:

1. **Click the Ekiga window shown in Figure 17-3.**

   If you've already closed the window, you can open it by selecting Internet⇨Ekiga Softphone from the GNOME Applications menu.

2. **Type 500@ekiga.net after sip: in the text box.**

   The address in the text box should be `sip:500@ekiga.net`.

3. **Click the Connect button to the right of the text box.**

   Ekiga connects to the test address, and you hear a voice that informs you of the test connection.

4. **Speak into your microphone.**

   You hear your voice after a short delay, and you're ready to use Ekiga.

Calling Other Ekiga Users

Using Ekiga is easy after you register and create an Ekiga user account and configure your Ekiga application: Just choose Internet⇨Ekiga Softphone from the GNOME Applications menu. The Ekiga window opens automatically.

✔ When you start Ekiga, it remains online until you explicitly stop it. You can send and receive messages at any time while Ekiga is running.

✔ To *stop* Ekiga and stop receiving any messages, just click the Call menu and select the Quit option.

Ekiga can run in the *background* when you aren't sending or receiving messages:

✔ Close the *dialog* but keep the *application* running with either of these options:

   • Click the Call menu and choose the Close option.

   • Click the Close Window button at the upper-right corner of the window.

   The dialog will automatically open if an Ekiga user contacts you.

✔ If you want to either quit or use Ekiga, first *reopen* the window by clicking the Ekiga telephone icon in the upper GNOME menu panel.

Finding other users

An Ekiga user must be online before you can speak with him or her. Likewise, you must be online before another Ekiga user can speak with you.

Ekiga provides useful tools to remember other users and find online users.

Using the address book

Ekiga provides an address book you can use to find and record other Ekiga user's SIP addresses. You simply use the address book's search function to find the person's SIP address and then save the address. Once saved, you can use the address book to call the person at any time.

The following instructions use the address book to find and remember other Ekiga users, even if they aren't logged into the service. When you're using Ekiga, follow these steps to use the address book:

1. **Click the Tools menu and select the Address Book option.**

   The Address Book dialog opens.

2. **In the Address Book window, type part or all of the person's name you're searching for in the Name Contains text box.**

3. **Click the Find button.**

   The address book sends the name to Ekiga's white pages search engine and displays a list of all matching Ekiga subscribers.

4. **Click the person's name and click the Contact menu — near the top-left of the Ekiga window — and choose the Add Contact to Address Book option.**

   The Edit the Contact information dialog opens.

5. **Click the OK button.**

   The person's name, SIP address, and e-mail address are saved in the Local Contacts section of the Ekiga address book.

6. **Click the Personal option in the Local Contacts section of the Ekiga window (the menu on the left side of the Ekiga window).**

   Ekiga displays the contact you just saved in the Address Book window.

You can call anyone who's listed in your address book. The section "Calling other Ekiga users" describes how to use the address book to call people.

Finding online users

The Ekiga Web page provides a service to determine whether another Ekiga user is currently available. Open a Firefox Web browser and follow these steps:

1. **Type `www.ekiga.net` in the Firefox Location text box near the top, center of the window.**

   The Ekiga.net Userlogin window opens.

2. **Type your Ekiga username and password and click the Login button.**

   Some of your user account information is displayed.

3. **Click the Phone Book tab near the upper-left side of the window.**

   The next Web page displays input text boxes where you can input the Ekiga user's first name, last name, and SIP address.

4. **Give Ekiga information to find the user you want.**

   You can search for the person you want to call by typing any combination of *first name, last name,* and *SIP address.*

5. **Click the Find button.**

   Ekiga displays a list of all the Ekiga user's names and SIP addresses that match your search information.

6. **Click the Add to Phonebook link next to the person you want to call.**

   The Ekiga Web page returns to the Phone Book tab and displays the user's name, SIP name, and online status.

PC-to-PC calling

Ekiga makes it very easy to talk to other Ekiga users over the Internet. The steps depend on whether you start the call.

The section "Using the address book" shows how to find Ekiga users and add them to your contact list.

Calling other Ekiga users

To call another Ekiga user, open the Ekiga window and follow these steps:

1. **Click the Tools menu and select the Address Book option.**

   The Address Book dialog opens.

2. **Click the Personal option under Local Contacts on the left side of the Ekiga window.**

   The personal contacts you saved in the "Using the address book" section are displayed in the main Ekiga window pane.

3. **Select the Ekiga user you want to call.**

   There are two ways to select an Ekiga user:

   • *Double-click the user's entry in the Ekiga address book and select the Call Contact option.*

   • *Type the user's Ekiga username next to the* sip: *prefix in the text box immediately below the menu bar and click the icon to the right of the text box.*

   Ekiga tries to connect to the other user. You can speak to the other Ekiga user if he accepts the call.

Receiving Ekiga calls

When you (or another active Ekiga user) receive an Ekiga call, the Ekiga client produces a ringing sound like a traditional telephone:

✔ To accept the call, click the button to the right of the text box.

   The Ekiga client answers the call and you can speak.

✔ To *end* the call, click the button to the right of the text box.

You can configure Ekiga to *automatically accept* incoming calls. Open the Ekiga window and follow these steps:

1. **Click the Call menu.**

2. **Choose the Auto Answer radio button.**

Viewing your call history

Ekiga records all *incoming, outgoing,* and *missed* calls.

The call history function is easy to use when an Ekiga window is open:

1. **Click the Tools menu and choose the Calls History option.**

   The Calls History window opens. You can view all the calls you've received from this window.

2. **In the Calls History window, select the tab for the *type* of calls to list:**

   • *Received Calls:* All the incoming calls you've *accepted.*

     This is the default.

   • *Placed Calls:* All the outgoing calls you've *made.*

   • *Missed Calls:* All the incoming calls you've *missed* or *ignored.*

To close the Calls History window, click the Close button.

Text messaging

Ekiga provides a very nice instant messaging system. You can easily carry on a text-based conversation using this system with Ekiga users who are running the Ekiga client.

If you'd rather use another message system, such as AOL or MSN, you can send messages with *Gaim.* Chapter 18 shows you how.

Opening a chat window

To start the Ekiga instant messaging service and begin messaging, open an Ekiga window and follow these steps:

 1. **From the Ekiga menu bar, choose Tools⇨Chat Window.**

    The Chat Window, as shown in Figure 17-4, opens.

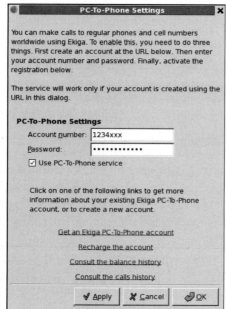

Figure 17-4:
The Chat
Window.

 2. **Type the Ekiga user's URL after the `sip:` prefix in the text box at the top of the window and click the Call button.**

    If you don't know the Ekiga user's URL, you can look it up in the Ekiga white pages phone book. See the "Using the address book" section for instructions.

After you connect, the Call button turns into the Hang Up button. Click the Hang Up button when you're finished text messaging.

Accepting an invitation

Anyone can text message you as long as your Ekiga client is set as Available; this is the default Ekiga state. Click the Ekiga Call menu and select the Available radio button if necessary to allow people to contact you.

When someone is trying to text message message you, Ekiga announces the contact with a quick, three tone (like a guitar) alert. You can join the exchange by clicking the Tools menu and selecting the Chat Window option. The Chat Window dialog opens and displays the other person's text message.

Sending and receiving messages

Type your message in the text box near the bottom of the window and click the Send button. Messages from the other user are displayed in the text box in the middle of the window.

To close the Ekiga Chat Window, click the Close Window icon in the upper-right corner of the window. (The icon looks like an X.) The Chat Window closes and you return to the Ekiga window.

When you're finished text messaging, click the Hang Up button.

Calling Real Telephones

You aren't limited to calling other Ekiga clients on their computers. Ekiga provides a service that enables you to call land-line telephones and cellular phones throughout the world. This isn't a free service, but it's less expensive than traditional telephone service.

The PC-to-phone option provides a wonderful opportunity to drop your plain old telephone service (POTS). I've just put my telephone on temporary hiatus as I wean myself from this expensive and, hopefully, unnecessary service.

The rest of this chapter shows how to set up and use Ekiga for phone calls.

Creating a PC-to-phone account

You must *register* and *verify* an account with Ekiga before using their PC-to-phone service.

Registration

To create an Ekiga PC-to-phone account, begin by following these steps:

1. **Browse to `www.diamondcard.us/exec/voip-login?act=sgn&spo=ekiga` and select the payment method.**

2. **Select the amount you want to add to your account.**

   If you want to *manually* add money to your account when it starts to run low, deselect the Recharge My Account Automatically check box

   Ten dollars is the minimum amount you can select. You can select a higher recharge amount.

3. **Type your personal information (including your payment information) and click the Submit button.**

   The e-mail address you enter here will be used later to *verify* your account.

   You're directed to a second registration page, where you select your username and password.

4. **Select your username and password and click the Submit button.**

   Don't click the Submit button more than once!

   Keep your username and password handy. You'll need them to log into and manage your DiamondCard.com account.

After you register your account, you must verify it. The following instructions show you how.

Verification

Use the following instructions to verify your new Ekiga PC-to-phone account:

1. **Open the e-mail account that you used for registration.**

2. **Reply to the first e-mail message from DiamondCard.us.**

   DiamondCard.us needs to verify that you started the registration process.

   After you reply, DiamondCard.us processes your payment and sends a second e-mail.

3. **Open the second e-mail message from DiamondCard.us and click the Click Here to Administer Your Account link.**

   The DiamondCard.us Administration Center Login after page opens.

4. **Type your username and password and click the Login button.**

   The DiamondCard.us Administration Center after page opens. You're presented with

   • Your account number and PIN (personal identification number) code

     Keep the account number and PIN handy; you'll need them to make PC-to-phone calls. (Use the PIN as Ekiga's *password.*)

   • Your account balance and basic information about your account

   • Links to management options

Ekiga calls the number that the DiamondCard.us Web page refers to as a PIN, a *password.*

Placing calls to telephones

After you verify your PC-to-phone account, you can use Ekiga to call real telephones. Open an Ekiga window and follow these steps:

1. **From the Ekiga menu bar, choose Tools➪PC-to-Phone Account.**

   The PC-to-Phone Settings dialog opens. Figure 17-5 shows the window.

Figure 17-5:
PC-to-
Phone
Settings
dialog.

2. **Type your account number and password in the corresponding text boxes.**

   You obtain your account number and password from your DiamondCard.us account Web page. (The DiamondCard.us Web page calls this password a *PIN*.)

3. **Click the Apply and the OK buttons.**

   The PC-to-Phone Settings dialog closes, and you return to the Ekiga window.

4. **Type 00 plus the country code followed by the area code and phone number of the person you're calling after the sip: prefix in the Ekiga text box.**

   You can find your country code at www.countrycallingcodes.com.

   For example, if I want to call someone in the United States whose phone number is 505-555-5301, I'd type: 0015055555301; the complete address is sip:0015055555301.

   Figure 17-6 shows an example window.

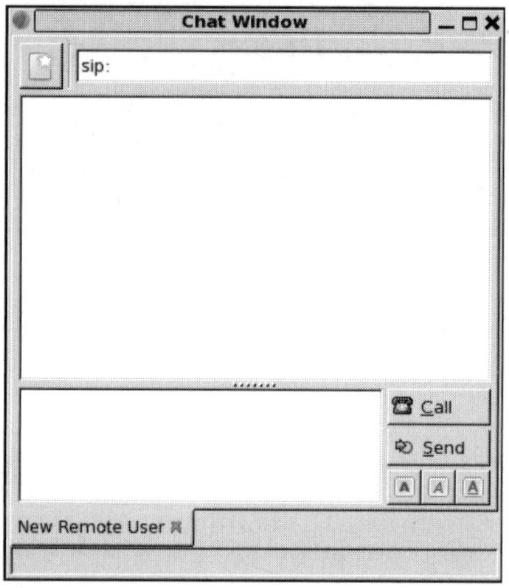

Chat Window

sip:

☎ Call

🔊 Send

A A A

New Remote User

Figure 17-6: Dialing a telephone number.

5. Click the button to the right of the SIP input text box, and Ekiga calls the telephone number.

You can talk to your party as if you were using a traditional telephone.

To end the call, click the button to the right of the SIP input text box.

Chapter 18

Instant Messaging

● ●

In This Chapter

▶ Considering instant message service providers

▶ Registering with Gaim-compatible instant message services

▶ Signing in to and messaging with Gaim

● ●

*I*nstant messaging is a popular Internet communication method based on the quick exchange of text-based messages. You contact another person — your *buddy* — and type a quick message. The other person sees your message and responds in kind. The exchange shows up instantly on your screen.

Gaim is an open source instant messenger (IM) application that lets you chat on your Ubuntu computer through these message services:

✔ AIM (AOL Instant Messenger, the Gaim default service)

✔ MSN Instant Messenger

✔ Yahoo! Messenger

✔ Jabber

✔ ICQ

✔ Google Talk

The name *Gaim* is unusual in a world filled with technical acronyms. Gaim is not an acronym. According to its creators, Gaim doesn't stand for anything but *freedom* (an open source application that helps the world communicate).

Configuring Gaim

To use Gaim, you must

✔ Tell Gaim which IM service provider to use.

You need an *account* to use an IM service. If you don't have an account for an IM service you want to use, go to the service's Web home page and sign up.

✔ Provide your IM username and password.

Gaim uses the information you provide to log in to the IM service provider. When you're logged in, you can communicate with other people who use that service.

There's no limit to how many IM service providers you can use. Just register with the IM service and then configure Gaim to use it. After you've registered and configured it, you can start up a separate instance of Gaim for each service.

The following section describes how to register with the default Gaim IM service provider. The section after that shows you how to configure Gaim to use other service providers; Gaim takes care of the actual default registration, but you must register with everyone else.

You can configure and use Gaim when running Ubuntu live from an Ubuntu CD-ROM (or DVD), which is described in Chapter 2. However, any configurations you make won't be saved after you reboot your Ubuntu computer. All settings are saved when running Ubuntu from a hard drive as described in Chapter 4.

Registering with Instant Message services

Let's start by starting Gaim, configuring its basic stuff, and connecting to an IM service provider:

1. **Choose Applications⇨Internet⇨Gaim Internet Messenger from the GNOME menu bar.**

   Two windows open:

   • Figure 18-1 shows the Gaim Login window.

   • Figure 18-2 shows the Gaim Accounts window.

2. **Click the Add button in the Accounts window.**

   The Add Account dialog, as shown in Figure 18-3, opens.

3. **Click the Protocol drop-down menu and select your IM service provider.**

Using compatible service providers

You can connect to multiple IM sessions at once with Gaim. For example, you can simultaneously chat with friends using Gaim (AIM), Yahoo!, and MSN.

Configuring and using Gaim is straightforward, as you'll see in this chapter. You need only select these Gaim options before you can start using it:

✔ A unique screen name (the account name you're registered with by the IM service provider)

✔ A password (which prevents anyone else from using your account)

✔ A local alias (the name that Gaim knows you as on your Ubuntu computer)

Figure 18-1:
The Gaim
Login
window.

The default service provider is AIM, but you can choose from any of the other available ones.

4. Type your screen name in the Screen Name text box.

You'll be known as your screen name while chatting.

5. Type your screen name password in the Password text box.

You can select options to simplify startup and stay in touch with Gaim.

- If you want Gaim to remember your password, select the Remember Password and/or the Auto-Login check box.

- If you want Gaim to notify you when you receive a message to your IM provider e-mail account, select the New Mail Notifications radio button.

Figure 18-2:
The Gaim
Accounts
window.

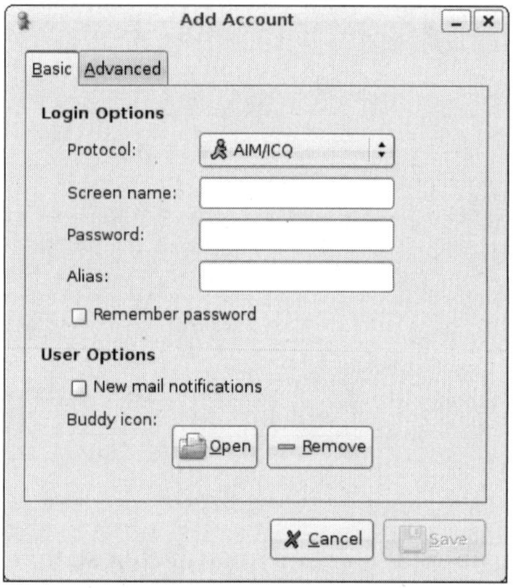

Figure 18-3:
Gaim Add
Account
dialog.

6. **Click the Save button.**

   Control returns to the Account window.

7. **Click the Close button.**

Your screen name and alias are displayed in the Account drop-down menu in the Gaim Login window. You're ready to chat.

Adding other IM services

If you want to add an IM service to Gaim, follow these steps:

1. **Open Gaim by choosing Internet⇨Gaim Internet Messenger from the GNOME Applications menu, if it isn't already running.**

2. **Click the Accounts menu (from the Buddy List dialog) and select the Add/Edit option.**

   The Accounts dialog opens.

3. **Click the Add button.**

   The Add Account dialog opens.

4. **From the Protocol drop-down menu, select an IM service provider.**

   For example, select Yahoo! to chat with people using Yahoo! Messenger.

5. **Type your screen name, password, and alias in the appropriate text boxes.**

   You must use the screen name and password that you selected when registering your Gaim account with the IM service provider.

6. **Click the Save button.**

   The Add Account dialog closes and your settings are saved.

7. **Click the Close button in the Accounts dialog.**

   The Accounts dialog closes. Now you're ready to converse with people using the particular IM service.

Communicating through Gaim

Using Gaim to communicate with other IM clients is a straightforward process. The following instructions show how to use Gaim to communicate with Gaim's default service, AIM (AOL Instant Messenger).

Sending messages

The following instructions use Gaim to contact and start communicating with others using AIM:

1. **Open the Gaim application, if necessary, by choosing Internet⇨Gaim Internet Messenger from the GNOME Applications menu.**

   The Gaim Buddy List window opens. Another Gaim dialog, showing a text box in which you type your IM account password, opens if you chose not to save your IM account password when configuring Gaim; the section "Registering with Instant Message services" describes the configuration process.

2. **If necessary, type your password in the Enter Password text box, immediately below the Enter password for User heading, in the Gaim dialog.**

   Gaim logs in to your AIM account and displays a message in the bottom of the Buddy List window telling you that your account is available.

3. **Click the Buddies menu and select the New Instant Message option.**

   The New Instant Message dialog opens, as shown in Figure 18-4.

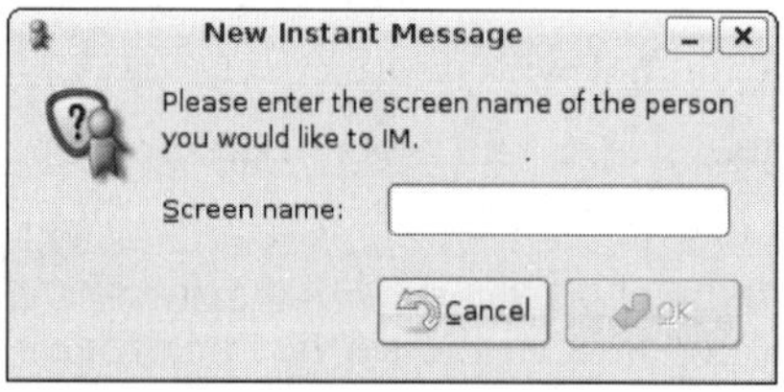

Figure 18-4:
Tell Gaim who you want to talk to.

New Instant Message

Please enter the screen name of the person you would like to IM.

Screen name:

Cancel   OK

4. **Type the name of the person (buddy) you want to contact and click the OK button.**

   The Gaim window, shown in Figure 18-5 opens. (The name tope43 in the title bar is my username.)

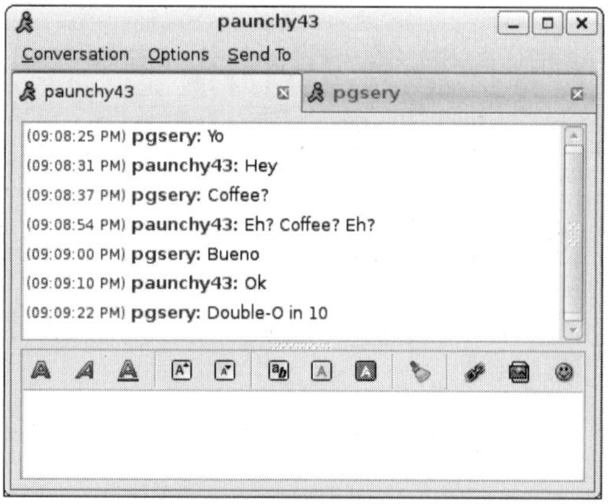

paunchy43

Conversation   Options   Send To

paunchy43   pgsery

(09:08:25 PM) **pgsery:** Yo
(09:08:31 PM) **paunchy43:** Hey
(09:08:37 PM) **pgsery:** Coffee?
(09:08:54 PM) **paunchy43:** Eh? Coffee? Eh?
(09:09:00 PM) **pgsery:** Bueno
(09:09:10 PM) **paunchy43:** Ok
(09:09:22 PM) **pgsery:** Double-O in 10

Figure 18-5:
Using Gaim to chat up a storm.

5. **You can start chatting:**

   a. Type a message in the lower subwindow.

   b. Press the Send button in the lower-right corner of the Gaim window.

TIP

Testing, 1-2-3-4, testing. If you're new to IM and don't know anyone who uses it, you can simply talk to yourself. (Chatting with yourself might not be particularly interesting, but it does demonstrate how the system works.) Follow these steps:

   a. *Open a Gaim window and sign in as described in these instructions.*

   b. *Select your own name in Step 4.*

   A second Gaim window opens. Whatever message you type in one window is displayed in the other window.

Adding buddies

You'll accumulate contacts as you use Gaim. Gaim provides a convenient method for saving contact information with AIM (the default Gaim service). Here's how to use it:

1. **In the Buddy List window, click the Buddies menu and select the Add Buddy option.**

   The Add Buddy dialog, shown in Figure 18-6, opens.

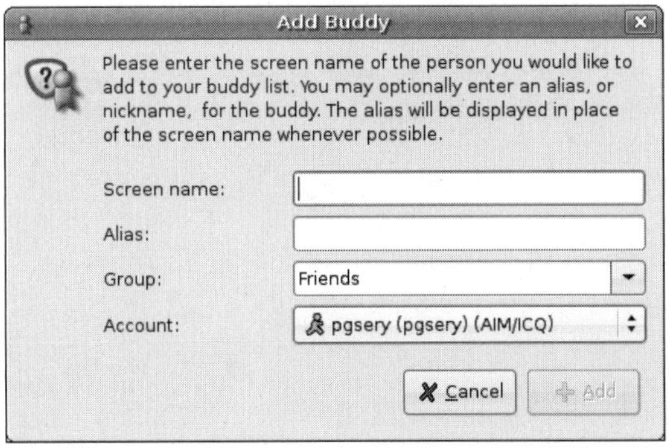

Figure 18-6:
Add Buddy
dialog.

> **Add Buddy**
>
> Please enter the screen name of the person you would like to add to your buddy list. You may optionally enter an alias, or nickname, for the buddy. The alias will be displayed in place of the screen name whenever possible.
>
> Screen name:
>
> Alias:
>
> Group: Friends
>
> Account: pgsery (pgsery) (AIM/ICQ)
>
> ✗ Cancel   ✚ Add

2. **Type the screen name and the alias for your contact.**

   The screen name is valid only for the IM service the person is registered for. The alias is the name Gaim knows the contact as; that is, Gaim uses the alias to locate the contact on your Ubuntu computer.

3. **If you want to categorize your new Buddy, select your contact's category from the Group drop-down menu.**

For instance, Friend is the default.

4. **Select the IM service provider from the Account drop-down menu.**

5. **Click the Add button.**

6. **In the Buddies window, click the Buddies menu and select New Instant Message.**

   The New Instant Message dialog opens, and you can type the contact's alias in the Name text box to contact that person.

Chapter 19

Connecting to the Dark Side: Working Remotely on Windows

reating Ubuntu Linux is all about creating a platform that encourages and helps you to access and share information. Your Ubuntu computer is based on open source software that lets you use and modify it as you wish. Open source is a brilliant concept that has changed the world by allowing the free exchange and use of ideas.

However, just because Ubuntu is based on open source doesn't mean it can interact with proprietary operating systems and software. Open source doesn't preclude using closed source when necessary and appropriate. Ubuntu provides many tools for such interaction, and I've found one such tool useful when I need to remotely access and control Windows computers.

Proprietary software — including applications and operating systems — is owned and protected by the owner of the operating system and software. The owner can be a company or an individual. Typically the owner licenses but doesn't sell the software for others to use. For instance, when you purchase a computer, it usually comes with Microsoft Windows installed. You own the computer but not Windows or the applications, such as Word, that come with it. Microsoft's license gives you the right to use their software but not to modify it or even to understand how it works.

Having the ability to connect to remote Windows computers is useful because it saves you time. You don't have to be in the same location as the Windows computer anymore to work on it or manage it. I have to manage some Windows computers, and being able to remotely work on them from my office or from home makes life easier and saves many trips.

Introducing the Remote Desktop Protocol

This chapter describes how to use the Remote Desktop Protocol (RDP) to connect, authenticate, and work on remote Windows servers. This is a very useful capability because, in general, Windows is difficult to work with remotely.

The RDP is designed to communicate with Windows Terminal Services. *Terminal Services* allow data and applications stored on a Windows computer to be accessed *remotely* (from another computer). Using RDP on your Ubuntu computer lets you communicate with Terminal Services on the Windows computer. That combination makes your Ubuntu computer into a window into Windows, so to speak. You see everything on the remote Windows computer as if you were sitting at its console. You control the remote computer and can do anything on it you wish.

RDP is a very cool and useful system. It saves me a lot of shoe leather — okay, it saves my worn out Adidas Sambas from totally falling apart — walking to and from every Windows box that I have to administer.

Configuring Your Windows Remote Desktop Server

Microsoft doesn't provide the Remote Desktop server on its home-based operating system. You can get the server version on only the Professional versions of Windows. You must have one of the following Windows operating systems to use RDP:

- ✔ **Vista Business**
- ✔ **Vista Small Business**
- ✔ **Vista Enterprise**
- ✔ **Vista Ultimate**
- ✔ **Server 2003**
- ✔ **XP Professional**
- ✔ **2000 Server**
- ✔ **2000 Advanced Server**
- ✔ **2000 Datacenter Server**

Windows XP Home Edition and Windows Vista Home Edition provides the RDP client but not the server. You can connect to an RDP server using the client, but not the other way around.

Let's configure the Windows RDP server:

1. **Log on to a compatible Windows computer:**
    - Windows XP Professional
    - Windows Vista Business
    - Windows Vista Enterprise
    - Windows Vista Ultimate
    - Windows 2003 Server

2. **Click the Start button and select Control Panel.**

    The Control Panel dialog opens.

3. **Use either of the following actions to open the System Properties window:**
    - Double-click the System icon.
    - Right-click and select Open.

    The System Properties dialog opens.

4. **Click the Remote tab.**

    The System Properties dialog, as shown in Figure 19-1, shows the RDP options.

5. **Select the Allow Users to Connect Remotely to This Computer check box.**

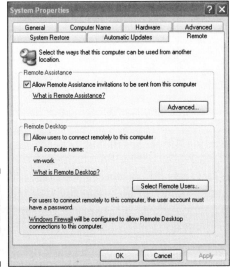

Figure 19-1:
The System Properties dialog RDP options.

6. Click the Select Remote Users button.

The Remote Desktop Users dialog opens. You need to specify which people can use RDP on your computer.

Windows automatically provides remote RDP access to the user account you're logged in as. If I'm logged in as Betty, Betty can connect using RDP without adding her explicitly through the Remote Desktop Users dialog.

7. Click the Add button.

The Select Users dialog opens.

8. Type the username you want to give RDP access to in the Enter the Object Names to Select text box.

You must specify the name of an existing user account. The Select Users dialog doesn't let you enter a nonexistent account name. You can click the Check Names button to check if a name is valid.

9. Click the OK button.

Control returns to the Remote Desktop Users dialog, in which the username appears. (See Figure 19-2.)

Figure 19-2:
Adding a username to the RDP remote access list.

10. Click the OK button.

Control returns to the System Properties dialog.

11. Click the OK button.

You've configured your Windows computer for remote access. You'll be able to connect to your Windows computer over a network or the Internet and use it as if you were sitting at its screen.

The account you configure to remotely access your Windows computer must have a password assigned to it. Follow these steps to create a password for the account, if necessary:

1. **Select Start⟶Control Panel.**

   The Control Panel dialog opens.

2. **Double-click the User Accounts icon.**

   The User Accounts dialog opens.

3. **Click the Create a password option.**

4. **Type your password in the Type a New Password text box.**

5. **Retype the password in the Type a New Password Again to Confirm text box.**

6. **Click the Create Password button.**

   The account is password protected.

Using Terminal Server Client

Connecting to your Windows computer requires you to start the Terminal Server Client on your Ubuntu computer. Proceed as follows:

1. **Choose Applications⟶Internet⟶Terminal Server Client from the GNOME menu bar.**

   The Terminal Server Client window opens, as shown in Figure 19-3.

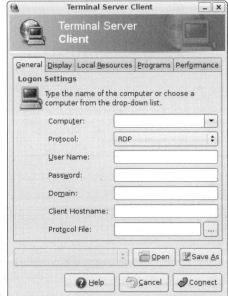

Figure 19-3:
Connecting
to a
Windows
computer
remotely.

2. **Type the name (or numeric IP address) of your Windows computer in the Computer text box.**

3. **Type your username in the User Name text box.**

4. **Click the Connect button.**

   The Terminal Server Client connects to your Windows computer and prompts you for your password, as shown in Figure 19-4.

Figure 19-4:
Your
Windows
computer
prompts you
for your
password.

5. **Type your password in the Password text box.**

6. **Click the OK button.**

The Terminal Server Client logs you in to your Windows account and displays the exact same screen you would see if you were sitting at the computer itself. You can now work on the remote Windows computer as if you were sitting at it. RDP and Ubuntu's Terminal Server Client provide this great capability. You can get your work done from Tahiti if you want.

Unfortunately, getting to Tahiti is not as easy as setting up RDP and the Terminal Server Client. Oh well.

Chapter 20

Lyrical Ubuntu: Using Multimedia Applications

*I*t used to be that computers were all about work. Then came graphical interfaces, and computers very quickly became multimedia machines. There's not much that you can't do with computers when it comes to multimedia.

Ubuntu is able to do all the fun things that you expect from today's computers. This chapter shows you how to have fun with Ubuntu. I talk about using audio CDs, playing Internet *audio streams* (continuous music or voice transmitted over the Internet), and more.

The first three sections in this chapter describe how to play audio CDs, play audio files using various formats, and listen to Internet radio. The last sections describe how to rip and burn music CDs.

Playing CDs

Ubuntu plays CDs if you want. Here's all you have to do:

1. **Pop an audio disc in your Ubuntu computer's CD player.**

   The Sound Juicer window opens, showing all the tracks on the CD.

By default, all the tracks are selected to play. You can deselect any tracks that you don't want to play: Click the check box next to the track.

2. **Click the Play button to start playing the selected CD tracks.**

That's all there is to playing a CD. Simple.

Playing MP3s with XMMS

MP3 is a popular audio-encoding protocol. Ubuntu provides an MP3 player called XMMS (X Multimedia System), which you can use to play MP3 files on your computer.

XMMS can play the following audio sources:

- ✔ MP3, Ogg, and WAV audio files
- ✔ Audio CDs
- ✔ MP3 Internet radio streams

Installing XMMS

You need to install XMMS before using it. The following instructions use the Synaptic Package Manager to find and install XMMS:

1. **Click the GNOME System menu and choose Administration➪Synaptic Package Manager.**

   The Enter Your Password to Perform Administrative Tasks dialog opens if you haven't performed an administrative task within the last 5 minutes.

2. **If prompted, type your user account password in the Password text box.**

   The Synaptic Package Manager dialog opens.

3. **Scroll down through the packages in the Packages menu and click the check box next to the XMMS package.**

   An unnamed submenu opens.

4. **Click the Mark for Installation option.**

   The Mark Additional Required Changes? dialog opens.

5. **Click the Mark button.**

   The Mark Additional Required Changes? dialog closes and control returns to the Synaptic Package Manager window.

6. **Click the Apply button.**

   The Summary dialog opens.

7. **Click the Apply button in the Summary dialog.**

The XMMS package is installed on your Ubuntu computer.

Playing audio files with XMMS

XMMS is easy to use. To get started, click the GNOME Applications menu and choose Sound & Video⇨XMMS Music Player. XMMS, as shown in Figure 20-1, opens.

Continue reading to find out how you can use XMMS to play audio files, CDs, and Internet radio.

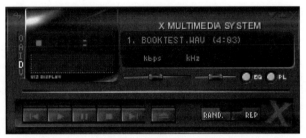

Figure 20-1:
The XMMS
Music
Player.

After you open XMMS, here's how to use it to play MP3, Ogg, and WAV audio files:

1. **Click anywhere on the right side of the XMMS window.**

   The About XMMS drop-down menu opens.

2. **From the About XMMS drop-down menu, select the file option you want.**

   To play a single file, follow these steps:

   a. Choose Play⇨Play File.

     The Play Files dialog opens.

   b. Find and select the audio file you wish to play.

   If you want to play a whole directory of files, follow these steps:

   a. Choose Play⇨Play Directory

     The Play Files dialog opens.

   b. Find and select the directory of files you wish to play.

3. Click the Play button.

The Play Files dialog closes and XMMS plays the selected recordings.

Playing Internet radio streams

XMMS fulfills its ace-of-trades reputation by playing Internet radio streams. The process requires you to find and select your Internet radio stream and then use XMMS to play it.

Recording a stream

Follow these steps to find a stream and save its address (but not its content):

1. Browse to your favorite Internet radio station.

For instance, go to `www.virginradio.co.uk` (Virgin Radio) or `www.wrti.org`.

2. Click the Listen Live or Windows Media link.

XMMS can also play Windows Media.

The Opening *Wrti.asx* dialog opens.

3. Select the Save to Disk radio button and click the OK button.

The Enter Name of File to Save To dialog opens.

4. Click the Save button.

The Downloads dialog opens.

Selecting the Open With option lets you open the audio stream directly with XMMS (or any other application you care to use). However, I like to save the audio stream's location in a file for future easy access.

5. Click the Clean Up button and close the dialog.

The saved file contains the Internet URL (uniform resource locator) of the Internet radio stream.

Playing a stream

When you know the audio you want, you can play it with XMMS. Follow these steps:

1. Click anywhere on the right side of the XMMS window.

The About XMMS drop-down menu opens.

2. **From the About XMMS drop-down menu, select the audio source option you want.**

   To play a *saved file* (such as the files saved with the preceding steps), follow these steps:

       a. *Choose Play⇨Play File.*

         The Play Files dialog opens.

       b. *Find and select the downloaded Internet radio file (such as the file downloaded by the preceding section of this chapter).*

   To play a *live stream,* follow these steps:

       a. *Choose Play⇨Play Location.*

         The Enter Location to Play dialog opens.

       b. *Type the URL in the text box.*

3. **Click the Play button.**

   The dialog closes and XMMS plays the stream. I love it!

Playing Ogg Files with Rhythmbox

Rhythmbox plays audio files and audio streams encoded with Ogg. Ogg-formatted audio files — use the suffix .ogg — are common in the Linux world because there are so many tools to record with (for instance, Audacity). Ogg-formatted audio streams are advertised as such on the provider's Web page. There are fewer Internet audio sources using Ogg versus MP3, but the list is growing.

Even though the Internet is dominated by MP3-encoded radio streams, Ogg is making progress and penetrating the market. As Linux proliferates the desktop, more listeners have access to applications compatible with the nonproprietary Ogg format. More potential listeners means more sources.

Virgin Radio is one popular Internet radio source that speaks Ogg.

Follow these steps to play Virgin Radio using Rhythmbox:

1. **Open a Firefox window by clicking the GNOME Applications menu and choosing Internet⇨Firefox Web Browser, and browse to your favorite Internet radio station.**

   For example, I usually go to www.virginradio.co.uk.

2. Click the Listen Live Now button near the upper-right side of the browser window.

The names and locations of the links vary by Web site, but they usually include the word *listen,* or something equally intuitive.

Your browser opens a Web page, which might look something like the one in Figure 20-2.

3. Click the Listen Live Now button under the Virgin Radio on Ogg Vorbis heading.

The Opening Live.pls dialog opens, showing the Open with radio button selected and the Rhythmbox Music Player (default) option also selected by default.

4. Click the OK button.

The first time you start Rhythmbox, the Rhythmbox dialog opens and displays the Welcome to Rhythmbox heading.

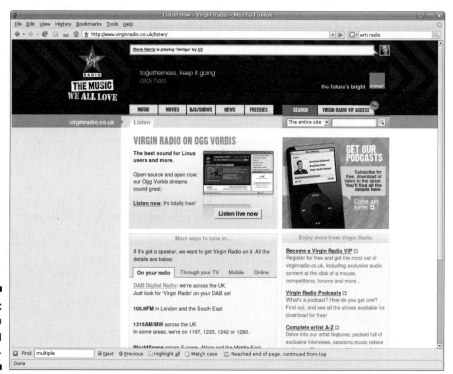

Figure 20-2:
Virgin Radio digs Ogg Vorbis.

5. **Click the Forward button in the Welcome to Rhythmbox dialog.**

   The Rhythmbox dialog shows the Music Library heading.

6. **Click the Skip This Step radio button and click the Forward button.**

   The Rhythmbox dialog shows the Finish heading.

7. **Click the Apply button.**

   The Rhythmbox dialog closes and the Music Player window, as shown in Figure 20-3, opens.

Figure 20-3:
The
Rhythmbox
Music
Player
window.

The following instructions use the Rhythmbox application to listen to an Internet radio station:

1. **Click the Radio option in the Source subwindow.**

   The main window shows a list of Internet radio stations you can select.

2. **Click to select any of the Internet radio stations displayed in the main window.**

   For instance, select the Virgin Radio Classic Rock option.

3. **Click the Play button on the Rhythmbox toolbar.**

   Rhythmbox opens and plays the radio station.

You can play Ogg audio files with Rhythmbox, of course. Follow these steps:

1. **From the GNOME menu bar, choose Applications⇨Sound & Video⇨ Rhythmbox Music Player.**

   The Rhythmbox Music Player window opens.

2. **Choose Music⇨Import File from the main menu bar.**

   The Import File into Library dialog opens.

3. **Find and select the audio file you want to play by clicking the folder and file in the Import File into Library dialog.**

   Figure 20-4 shows an example window.

4. **Click the Open button in the Import File into Library dialog.**

5. **Click the Play button.**

You might be surprised that neither Ogg nor Vorbis is an acronym. The terms come from science fiction characters. For more information about Ogg Vorbis and similar open source multimedia systems, go to www.vorbis.com.

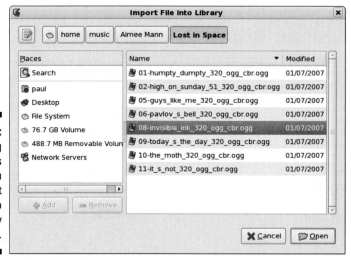

Figure 20-4:
Selecting
audio files
to play from
the Import
File into
Library
dialog.

Ripping Music with Sound Juicer CD Extractor

I have a lot of old audio CDs that don't get used much. I sit at my computer most of the day and I'm too lazy to get up and choose a disc, open the jewel case, take the disc out of the jewel case. . . . Sad.

But I listen to a lot of music — albums that I've put onto my computer. I don't have to get up and find the disc and play the disc. I can still — in spite of my middle-aged lack of inertia — point and click a mouse. (Yes, there was music when I was young.) By copying and formatting the audio on a CD, I can sit here and listen to tunes. The process is called ripping.

Ubuntu makes it easy to rip CDs. Here's all you need to do:

1. **Find your audio disc and put it in your Ubuntu computer's CD player.**

2. **From the GNOME menu bar, choose Applications⇨Sound & Video⇨ Sound Juicer CD Extractor.**

   Sound Juicer opens, displaying the title and tracks of your CD. Figure 20-5 shows a sample Sound Juicer dialog.

 You can manually enter the title, artist, and genre (or *kind of music,* for those of you who aren't used to seeing that word in print) by typing into the corresponding text boxes in the Sound Juicer dialog. Older CDs often don't include such information, so you can add it yourself. When you specify the title and artist, the files are organized according to the title and artist.

   All tracks are selected, by default (as shown by the check box to the left of each track number). You can deselect any that you don't wish to record.

	Sound Juicer	_ □ ✕

Disc   Edit   Help

Title: Dos Dedos Mis Amigos

Artist: Pop Will Eat Itself

Genre:

Duration: 46:35

Track	Title	Artist	Duration
☑ 1	Ich Bin Ein Auslander	Pop Will Eat Itself	3:59
☑ 2	Kick to Kill	Pop Will Eat Itself	3:24
☑ 3	Familus Horribilus	Pop Will Eat Itself	4:03
☑ 4	Underbelly	Pop Will Eat Itself	3:58
☑ 5	Fatman	Pop Will Eat Itself	3:17
☑ 6	Home	Pop Will Eat Itself	3:36
☑ 7	Cape Connection	Pop Will Eat Itself	4:59

▷ Play   ◉ Extract

Figure 20-5: Sound Juicer, ready to rip.

3. **Click the Extract button.**

   The dialog starts to rip the selected tracks onto your computer. A progress bar shows the percentage finished and an estimated time to completion.

An Information dialog opens when the job finishes, telling you that, yes, the job is finished.

4. **When the job finishes, click the Open button.**

A Nautilus window opens, showing the extracted tracks. Double-clicking an icon opens the Totem Movie Player, which plays the track while showing nifty graphics. Psychedelic, man.

5. **When you're finished listening to the music, click Movie and Quit to leave the Totem Movie Player.**

You return to the Sound Juicer window.

6. **Click the Disc from the main menu and select Quit to exit from Sound Juicer.**

You can use Sound Juicer to play your audio CD. From the GNOME menu bar, choose Applications⇨Sound & Video⇨Sound Juicer CD Extractor and do one of the following:

- *Click the Play button to start the whole album from the first track.*

- *Click a track number and then click the Play button to play just one track.*

By default, Sound Juicer converts your audio CD tracks into Ogg-encoded files. The files are stored in a directory (folder) named after the artist, in your home directory.

Ogg and Vorbis are the open source world's answers to MP3:

✔ *Ogg* is a protocol to format audio streams.

Ogg is quickly being adopted by people, businesses, and organizations who don't want to be beholden to proprietary formats such as MP3.

✔ *Vorbis* compresses audio streams.

✔ *Ogg Vorbis* (combined) provides better audio quality and compression than other proprietary formats.

You can play your album from the saved files you ripped. Follow these steps:

1. **From the GNOME menu bar, choose Places⇨Home Folder.**

A Nautilus window opens, showing the contents of your home folder.

2. **Double-click the artist's folder.**

Nautilus opens the folder and shows the album title.

3. **Double-click the album folder.**

   Nautilus opens the folder and displays the album tracks.

4. **Click any icon.**

   The Totem Movie player opens and plays the track.

Burning Audio CDs

While I'm too lazy to listen to my old CDs, I'm not too lazy to purchase audio files on the Internet. I often need to burn my downloaded music to CD or DVD, so I can put a stack of discs in my car.

You can have your music and listen to it, too. See the section "Playing MP3s with XMMS" for instructions.

Unless you want to record audio files that you ripped from another CD (for instance, to back up an album), you most likely need to convert the file formats. Most CD players recognize only WAV-formatted audio, so you need to convert to that format.

Converting MP3-formatted files to WAV format

Let's say you purchase an album, or album tracks, from any of the growing number of online music vendors. You most likely download the music files encoded in MP3 format. (MP3 is shorthand for MPEG-1 Audio Layer 3; MPEG stands for the Moving Picture Experts Group.) You need to convert from MP3 to WAV to ensure your CD player can play the music.

After you convert the file from MP3 to WAV, you can use the Serpentine Audio CD Creator utility, described later in this section, to burn the CD.

Installing the Audacity sound editor

Ubuntu provides the utility necessary to convert an MP3 file to a WAV-formatted one so that you can burn it to a CD.

The Audacity sound editor utility isn't installed by default, but you can readily install it by following these instructions:

1. **From the GNOME menu bar, choose System⇨Administration⇨ Synaptic Package Manager.**

   The Package Manager window opens.

2. **Scroll down and select the check box for the Audacity package.**

3. **From the unnamed drop-down menu that opens, choose the Mark for Installation option.**

   The Mark Additional Required Changes? dialog opens. The dialog informs you of the additional software that will be installed to satisfy Audacity's dependencies.

4. **Click the Mark button.**

   The Apply button in the package manager activates.

5. **Click the Apply button.**

   The Summary dialog opens.

6. **Click the Apply button in the Summary dialog.**

   The Applying Changes dialog opens, showing the progress of the package download and installation. Audacity is installed and the dialog closes.

7. **Click File and select Quit to close the package manager window.**

   An Audacity option is added to the Sound & Video menu.

Configuring Audacity

You need to configure Audacity before using it. But you don't need to change much. Just tell Audacity to record in stereo, rather than mono, by default. Follow these steps:

1. **From the GNOME menu bar, choose Applications⇨Sound & Video⇨ Audacity.**

   The Audacity First Run dialog opens.

2. **Select your language as necessary and click OK.**

   The Audacity window (Figure 20-6) opens.

3. **Click the Edit menu and select Preferences.**

   The Audacity Preferences dialog opens.

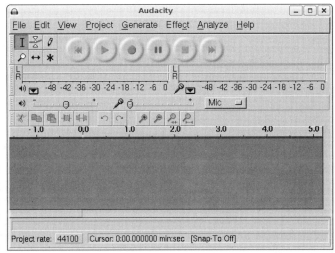

Figure 20-6:
The
Audacity
window.

4. Click the Channels button and select 2 (Stereo).

Nostalgia is good, but we don't want to return to the 1950s.

5. Click OK.

You exit the Audacity Preferences dialog and return to the main window.

Now you can use Audacity to convert Ogg and MP3 files to WAV. The following section shows you how.

Converting from one format to another

Audacity can convert to WAV files from either MP3 or Ogg.

Repeat these steps for each file you want to convert:

1. Click File in the Audacity main menu and select the Open option.

2. Select the folder containing the audio files you want to burn to CD.

For instance, if you want to re-record tracks you ripped using Sound Juicer, double-click the artist's folder and then the album folder.

3. Click to select any individual track.

4. Click OK.

A new Audacity window opens, along with the Import dialog. The Import dialog displays the progress as the track is imported.

5. **In the new Audacity window, click File and select the Export as WAV option.**

   The Save WAV (Microsoft) File As dialog opens, displaying the contents of your home directory (folder). This is a simple file manager that you use to select the name and location for the WAV files you export.

6. **Select the folder, if any, to save the new converted files to.**

7. **Click OK.**

   The Export dialog opens, showing the progress of the export process. The Export dialog closes, when the export process completes, and control returns to the Audacity dialog.

8. **Click the Audacity File menu and select Exit.**

   The Save Changes dialog opens.

9. **Close the new Audacity dialog and select No (don't save changes) when prompted.**

   You don't need to save the changes because you accomplished the process of converting from MP3 to WAV format. There's no need to instruct Audacity to remember that process.

Burning an audio CD with Serpentine

It's simple to burn (write) computer WAV files to a CD disc.

If you haven't converted your MP3 files to WAV files, take a step back and go through the "Converting MP3-formatted files to WAV format" section in this chapter.

To write computer WAV files to a CD, follow these steps:

1. **Put a blank, writable CD in your CD-ROM writing drive.**

   Ubuntu detects that a blank CD was inserted and opens the Choose Disc Type dialog. (See Figure 20-7.)

   You can manually open Serpentine by clicking the Applications menu from the GNOME menu bar and choosing Sound & Video⇨Serpentine Audio CD Creator.

2. **Click the Make Audio CD button.**

   The Serpentine dialog, shown in Figure 20-8, opens.

Figure 20-7:
The Choose
Disc Type
dialog.

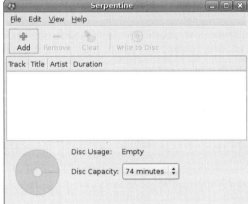

Figure 20-8:
The
Serpentine
Audio CD
Creator
window.

3. **Click the Add button.**

   A file manager window opens.

4. **Select the folder that contains the WAV music files you want to record.**

5. **Select PCM Wave Audio from the drop-down menu near the lower-right side of the window.**

   Selecting this option displays only WAV-formatted files and makes it easier to make your selections.

6. **Hold down the Shift key while selecting one or more files.**

   Holding down the Shift key lets you select multiple files.

7. **Click Open.**

   Serpentine imports the files you selected.

8. **Click the Write to Disc button.**

   A warning dialog opens, asking you if you really want to make this earth-shattering decision.

9. **Click the Write to Disc button.**

The Writing to Disc dialog opens, showing the progress.

10. **Click the Close button in the Writing to Disc Finished dialog when it opens.**

Your disc is automatically ejected.

11. **Click the File menu and select Quit to exit from Serpentine.**

You now have yourself a recording studio and can burn as many music discs as you want.

I remember in the mid-1980s when music CDs first hit the market. The discs were a little more expensive than they are today (much more expensive if you account for inflation). However, the factories that produced the discs were very expensive. Today, we have micro CD factories that cost less than filling your car with gas. Ain't technology amazing!

Chapter 21

Graphical Ubuntu

· ·

· ·

*U*buntu provides several graphical manipulation tools. You can save photos from your digital camera and create, manipulate, and view the photos using these tools. Ubuntu covers all bases when it comes to multimedia.

This chapter describes how to work with digital cameras, graphical images, and more.

Transferring Photos from your Digital Camera to Your Ubuntu Computer

Digital photography lets you take pictures and store them on a computer for viewing and reproduction. Doing away with traditional film is a great convenience. Ubuntu Linux provides the tools to download photos from a camera.

Most digital cameras provide software to transfer photos from the camera to a computer. However, most such software is incompatible with Linux and your Ubuntu computer. Fortunately, you can still easily transfer photos to your Ubuntu computer using generic Linux utilities. This section describes how to perform such transfers.

So go out and take your shots. Later, you can download your photos to Ubuntu as follows.

1. **Connect your camera to your Ubuntu computer using a USB (or FireWire) cable.**

   Ubuntu recognizes the device and launches the Photo Import dialog, shown in Figure 21-1.

Figure 21-1:
The Photo Import dialog.

2. **Click the Import Photos button.**

   Ubuntu *mounts your camera* (makes the photographs it contains available to your computer) as a USB disk and shows its contents. Figure 21-2 shows an example using a Fuji camera.

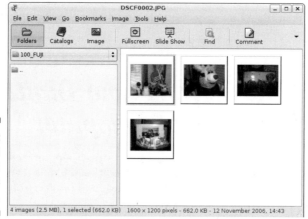

Figure 21-2:
My Fuji camera mounted as a USB disk.

Digital cameras use the same flash memory as USB pen drives. Your camera appears as a memory device to your computer.

3. **Select the photos you want to import to your Ubuntu computer:**

   • *To select a single image to import, click it.*

   • *To select multiple images, press and hold the Shift key and click each image.*

4. **Click the Edit menu and select the Copy option.**

   A Choose the Destination Folder dialog opens.

5. **Click the Browse button.**

   The Choose the Destination Folder dialog displays the camera's storage folder (typically, the camera's storage folder is in the `/media/usbdisk` directory).

6. **Designate a folder (directory) to save your photos.**

   There are a couple of ways to select a directory:

   - *Click an existing directory (folder), such as your home directory.*

   - *Create a new directory for your photos. (Click the Create Folder button and type the name of the new folder to create.)*

7. **Click the Open button.**

   The folder you select is displayed in the Choose the Destination Folder window.

8. **Click OK.**

   Your photos are copied to the selected folder.

You can edit the names using the Nautilus file manager's Rename function. Follow these steps:

1. **Right-click the icon.**

2. **Select the Rename option in the menu that opens.**

3. **Type the new name at the prompt.**

You can edit your photos using The GIMP image editor. (See the "Improving Your Images with The GIMP" section in this chapter.)

Viewing Your Pictures

Ubuntu provides numerous tools for viewing images. I describe a couple of them in this section:

One application (gThumb) provides quick, thumbnail-sized images in Nautilus or the GNOME desktop. The second application (Eye of GNOME) displays the full-blown image.

Displaying thumbnails with gThumb

Ubuntu makes it easy to store graphical images on disk. You can download images from your camera or from the Internet. Those images are stored as files — typically in your home directory — on your computer.

It's easy to build up large numbers of images but difficult to keep track of them. That's where gThumb comes to the rescue. gThumb displays thumbnails of the full-size images inside Nautilus or its own file manager; you can see at a glance the image contained in a file.

Thumbnails are icons containing low-resolution versions of an image file.

Ubuntu provides standard icons you can use to add application launchers to the *GNOME panel,* which is a menu bar described in Chapter 11. The following instructions use Nautilus and gThumb to view thumbnails of numerous images:

1. **From the GNOME menu bar, open a Nautilus window by choosing Places⇨Home Folder.**

2. **Click the Go menu in the menu bar along the top of the Nautilus window and select Location.**

3. **Type `/usr/share/pixmaps` in the Location text box and press the Enter key.**

4. **Scroll down until you start seeing images (instead of generic folder icons).**

 What you're seeing are files that contain images. The images are simple ones used to identify icons. If you use Nautilus to view photographic images that you've downloaded to you computer, gThumb displays those images.

Displaying images

Viewing an image is as easy as clicking on it.

1. **From the GNOME menu bar, open a Nautilus window by choosing Places⇨Home Folder.**

2. **Navigate to a directory (folder) where you have images — photos or other types of pictures.**

 You see thumbnails of the images.

3. Click a thumbnail.

The full image is displayed. For instance, Figure 21-3 shows a picture from the 2006 Albuquerque International Balloon Fiesta.

Nautilus calls on the Eye of GNOME application to display images. Eye of GNOME provides some simple manipulation capabilities, including

✔ **Zoom In or Out:** Enlarge or shrink the image.

✔ **Rotate Left or Right:** Rotate the image 90 degrees to the left or right. Figure 21-4 shows the previous figure rotated 90 degrees to the right.

✔ **Fit:** Force an image to take up the entire Eye of GNOME window.

✔ **Normal:** Return an image to its original orientation and size.

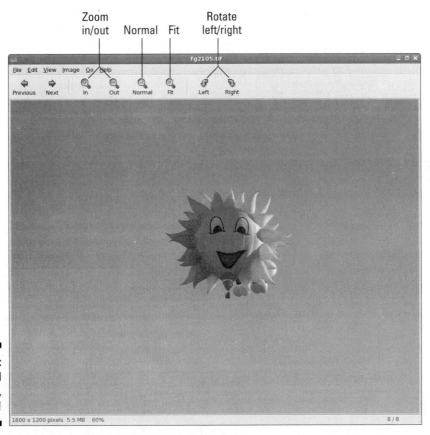

Figure 21-3: Good morning, Albuquerque!

Each image viewing selection is accessible via a labeled button near the top of the Eye of GNOME window.

The Eye of GNOME also lets you sequentially view a series of images. Click the Previous or Next button to go to another image.

Figure 21-4:
Rotating the previous image 90 degrees to the right.

Improving Your Images with The GIMP

The GIMP (GNU Image Manipulation Program — yet another nerdy acronym) provides power image editing capabilities similar to the commercial (and infinitely more expensive) Adobe Photoshop.

Any number divided by zero equals infinity. Since The GIMP costs *nothing* and similar commercial applications cost *something*, commercial applications are infinitely more expensive than The GIMP.

Some of The GIMP's capabilities include the following:

- ✔ **Painting:** You can set brush strokes, erasers, colors, and so on. Set your brush stroke size, edge, and type, or create your own brush stroke. You can mix your own colors or select them from the image you're editing.

- ✔ **Editing:** Select rectangles, ellipses, and circles to manipulate images.

- ✔ **Resizing:** Change the size of a photograph to make it fit your needs.

- ✔ **Layering:** You can edit one or more transparent image layers to, yes, create a layered effect.

- ✔ **Creating paths:** Create and edit line segments. Use mathematical tools such as Bezier curves or use simple straight lines to create diagrams and drawings.

- ✔ **Creating FX:** Create special effects (FX) with the filters that The GIMP provides. The GIMP helps you to create such special effects as shadows, blur lines, and noise.

- ✔ **Scripting:** The GIMP lets you automate image creation by providing a scripting system. You can program The GIMP with its internal scripting language.

The GIMP requires an entire book to do it justice. But I can give one simple example to demonstrate its power. I take Figure 21-3 and eliminate the two balloons at the top and bottom of the picture.

From the GNOME menu bar, choose Applications⇨Graphics⇨GIMP Image Editor. Two GIMP windows and a handy tip-of-the-day dialog opens. Figure 21-5 shows an example of the primary — business — end of The GIMP system.

Now I'll show an example where I edit Figure 21-3 to edit out the balloon images in the lower left and upper center of the image to leave just the single sunny balloon in the center.

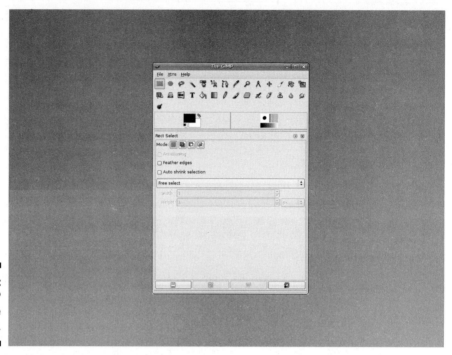

Figure 21-5:
The GIMP
Image
Editor.

You can follow the steps and perform the same type of editing on one of your own photos:

1. **Click The GIMP File menu and select Open.**

   The Open Image dialog opens.

2. **Select the image file (for example, I select the image from Figure 21-3) and click the Open button.**

   The GIMP opens another window displaying the image.

3. **I repeat these steps to remove the partial images of the balloon in the lower-left corner and upper-center area of the figure:**

   a. Click Tools and choose Selection Tools⇨Rect Select.

   The cursor turns into a square next to the normal arrow pointer.

   b. Click the background near the balloon and drag the mouse so it traces a rectangle about the same size as the balloon.

A dotted line outlines the rectangle you selected.

c. *Right click and choose Edit⇨Copy.*

d. *Choose Edit⇨Paste.*

The blue rectangle is placed directly over the area you just copied.

e. *Click on the newly pasted rectangle and drag it over the balloon.*

The balloon is replaced by a nearly perfect sky background, as shown in Figure 21-6.

One of The GIMP's most useful capabilities — especially for *For Dummies* authors — is taking *screen shots* (pictures of the stuff on your computer screen). I've used The GIMP to take every image in this book, and many others. Here's a trade secret:

1. **Click File and select Acquire⇨Screen Shot.**

2. **Click the Grab button and the cursor turns into a plus (+) sign.**

The GIMP can take a screen shot of any window you point and click your mouse on.

Figure 21-6:
Editing out the unwanted balloons using The Gimp.

The GIMP's default action is to capture a single window. Select the Whole Screen radio button to capture your entire computer screen.

3. **Point and click the mouse on the window you want to capture.**

The GIMP grabs the window and displays the image in a new window.

You can edit, manipulate, and save the image as a file.

Part V
The Part of Tens

The 5th Wave   By Rich Tennant

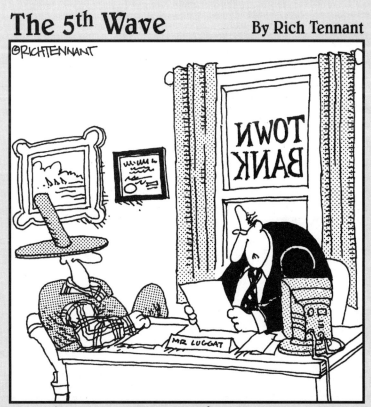

"We have no problem funding your Web site, Frank. Of all the chicken farmers operating Web sites, yours has the most impressive cluck-through rates."

In this part . . .

Part V completes my Ubuntu coverage by showing how to find helpful information about Ubuntu and Linux in general. It also describes how to tackle common problems.

Chapter 22 introduces you to help and documentation sources. You're initiated into system administration functions in Chapter 23.

Chapter 22

Almost Ten Ubuntu Resources

· ·

· ·

*U*buntu Linux is easy to use. Sometimes, however, you encounter a topic or run up against a problem that you need to learn more about. No problem. Ubuntu comes with a wealth of resources, including great and abundant documentation. Ubuntu documentation comes in a variety of forms and can be found in many locations.

This chapter outlines the most useful information that you can find within Ubuntu itself, on the Internet, and from other locations. The following sections describe what the Ubuntu informational resources are and where you can find them.

Accessing Local Documentation

Ubuntu provides numerous information resources on your computer.

Looking at man pages: Read the manual

Despite their moniker, man pages (manual pages) are gender neutral. *Manual pages* provide concise, easy-to-use information and are an age-old Linux standby — originating from the UNIX operating system, which came into widespread use during the 1970s. There's a man page for everyone, with topics ranging from programs and utilities to libraries and almost every conceivable aspect of Linux.

You access man pages from the Linux command line. Open a GNOME Terminal window by clicking the Applications menu and choosing Accessories⇨ Terminal. A Terminal window opens, and you type man `topic`, where the `topic` can be anything from a GNU program to a configuration file format or protocol.

The following example demonstrates getting information about the list directory (ls), concatenate (cat), interface configuration (ifconf), and the /etc/passwd file.

From the GNOME menu, choose Applications⇨Terminal. A Terminal Emulator window opens. (If you need a refresher on how to enter a command, flip back to Chapter 5.) Type the following command:

```
man ls
```

You see the ls man page listing. Type the next commands to see man pages for the cat, ifconfig, and passwd commands.

```
man cat
man ifconfig
man passwd
```

Man pages are organized by section. (See Table 22-1 for more information.) The sections are stored in the /usr/share/man directory by default. List that directory (ls /usr/share/man), and you see man page sections 1 through 9. You can specify the topic by adding the section number to your man command line before the topic:

```
man section-number topic
```

For instance, there is a man page for the passwd command, and one for the passwd file. Type man 1 passwd to see information about the passwd command. Alternatively, type man 5 passwd to see the man page for the /etc/passwd file.

You see the man page for the password command if you don't specify a section number. (The man program defaults to the lowest section number by default.)

The nine sections are listed in Table 22-1.

Table 22-1		Man Page Section Descriptions
Topics	*Section*	*Description*
Commands	1	Displays information about programs, utilities, and shell scripts, all of which are executable.
System Calls	2	Provides access to kernel-space functions. User-space programs use system calls to ask the Linux kernel to provide information and perform tasks.
Library Calls	3	Gives user-space programs access to common tasks and information. Using library calls reduces the need to reinvent the wheel.

Topics	Section	Description
Special Files	4	Shows information about Linux files that act as an interface to hardware subsystems like disk drives.
File Formats	5	Describes the file formats used to operate Linux.
Games	6	Text-based Linux games might not entice Kyle, Stan, Kenny, and Cartman to rack up hundreds of hours of World of Warcraft quests, but they can help pass the odd ten minutes or so.
Miscellaneous	7	Provides information about general topics that don't fit into any other category.
Administration	8	Gives information about commands used to manage the computer.
Kernel	9	Lists kernel-related commands and systems.

Use the up-arrow and down-arrow keys on your keyboard to move up and down one page at a time. Use the slash (/) character to search for text strings. Typing the letter Q exits the man page.

By default, the man command shows the first section of a topic. For instance, there's a section for the passwd command and the passwd file (found in /etc/passwd). Typing man passwd shows information on the passwd command. You can view information about the passwd file by typing man 5 passwd.

If you can't remember the name of a man page topic, you can use the man command to find it. Type man -k search-string, and man will return a list of all the man pages that match or partially match the search string. For instance, typing man -k passwd returns a long list of passwd-related man pages.

Figure 22-1 shows a terminal emulator window showing the man -k passwd command and the list of man pages it produces.

Pulling up the info documents

Information documents, commonly referred to as *info docs,* are similar to man pages. Info docs augment the information provided by man pages.

To view information about a topic, type the following in a terminal window:

```
info topic
```

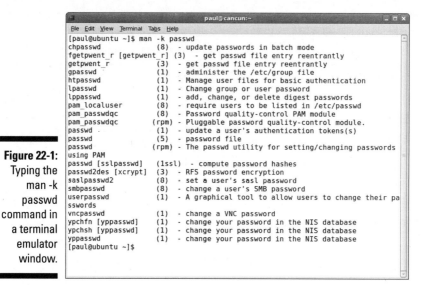

Figure 22-1:
Typing the
man -k
passwd
command in
a terminal
emulator
window.

For instance, to see information on the `/etc/passwd file`, which contains local user account information, type this:

```
info passwd
```

The first page of information about the topic is displayed. Press the spacebar or the N key (for *Next*) to move down one page and the U key to maneuver up one page. Pressing the H key brings up help information, and pressing Q exits (quits) the information utility.

Finding Debian package–based documentation

Your Ubuntu Linux computer is constructed from many, many individual pieces of software. Ubuntu uses Debian packages to install all those pieces of software. The Debian packaging system combines the program, library, and configuration files that make up a software system into a single file, which is called a *package*. The package concept is a wonderful piece of engineering, without which it would be impossible to construct a Linux distribution like Ubuntu.

Package management is discussed in Chapter 4 and Chapter 23.

Debian packages store the individual software pieces that make up the particular system. The pieces include the executable — when appropriate — programs, configuration files, and documentation. The documentation files are stored in a subdirectory of /usr/share/doc; the subdirectory takes the name of the Debian package.

Use the following command to find the documentation file belonging to a package:

```
dpkg -L package-name
```

For instance, typing dpkg -L wireless-tools lists the files belonging to the package. The following output shows a snippet of a listing that includes the documentation for the wireless-tool package:

```
/usr/share/doc
/usr/share/doc/wireless-tools
/usr/share/doc/wireless-tools/PCMCIA.txt.gz
/usr/share/doc/wireless-tools/HOTPLUG.txt.gz
/usr/share/doc/wireless-tools/README.gz
/usr/share/doc/wireless-tools/README.Debian
/usr/share/doc/wireless-tools/copyright
/usr/share/doc/wireless-tools/changelog.gz
/usr/share/doc/wireless-tools/DISTRIBUTIONS.txt.gz
/usr/share/doc/wireless-tools/changelog.Debian.gz
```

The chnagelog file provides information about the changes made to the wireless-tools system over time. The README file provides general information about the package and the utilities it contains. All such files can be useful.

The dpkg command also provides a quick synopsis of what function a package performs or what service it provides. Typing dpkg -L package-name not only lists the files belonging to the package, but also a short description of the package function. For instance, typing dpkg -L wireless-tools gives the following synopsis at the very end of the listing:

```
ii  wireless-tools 27+28pre13-1ub Tools for manipulating
           Linux Wireless Extensions
```

Asking for Ubuntu help

Ubuntu can help you. Click the System menu and choose Help⇨System Documentation. The Ubuntu Help Centre window, shown in Figure 22-2, opens.

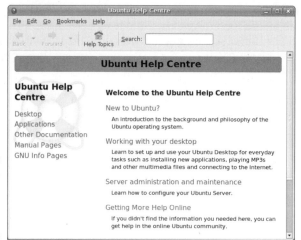

Figure 22-2:
The Ubuntu
Help Centre
window.

The Ubuntu Help Centre window gives you access to both local and Internet-based information. I focus on the local information in this section. The "Finding Online Documentation" section, later in this chapter, shows how to get information from the Internet.

You have access to the following information from the Help Topics window:

- ✔ **About Ubuntu:** Displays useful information about the Ubuntu Linux distribution.

- ✔ **Desktop Guide:** Shows how to use the Ubuntu GNOME desktop and applications. (See Chapters 11 through 16.) It also shows how to add and remove software packages to/from Ubuntu by using graphical and command line tools. And the Desktop Guide describes how to update existing software packages from Internet software repositories. (See Chapter 23.)

- ✔ **Server Guide:** If you want to experiment with the Ubuntu Linux Server distribution, these documents can help you. Selecting this option opens a document that describes how to use and configure the Ubuntu Linux Server distribution.

- ✔ **Packaging Guide:** The great thing about open source software is that you can jump right in and start contributing. You can design and build your own software packages. If they turn out to be useful, you might even get them included in a future version of Ubuntu!

- ✔ **Applications:** Provides access to the manuals of applications installed by Ubuntu.

- ✔ **Other Documentation:** Includes various documents describing various Linux systems and utilities. For instance, if you want to find out more about network address translation (NAT), select the Linux NAT HOWTO option included in Other Documentation.

✔ **Command Line Help:** You can view all the man pages and info documents in Command Line Help. Click a man page and you see the same information you would if you selected the command line man page described in the "Looking at man pages: Read the manual" section earlier in this chapter.

Opening application-based help

Most applications found on your Ubuntu computer provide their own help systems and documentation. Start the application and click the Help menu to find the information you need. The Help menu for an application typically shows several options, including the following:

✔ **OpenOffice.org Help:** Select this option, and the OpenOffice.org Help window dedicated to the particular application — Writer, Calc, and so on — that you're using opens. The window provides a table of contents of OpenOffice.org documents and also lets you view the index or search for topics.

✔ **What's This?:** Provides information about specific OpenOffice.org objects. Select What's This? and the mouse cursor changes to a question mark. Place the question mark cursor on any part of the OpenOffice.org application window and a small informational dialog pops up describing the purpose of the object.

✔ **Get Help Online:** Opens Firefox to a Web site providing additional OpenOffice.org information.

✔ **Translate This Application:** Opens Firefox to a Web site dedicated to translating OpenOffice.org to languages other than English.

✔ **About OpenOffice.org:** Opens a dialog showing the basic information about OpenOffice.org, including copyright and version number.

Application-based help often provides complete and thorough information about the application. I rarely have to search elsewhere when using information provided by OpenOffice.org, Firefox, and other applications.

Finding Online Documentation

In addition to the local documents that Ubuntu provides, you can find more help and information online via the Internet. This section outlines some of the most useful resources available on the Internet.

Reading Ubuntu documentation

The Ubuntu Web site — `http://help.ubuntu.com` — provides a wealth of information for the Ubuntu user. You can browse directly to the Web site from Firefox or from the GNOME menu bar — choose System⇨Help⇨ Online Documentation. Figure 22-3 shows the Web page.

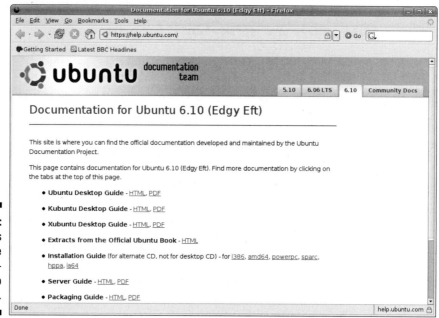

Figure 22-3:
Ubuntu's online documentation Web page.

This Web page provides access to essentially the same documents that you can access locally on your Ubuntu computer by choosing System⇨Help⇨ System Documentation from the GNOME menu bar. The documentation found online, however, might be more up to date than that found on your computer.

Talking to other Ubuntu users: Community support

Ubuntu Linux is all about adhering to the philosophy of one being a better person by being part of and contributing to a community. That's also very much the ideal of the open source movement. Open source and Ubuntu rely on the community of software developers and software consumers — often the two are indistinguishable — helping one another.

You can plug into the Ubuntu community for support and information. Ubuntu, of course, makes it very easy to access this support and even has a "button" for it. From the GNOME menu bar, choose System⇨Help⇨ Community Support. Figure 22-4 shows the Web page.

This Web page provides links to the following types of support:

- ✔ **Local Language Support:** Click the Local Language Support link under the Free Technical Support heading and a Web page opens with links to Ubuntu help in numerous languages.

- ✔ **Documentation:** Provides another link to `http://help.ubuntu.com`.

- ✔ **Community Support Chat:** Gives you an interactive IRC (Internet Relay Chat) to communicate with other enthusiasts.

- ✔ **Web Forums:** Delivers you into the very helpful world of Ubuntu-based forums. Register with Ubuntu forums and you gain interactive access to Web-based forums. You can submit questions within numerous threads and receive answers via the forum; you can also search existing threads for answers.

Figure 22-4:
Ubuntu's
support
Web page.

✔ **Mailing Lists:** These are similar to Web forums except all interaction is carried out via e-mail. You can submit a question to a list, and someone with an answer can respond to the list; just like with Web forums, you can also search existing threads for answers.

✔ **Tech Support System:** Submit questions as well as feature and bug requests directly to the Ubuntu community. Ubuntu provides a Web-based system for responding to community-based requests.

Hiring commercial support

Ubuntu, at its heart, is an open source and community-based Linux distribution. However, Ubuntu also offers a commercial conduit to support and service.

When individuals like myself use Ubuntu, we do so to enhance our own productivity and also for fun and the sheer beauty of the system. Ubuntu works for us as individuals, but it also works for small, medium, and large organizations.

However, commercial organizations often require more in-depth support than individuals require. Ubuntu and its overseer, Canonical, provide such support for a fee through the Ubuntu Marketplace. From the GNOME menu bar, choose System⇨Help⇨Commercial Support. Firefox opens to the Ubuntu Marketplace Web page, where you can find both global and local support providers.

Google, google!

There's lots of additional Ubuntu information beyond that provided by the Ubuntu community. In fact, there's too much to even start to describe. Just submit a search string or phrase to `www.google.com` (or your favorite search engine) and you'll receive as many links to information sources as you can handle.

Chapter 23

Almost Ten System-Administration Functions

Sure, you didn't sign up to be a system administrator when you decided to use an Ubuntu computer. Even though system administrators lead lives of excitement and get paid huge salaries — not!! — that profession is not for everyone.

But anyone who owns and uses a computer is by default a sysadmin. System administration is actually very easy. You need to perform several simple tasks and perform them regularly, and you're a sysadmin.

Being a professional system administrator is basically like being the sysadmin of your own computer. The primary difference is that you perform system-administrator tasks for others as well as for yourself. You also have to know a wider range of tasks.

This chapter describes the most common, and also most important, system-administrator tasks. Those jobs are pretty basic, if not simple. The easy part is learning what they are. The hard part is regularly doing the jobs.

Updating Debian Software Packages

Ubuntu maintains repositories that let you update your Ubuntu computer with the software. In the bad old days, you had to manually find, download, and install updated software; in the bad, really old days, you had to find, download, and recompile the bloody things. Rather than rely on and require computer users to update their computers, software repositories make the process painless and easy as pie.

The Ubuntu support system includes all the documentation and help material, described in Chapter 22, plus *software package repositories* designed to keep your Ubuntu workstation updated with the latest patches and bug fixes.

Computer operating systems and applications are complex beasts. Software developers are constantly improving their systems' capabilities and fixing problems that inevitably pop up. Change is part of life and software, and computer users must keep up with the change or be left with outdated software. The software package repository was invented to help you keep up with software updates, but keeping up with life is another thing.

You need to be connected to the Internet or to a network with Internet access to update your computer. See Chapters 6–9 for information about Ubuntu networking.

When an update to a software package is approved by Ubuntu, the software is posted to the repository and also to numerous mirrors around the world. (Mirrors are computers that hold duplicate — mirror images — Ubuntu repositories. Ubuntu uses mirrors to distribute software and eliminate bottlenecks.) Your Ubuntu computer automatically checks the mirrors for updates and informs you of them by showing the Software Updates Available icon on your screen. Figure 23-1 shows such a notification icon.

Figure 23-1:
Ubuntu notifies you that software updates are available.

Software updates available
Click on the notification icon to show the available updates.

To install updates, follow these steps:

1. **Click the update icon — the white star with an orange background on the GNOME menu bar (see Figure 23-1) that the Software Updates Available icon points to.**

   The Software Updates dialog opens, prompting you to enter your user account password.

2. **Type your password in the Password text box and click the OK button.**

   The Software Updates dialog opens, showing a list of the available updates. Figure 23-2 shows an example.

3. **Click the Install Updates button.**

   The Downloading Packages dialog shows the package download process, and the Applying Changes dialog shows the progress of the installation. When the process finishes, the Changes Applied dialog opens.

Figure 23-2:
The
Software
Updates
dialog.

4. **Click the Close button.**

Control returns to the Software Updates dialog.

5. **Click the Close button.**

Your Ubuntu computer's software is now up to date.

You can also use the `apt-get` utility to update packages. Follow these steps:

1. **Open a Terminal window by choosing Accessories⇨Terminal from the GNOME Applications menu.**

2. **Type `apt-get update`.**

This command tells `apt-get` to get a list of packages that need to be updated.

3. **Type `apt-get upgrade`.**

This second command selects packages to be downloaded, downloads them, and then installs them.

Installing New Software Packages

Ubuntu provides networked software package repositories that let you install new software packages. You perform the software package installation process as follows:

1. **From the GNOME menu bar, choose System⇨Administration⇨ Synaptic Package Manager.**

The Enter Your Password to Perform Administrative Tasks dialog opens.

2. **Type your password in the Password text box and click OK.**

The Synaptic Package Manager window and the Quick Introduction dialog open, with the introduction dialog on top.

3. **Read the introduction and click the Close button.**

Figure 23-3 shows the Synaptic Package Manager window open after closing the Quick Introduction dialog.

You can scroll through the list of available packages or use the search facility to find the package or packages that you want to install.

To search for packages, follow these steps:

a. *Click the Search button.*

The Find dialog opens.

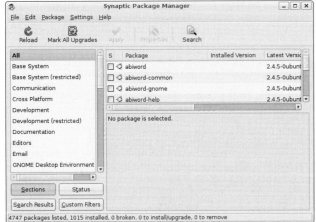

Figure 23-3:
The
Synaptic
Package
Manager.

b. *Enter a text string in the Search text box.*

c. *Click the Search button.*

> You exit the Find dialog, and the Synaptic Package Manager displays any packages that meet your search criteria.

4. Select the check boxes to the left of any packages you want to install.

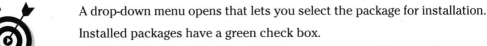

A drop-down menu opens that lets you select the package for installation.

Installed packages have a green check box.

5. Click the Mark for Installation option in the drop-down menu.

Another dialog opens, showing any additional packages that the one you just selected depends on. If you choose to install a package, its dependencies are installed, too.

6. Click the Mark button in the dialog.

Control returns to the Synaptic Package Manager.

7. Click the Apply button.

The Summary dialog opens, telling you what's about to happen.

8. Click the Apply button in the Summary dialog.

A dialog opens, telling you about the progress of the package or packages you're downloading. When downloading is complete, another dialog opens, displaying the status of the package installation process.

The Changes Applied dialog opens when the download and installation process finishes.

9. **Click the Close button in the Changes Applied dialog.**

   Control returns to the Synaptic Package Manager. You can install additional packages if you want.

10. **Click the File button and select Quit.**

You can use the Synaptic Package Manager to install packages from the companion Ubuntu disc or from Ubuntu Internet software package repositories.

You can also use the `apt-get` utility to install packages:

1. **Open a Terminal window by choosing Accessories⇨Terminal from the GNOME Applications menu.**

2. **Type `apt-get install` *package-name*.**

   `apt-get` downloads and installs the package.

Reading System Logs

Every time you do anything on your Ubuntu computer, Ubuntu records a log of the event. Every time Ubuntu performs a task, the event is logged. The records are called *system logs*.

When you start (boot) your Ubuntu computer, Ubuntu automatically runs the `syslogd` and `klogd` daemons that save system log events to files in the `/var/log` directory. The default — catch-all — system log file is `/var/log/messages`.

System logs are useful when you need to troubleshoot a problem, see what's happening on your computer, or investigate security issues. Reading your logs is one of the most under-appreciated and under-performed system-administration tasks. Unfortunately, reading logs is a boring, time-consuming process because log files contain a lot of information.

Worse, the information contained in log files is often repetitive and uninteresting. You have to wade through a lot of data before coming across something interesting.

Ubuntu provides two utilities to help you monitor your logs: System Log Viewer and Logcheck.

Using System Log Viewer

System Log Viewer graphically displays the contents of your log files. To open System Log Viewer, choose System⇨Administration⇨System Log from the GNOME menu bar. The System Log Viewer window opens; Figure 23-4 shows an example log excerpt. From here, you can look through your log files.

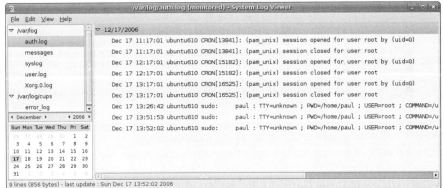

Figure 23-4:
A sample
log excerpt.

There are no tricks to using System Log Viewer. Using it regularly can, first, help you develop the habit of monitoring your computer, and second, help you develop the eye for what's normal and what's not normal. The human brain is wonderful at pattern recognition. With practice, you'll develop a feel for your computer and be able to identify problems when they occur. Practice makes perfect!

Using Logcheck

Logcheck is a utility that helps identify problems as recorded in your log files. Logcheck keeps a database of events — actually, it keeps a list of regular expressions, but that's beyond the scope of this book — that are considered normal. Any events that Logcheck finds in your log files that don't match the database are considered abnormal. Abnormal events are flagged and e-mailed to you.

Logcheck is a good tool for filtering out the noise that makes reading logs so difficult. By concentrating on unusual events, you can better monitor your logs.

Installing the Logcheck utility

Logcheck isn't installed by default on your Ubuntu computer. Here's how to install it:

1. **From the GNOME menu bar, choose System⇨Administration⇨ Synaptic Package Manager.**

   The Enter Your Password to Perform Administrative Tasks dialog opens.

2. **Type your password in the Password text box and click OK.**

   The Synaptic Package Manager window opens. So does the Quick Introduction dialog, if this is the first time you've used the Synaptic Package Manager. Click the Close button in the Introduction dialog if it opens.

3. **Scroll down to the Logcheck package.**

4. **Select the check box for Logcheck.**

5. **Select the Mark for Installation option from the drop-down menu.**

6. **Click the Mark button in the Mark for Installation dialog that opens.**

7. **Repeat Steps 4, 5, and 6 for the Logcheck-database package.**

8. **Click the Apply button in the Synaptic Package Manager window.**

9. **Click the Apply button in the Summary dialog when it opens.**

   The two packages are downloaded and installed.

   Installing Logcheck opens the Configuring Exim dialog that configures your Ubuntu computer to deliver e-mail messages.

10. **Click the Forward button in the Configuring Exim dialog.**

    The Synaptic Package Manager downloads and installs the package. The Changes dialog opens upon completion.

11. **Click the Close button.**

    Logcheck will now deliver e-mail locally on your Ubuntu computer.

Using the Logcheck utility

Logcheck is configured by default to run once per hour. You can also execute Logcheck manually by typing the following command from the GNOME Terminal Emulator window (choose Accessories⇨Terminal from the GNOME Applications menu):

```
sudo -u logcheck logcheck
```

When you run Logcheck, it searches your log files for log events it considers
to be potentially interesting and e-mails you the results. For instance, I got
the following listing on an Ubuntu machine I just installed:

```
From logcheck@ubuntu610 Sun Dec 17 22:03:03 2006
Envelope-to: paul@ubuntu610
Delivery-date: Sun, 17 Dec 2006 22:03:03 -0700
To: paul@ubuntu610
Subject: ubuntu610 2006-12-17 22:03 System Events
From: logcheck@ubuntu610
Date: Sun, 17 Dec 2006 22:03:03 -0700

This email is sent by logcheck. If you wish to no-longer receive it,
you can either deinstall the logcheck package or modify its
configuration file (/etc/logcheck/logcheck.conf).

System Events
=-=-=-=-=-=-=
Dec 17 22:02:02 ubuntu610 CRON[19584]: (pam_unix) session closed for user
               logcheck
Dec 17 22:02:27 ubuntu610 su[19657]: (pam_unix) authentication failure; logname=
               uid=1000 euid=0 tty=pts/3 ruser=paul rhost
= user=logcheck
Dec 17 22:02:29 ubuntu610 su[19657]: pam_authenticate: Authentication failure
Dec 17 22:02:29 ubuntu610 su[19657]: FAILED su for logcheck by paul
Dec 17 22:02:29 ubuntu610 su[19657]: - pts/3 paul:logcheck
Dec 17 22:02:34 ubuntu610 su[19661]: (pam_unix) authentication failure; logname=
               uid=1000 euid=0 tty=pts/3 ruser=paul rhost
= user=logcheck
```

There's nothing sinister in here, even though the su (switch user) command
failed. (Someone who breaks into a computer might try to get root privileges
by using the su command.) In this case, I just fat-fingered my password and
was denied root-level access. But this listing does prove that Logcheck is on
the watch. Had I not been using my Ubuntu computer during this time frame,
the failed su command would be very suspicious.

Use these tools to monitor your logs. Reading logs is becoming evermore
important in the world of system administration. Your best defense is information, and logs provide a lot of it. Using tools like Logcheck makes it easier
to sort the uninteresting information from the interesting.

Working with User Accounts

Ubuntu configures a user account when it's installed. However, you aren't limited to using this account. You can easily create additional accounts or modify and delete existing ones by using Ubuntu utilities.

The following instructions show how to modify a user account by having Ubuntu suggest a random password:

1. **From the GNOME menu bar, choose System⇨Administration ⇨ Users and Groups.**

   The User Settings dialog opens, as shown in Figure 23-5, showing the root (also called the *superuser*) account and the user account you created during the installation; in this case, the user account name (username) is paul.

Figure 23-5: The User Settings dialog.

2. **Click to highlight a user account.**

   In this case, I click the paul user account.

3. **Click the Properties button.**

   The Account Properties dialog opens. Figure 23-6 shows my account information displayed in the dialog. For instance, you can add or edit information about your home and office.

   In this case, I'd like to generate a random password to frustrate any hackers who might want to compromise my Ubuntu computer.

4. **Select the Generate Random Password radio button.**

   Ubuntu generates a random, eight-character password, including numbers plus lowercase and uppercase letters. (You can generate additional random passwords by clicking the Generate button.)

5. (Optional) Record the password on a piece of paper.

Recording your password is a double-edged sword. On one hand, your new password will not do you any good if you forget it. But writing the password on paper makes it possible for someone to steal it. I recommend writing your password on the back of a business card and keeping it in your wallet until you memorize it. After you memorize it, you should destroy the password. (I'm so paranoid that I rip the paper into tiny pieces and flush the pieces.)

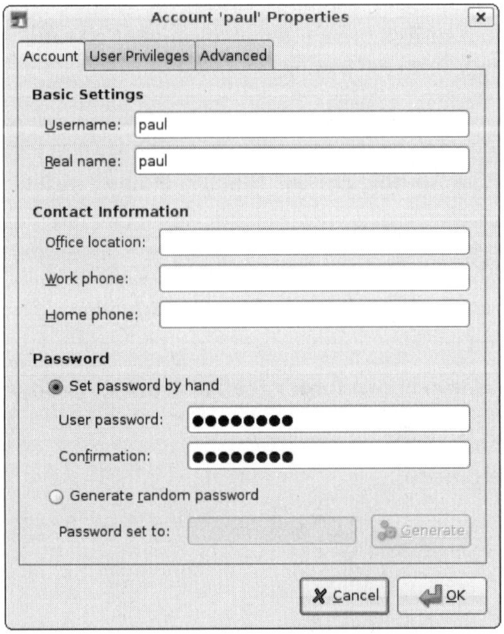

Figure 23-6:
Editing a
user
account's
properties.

6. Double-click the password.

7. Right-click the highlighted password and choose Copy.

8. Click the Set Password by Hand radio button.

9. Right-click the User Password text box and choose Paste.

10. Repeat Steps 8 and 9 for the Confirmation text box.

11. Click OK.

Control returns to the User Settings dialog.

12. Click the Close button.

You can also change user account options such as its home directory, numeric user ID, and group ID. You can use the User and Groups utility to add and delete user accounts.

Changing File Permissions

One fundamental, important, yet simple-to-perform system-administration process is changing file and directory (folder) access permissions. Changing permissions lets you provide or deny access to other users and processes. Limited access is especially important when multiple users have access to your Ubuntu computer — you might or might not want your fellow users to access your files.

Linux files and folders have three sets of permissions: owner, group, and others. You can use the Nautilus file manager to prevent anyone who doesn't own your home directory from accessing anything in it.

To change file permissions, follow these steps:

1. **From the GNOME menu bar, choose Places⇨Home Folder.**

   The File Browser dialog opens.

   When you build your Ubuntu computer, your home directory initially contains only one directory (folder), called the Desktop.

2. **Click the Up button.**

3. **Right-click your user account folder icon and select Properties.**

   The Desktop Properties dialog opens.

4. **Click the Permissions tab.**

   Figure 23-7 shows the Desktop Properties dialog showing the Owner, Group, and Others permissions. Each option shows the directories (folders) and file access options:

   • Change the Folder Access menu options to allow or deny access to the directory itself.

   • Change the File Access menu options to allow or deny access to individual files.

5. **Click the Others/Folder Access drop-down menu, near the bottom-half of the dialog and select one of these three options:**

   • *None:* You can't access or modify the folder, or the folder's contents, in any way.

   • *List Files Only:* You can see a listing of files in the directory, but not create, read, or delete files.

   • *Access Files:* This option lets you read but not modify or delete files.

   • *Create and Delete Files:* This option lets you create, modify, and delete files.

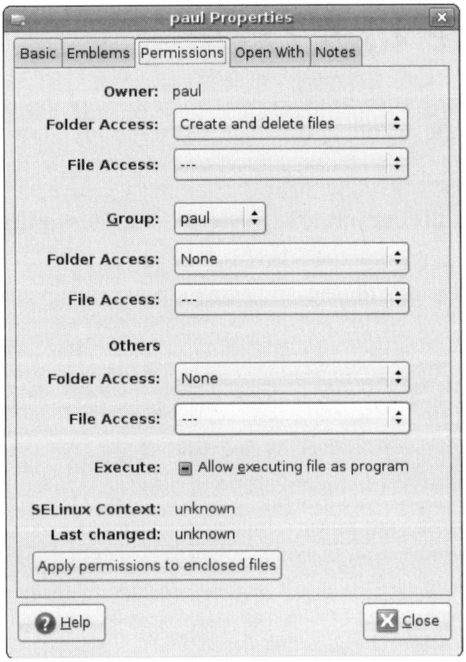

paul Properties

Basic | Emblems | Permissions | Open With | Notes

Owner: paul

Folder Access: Create and delete files

File Access: ---

Group: paul

Folder Access: None

File Access: ---

Others

Folder Access: None

File Access: ---

Execute: ☑ Allow executing file as program

SELinux Context: unknown
Last changed: unknown

Apply permissions to enclosed files

? Help   ✕ Close

Figure 23-7:
The
Properties
dialog
showing file
and folder
permissions.

For example, select the None option. Selecting the None option denies all access to anyone who does not own or belong to a group that owns the files.

You've changed your home folder (directory) access permissions to prevent anyone who is not you, and who doesn't belong to your group from accessing files in your home directory.

Alternatively, you could select options to let other users who belong to your group access your home directory.

6. Click the Close button.

Control returns to the original Nautilus file browser window.

7. Choose File⇨Close.

You can manually change file permissions by using a Terminal Emulator. From the GNOME menu bar, choose Applications⇨Accessories⇨Terminal. A GNOME Terminal window opens. Type `ls -l` to display all files and directories in your current working directory. Use the chmod program to change file permissions. For instance, type `chmod 700 /home/username` to deny access to everyone except yourself. In my case, I type `chmod 700 /home/paul`.

Changing the Time and Date

Time waits for no one, as the song goes. How true, but we're living in Ubuntu time and change it as we want. Follow these steps to modify your Ubuntu computer's time and date:

1. **From the GNOME menu bar, choose System⇨Administration ⇨ Time and Date.**

   The Time and Date Settings dialog opens, as shown in Figure 23-8.

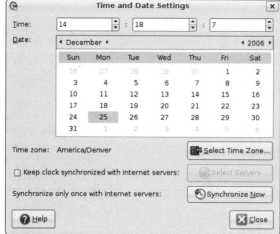

2. **Click the Select Time Zone button to change your time zone.**

3. **Select the Keep Clock Synchronized check box.**

   The NTP Support Not Installed dialog opens.

   Using the Keep Clock Synchronized option tells your Ubuntu computer to continually update its internal clock from very accurate — atomic clocks — time sources that are accessible via the Internet.

4. **Click the Install NTP Support button.**

   The Enter Your Password to Perform Administrative Tasks dialog opens.

5. **Type your user account password in the Password text box and click OK.**

   Ubuntu downloads and installs the necessary package. The Replace Configuration File /etc/ntp.conf dialog opens.

6. **Click the Replace button.**

7. **Click the Close button in the Changes Applied dialog.**

8. **Click the Select Servers button in the Time and Date dialog.**

   The Time Servers dialog opens.

9. **Select three servers closest to your area.**

10. **Click the Close button.**

11. **Click the Synchronize Now button.**

12. **Click the Close button.**

Your computer's clock will automatically be kept up to date.

Monitoring Your System

I like to keep tabs on what my Ubuntu computer hardware is doing. Ubuntu provides a utility for monitoring your computer. From the GNOME menu bar, choose System⇨Administration⇨System Monitor. The System Monitor dialog, shown in Figure 23-9, opens.

You can see at a glance how hard your CPU (central processing unit) is working. You also see how much memory and network is used.

You can put your CPU monitor information in any GNOME panel:

1. **Right-click a GNOME panel and select the Add to Panel option.**

   The Add to Panel dialog opens.

2. **Scroll down and click the System Monitor option.**

3. **Click the Add button.**

   The System Monitor icon appears on the panel.

4. **Right-click the System Monitor icon and select Preferences.**

   The System Monitor Preferences dialog opens, as shown in Figure 23-10.

5. **Select any or all of the Monitored Resources check boxes.**

6. **Click the Close button.**

7. Click the Close button in the Add to Panel dialog.

Your computer's real-time information is always displayed on your GNOME panel.

Placing your mouse cursor over any System Monitor icon shows the resource state in detail.

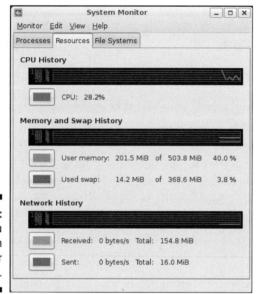

Figure 23-9:
The Ubuntu System Monitor dialog.

Figure 23-10:
The System Monitor Preferences dialog.

Starting and Stopping System Services

Out of the box, so to speak, Ubuntu runs a handful of system services (also known as *daemons*). For instance, Ubuntu runs the HAL (hardware abstraction layer) daemon that automatically detects and mounts storage devices when a device is plugged into your computer. You plug a USB flash drive into your Ubuntu computer, and HAL detects and mounts the device.

You can start and stop any service. Follow these steps:

1. **From the GNOME menu bar, choose System➪Administration➪ Services.**

   The Services Settings dialog, shown in Figure 23-11, opens.

2. **Select any deselected check box to start the service or deselect any selected check box to stop the service.**

3. **Click the Close button.**

Figure 23-11:
The
Services
Settings
dialog.

You can see what processes are running by using the ps command. Open a Terminal Emulator window and type either of these commands:

✔ ps -ef   Every running process is displayed.

✔ top   The processes using the most resources are continuously listed.

Managing Your Computer's Power Use

Ubuntu, go to sleep! You can make your Ubuntu computer hibernate, saving the time it takes to shut down and start up; this also saves money because a hibernating computer uses practically no power. Follow these steps:

1. **From the GNOME menu bar, choose System⇨Preferences⇨ Power Management.**

   Figure 23-12 shows the Power Management Preferences dialog that opens.

2. **Click the Put Computer to Sleep when It Is Inactive For slider and select a time between 1 and 60 minutes.**

3. **Click the Close button.**

Your computer will go to sleep after you haven't used it for the specified time. Your computer will wake up when you move the mouse or press any key.

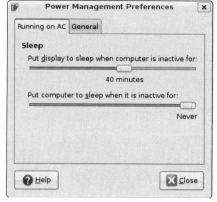

Figure 23-12:
The Power Management Preferences dialog.

Part VI
Appendixes

"We're much better prepared for this upgrade than before. We're giving users additional training, better manuals, and a morphine drip."

In this part . . .

The appendixes provide information that doesn't necessarily fit into the general flow of the chapters.

Appendix A introduces three Ubuntu projects: Kubuntu, Edubuntu, and Xubuntu; it also introduces the Server version of Ubuntu.

Appendix B shows how to use the powerful, flexible, and amazing OpenSSH (open source Secure Shell); this appendix also shows how to use OpenSSH to create a simple and easy-to-use virtual private network (VPN) on an unencrypted wireless network.

Appendix C is a brief technical summary of the *Ubuntu Linux For Dummies* CD-ROM.

Appendix A

Tutti-Fruti Ubuntu

ou say Ubuntu, I say Kubuntu. You say Edubuntu, I say Xubuntu. Why don't we just . . . Anyway, there's more to Ubuntu than just Ubuntu. As the song says, there are actually four variations of Ubuntu.

This appendix introduces them all. Ubuntu makes it easy to download each version and burn a CD-ROM. You can make and boot any or all discs. It's fun to experiment and explore the diverse Ubuntu world and make the decision as to which one best suits your needs.

Trying a Different Look: Kubuntu

Kubuntu is Ubuntu that uses the K Desktop Environment (KDE) graphical desktop in place of GNOME. KDE and GNOME are similar in many ways. However, KDE is considered to use more advanced technology than GNOME.

The ordinary computer user won't find that much difference between KDE and GNOME. Some people like KDE, others like GNOME, and yet others — like myself — don't care.

Kubuntu provides the same range of applications, such as Openoffice.org, that Ubuntu does. New Kubuntu releases follow the same six-month schedule, too. Please browse www.kubuntu.org for more information about this product.

The following instructions assume you're working from an Ubuntu computer with a writable CD-ROM or DVD drive.

You need to download a Kubuntu CD-ROM image from an Ubuntu mirror to a computer from which you can burn the image to a writable CD. Follow these steps:

1. **Click your Firefox browser icon on the GNOME panel.**

2. **Type `www.kubuntu.org/download.php` in the Location text box and press the Enter key.**

3. **Click the Download link for the latest version.**

4. **Click the link to your continent.**

   The menu of download sites expands to different countries.

5. **Click your country.**

   The menu expands to show universities and various organizations.

6. **Click any of the various university or organization links (that house Kubuntu mirrors).**

   The list further expands to one or more actual download sites.

7. **Click a download site.**

   The Opening Kubuntu-6.10 dialog opens.

8. **Click the Save File button.**

   The Downloads dialog opens, showing a progress meter.

9. **Click the Cleanup button and close the dialog when the download finishes.**

After you download the Kubuntu disc image, you'll want to burn a CD-ROM. Follow these steps:

1. **Insert a writable CD-ROM in your computer's CD burner drive.**

2. **From the GNOME menu bar, choose System➪Administration➪ Terminal.**

3. **Type the following command to burn the CD-ROM:**

```
sudo cdrecorder -v Desktop/kubuntu*iso
```

When the burn finishes, you can either reboot directly from the new disc or eject the disc and use it to boot another machine. Your computer boots from the Kubuntu CD-ROM, just like an Ubuntu disc. After the computer boots, you see the screen in Figure A-1.

If you're comfortable using Ubuntu, you should feel at home using the KDE interface in Kubuntu.

Figure A-1:
The
Kubuntu
screen.

An Operating System for Kids: Edubuntu

The Edubuntu project takes the concept of Ubuntu — humanity towards others — into the educational realm. The Edubuntu project takes the basic Ubuntu, which is based on Debian Linux, and adds educational tools to it.

Edubuntu is a cool variation on Ubuntu Linux. Edubuntu isn't just for kids, either. I enjoy the educational tools it provides and also the attractive, customized GNOME interface.

The following instructions assume you're working from an Ubuntu computer with a writable CD-ROM or DVD drive.

Downloading Edubuntu

You can download Edubuntu from one of Ubuntu's mirror sites. Follow these steps:

1. **Click your Firefox browser icon on the GNOME panel.**

2. **Type www.edubuntu.org/Download in the Location text box and press the Enter key.**

3. **Click the link to your continent.**

   The menu of download sites expands to different countries.

4. **Click your country.**

   The menu expands to show universities and various organizations.

5. **Click any of the various university or organization links (that house Edubuntu mirrors).**

   The list further expands to one or more actual download sites.

6. **Click a download site.**

   The Opening Edubuntu-6.10 dialog opens.

7. **Click the Save File button.**

   The Downloads dialog opens, showing a progress meter.

8. **Click the Cleanup button and close the dialog when the download finishes.**

Burning the CD

When you have the Edubuntu CD-ROM image, use the following instructions to burn a CD-ROM from this image:

1. **Insert a writable CD-ROM in your computer's CD-ROM drive.**

2. **From the GNOME menu bar, choose System⇨Administration⇨Terminal.**

3. **Type the following command to burn the CD-ROM.**

```
sudo cdrecorder -v Desktop/edubuntu*iso
```

When you complete burning the CD-ROM, you can use it to boot into Edubuntu. Insert the disc and reboot your computer. When it finishes booting, you see the screen shown in Figure A-2.

Running Edubuntu

Edubuntu uses GNOME, just like Ubuntu, and provides all the applications and utilities you get with Ubuntu; it also gives you a very colorful desktop and fun icons.

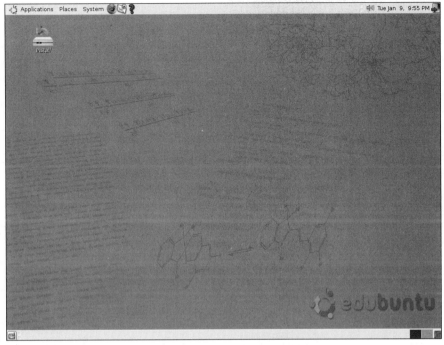

Figure A-2:
Your
Edubuntu
computer.

Some of the more interesting and useful educational applications that
Edubuntu provides are

- **Kalzium:** Displays an interactive periodic table from which you can click
  on the elements to see detailed information about them.

- **Kanagram:** Have fun experimenting with and guessing anagrams.

- **KmPlot:** Graphically plot mathematical functions using KmPlot.

- **KStars:** Enter your geographical location and see what stars and
  constellations you can see from your Edubuntu planetarium.

- **Tux Pain:** Provides a simple drawing program that kids of all ages can
  have fun using.

Everyone can learn and have fun using Edubuntu!

Follow these steps to access Edubuntu's educational tools:

1. **From the GNOME menu bar, choose Applications⇨Education.**

   The Education menu opens, where you can select from numerous
   educational-oriented applications.

The Lightweight Champ: Xubuntu

But wait, there are still more Ubuntu spin-offs. Xubuntu — pronounced *zoo-BOON-too* — is based on the Xfce Desktop manager, which uses less resources than GNOME or KDE. Using the "lighter-weight" Xfce means that you can install Xubuntu on that old PC or laptop you have that doesn't have the power to run heavy-weight systems like GNOME or KDE.

Xubuntu requires a minimum of only 64MB (although 128MB is recommended) of RAM and

1.5GB of disk space, compared to Ubuntu's 256MB of RAM and 3GB of disk space. You can find out more about the Xubuntu diet plan at www.xubuntu.org, and you can download the Xubuntu CD-ROM image from www.xubuntu.org/get.

The Xubuntu CD-ROM image is only 528MB. The image is almost 100MB smaller than the Ubuntu and Kubuntu images.

2. **Select applications (such as the Kalzium periodic table shown in Figure A-3).**

You can use Edubuntu to help your kids, or the child in you, learn more about periodic tables and the world.

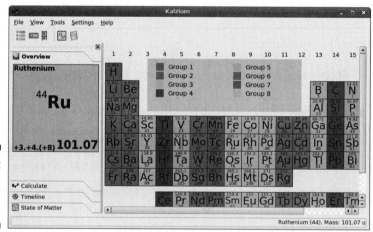

Figure A-3:
The Kalzium periodic table utility.

Appendix B

Stupendous OpenSSH Tricks

. . . .

In This Chapter

▶ Interactively connecting to a remote SSH server

▶ Installing and starting an OpenSSH server

▶ Noninteractively executing commands on remote computers

▶ Using OpenSSH port forwarding

▶ Using Public/Private Keys

▶ Using ssh-agent

▶ Creating an encrypted wireless network using OpenSSH

. . . .

Secure Shell (SSH) is a set of network protocols that lets you create a secure — encrypted — communication channel between two computers. Tatu Ylonen created SSH in 1995 to replace the nonencrypted communication applications then in use.

SSH creates an encrypted connection between two computers that protects your private communication. SSH enables you to securely communicate with other computers interactively and noninteractively.

OpenSSH is an open source version of the SSH protocol. OpenSSH is an amazing system that at first glance provides a simple and secure method for interacting with other computers. But dig a little under the surface and OpenSSH provides many more capabilities.

The open source OpenSSH suite of security communication tools is compatible with the commercial SSH suite. In this appendix, I say "connect to an SSH server" when describing the process of connecting to either an SSH or OpenSSH server.

This appendix shows you how to configure and use OpenSSH. It also describes how to use some of OpenSSH's lesser-known capabilities, such as authenticating without passwords and creating an encrypted wireless network using unencrypted access points. OpenSSH is a truly amazing piece of software.

Interactively Connecting to an SSH Server

Using the OpenSSH client to connect to an OpenSSH, or commercial SSH, server is simple. For instance, do the following if you want to use OpenSSH to connect to your computer account on another SSH server on another computer:

1. **Open a GNOME Terminal Emulator window by clicking the GNOME Applications menu and choosing Accessories⇨Terminal.**

2. **Type ssh** *username@computername*.

   For instance, I type ssh paul@ssh.swcp.com to connect to my Internet service provider's (ISP) account.

3. **Type your password when prompted.**

You can work on the remote computer at this point.

Using the OpenSSH Server

OpenSSH is based on a client-server model. You use the OpenSSH client to connect with an OpenSSH server. It's a conceptually simple system to configure and use; I show you how to do so in this section.

Installing the OpenSSH server

Ubuntu installs the OpenSSH client, by default, but not the OpenSSH server. Follow these steps to install the OpenSSH server:

1. **Click the GNOME System menu and choose Administration⇨ Synaptic Package Manager.**

   The Enter Your Password to Perform Administrative Tasks dialog opens.

2. **Type your password and press the Enter key.**

   The Synaptic Package Manager dialog opens.

3. **Click the Search button.**

   The Find dialog opens.

4. **Type openssh in the Search text box and click the Search button.**

5. **Click to select the openssh-server check box.**

6. **Select the Mark for Installation option in the drop-down menu that opens.**

7. **Click the Apply button.**

   The Summary/Apply the Following Changes? dialog opens.

8. **Click the Apply button.**

   The OpenSSH server package is downloaded and installed. The Changes Applied dialog opens when the installation is complete.

9. **Click the Close button.**

   Control returns to the Synaptic Package Manager window.

10. **Click the File menu and choose Quit.**

The OpenSSH server package is installed and the SSH daemon — sshd — is started automatically.

Testing your OpenSSH server

You can use the OpenSSH client on your Ubuntu computer to connect back to itself. Follow these steps:

1. **Click the GNOME Applications menu and choose Accessories⇨ GNOME Terminal.**

2. **Type ssh *username@localhost*.**

   For instance, I type ssh paul@localhost to log in to my user account on my Ubuntu computer.

3. **Type yes when prompted and press the Enter key.**

4. **Type your password when prompted.**

You log on to your computer using the SSH protocol. You can log in to your Ubuntu computer from any other computer that provides an SSH client.

You need to allow incoming SSH sessions if you set up a firewall using Firestarter in Chapter 10. Use the instructions in the section "Configuring Firestarter to allow incoming connections" to allow SSH connections.

Executing a Remote Command

SSH is primarily used to make secure, interactive connections to remote computers. However, SSH can also be used noninteractively to execute commands on remote computers. In the following example, I connect to an OpenSSH server installed in the previous section, "Installing the OpenSSH server." Here's how:

1. **Click the GNOME Applications menu and select Accessories↔ GNOME Terminal.**

2. **Type the following and press the Enter key; for example:**

```
ssh paul@localhost date
```

3. **Type your password when prompted.**

Your computer's time and date is displayed. You never interactively connected to your computer using OpenSSH. Instead, the OpenSSH client authenticated with the OpenSSH server and executed the date command.

System administrators find the remote command executing to be useful when managing many computers. For instance, you might want to automatically copy files to or from the remote computer in order to back up files to an external USB hard drive. You can use the following command to back up some files:

```
ssh username@remotemachine rsync -ru * /media/disk
```

Or for instance, if I want to connect to a remote machine called cancun and copy my home directory to a directory called backups on the USB disk:

```
ssh paul@cancun rsync -ru * /media/disk/backups
```

OpenSSH runs the command `rsync -ru * /media/disk`, which recursively copies all new files from your home directory to the USB hard drive mounted at `/media/disk`. (The `-r` option tells `rsync` to copy files recursively, and the `-u` option tells it to update files.) This process happens without you having to log into the remote computer and run the command yourself. All you have to do is enter your account password. Less work makes for better system administration.

Using OpenSSH Port Forwarding

OpenSSH lets you forward Linux network ports between machines. *Port forwarding* lets you set up specialized virtual private networks (VPNs). OpenSSH encrypts the information flowing between the two machines and also takes care of sending the information to and from the right ports.

Port forwarding provides a way to protect unencrypted network traffic. You can also use port forwarding to overcome barriers like firewalls that prevent you from connecting with services. I don't recommend using port forwarding to circumvent security features set up specifically to prevent you from being hacked from the Internet.

I illustrate port forwarding by example. Let's say a firewall prevents you from accessing your ISP e-mail account. You can use OpenSSH to overcome this limitation if you can log in to your ISP using SSH. Follow these steps:

1. **Click the GNOME Applications menu and select Accessories⇨ GNOME Terminal.**

2. **Type the following and press the Enter key:**

   ```
   ssh -L localport:remoteserver:remoteport
           username@localhost
   ```

   For instance, I type `ssh -L 1433:localhost:143 paul@myisp.com` to log in to my user account at my ISP.

   - I picked local port number 1433 at random — I can use any number above 1024.

     Using ports below 1024 requires `root` privileges.

   - The remote port 143 corresponds to the port IMAP listens to by default.

3. **Type yes if prompted to use the server's public key and press the Enter key.**

4. **Type your password when prompted.**

After you've authenticated to your ISP's user account, you can configure your e-mail client to work through the SSH connection. Follow these steps:

1. **Click the GNOME Applications menu and choose Internet⇨ Evolution (or Thunderbird Email, if that's your preference).**

   Your e-mail client opens.

2. **Click the Edit menu and choose Account Settings.**

   The Account Settings dialog opens.

3. **Click the Server Settings option.**

   The Server Settings tab opens.

4. **Type 127.0.0.1 in the Server Name text box.**

5. **Type the port number you selected in the Port text box.**

   For instance, type `1433` in the Port text box.

6. **Click the OK button.**

You can securely view your e-mail through the OpenSSH "tunnel."

OpenSSH can automatically forward X Window System connections back to your local machine using the -X option. Connect to the remote machine — ssh -X *username@remotemachine* — using the -X option, and any applications that use X to display output will automatically forward that output to your window. For instance, log in to a remote machine using the -X option, type the command /usr/bin/xclock, and you'll see the xclock display on your local machine.

Using Public-Private Key Authentication

We're all used to entering a password to gain access to user accounts, Web accounts, and so on. Type in your username and then enter your password when prompted, and you're in. However, passwords are becoming increasingly vulnerable to cracking, shoulder surfing, and good ol' yellow sticky notes. If someone learns your password, he has access to your account. This isn't good.

Fortunately, SSH provides an alternative to traditional static passwords. SSH lets you use a mechanism called *Public-key cryptography* (also known as *asymmetric keys) authentication.*

You generate a public- and private-key pair. Anything encrypted with a public key can be decrypted only with the private key. Conversely, anyone in possession of the public key can decrypt what has been encrypted with the private key. This *asymmetric relationship* allows the SSH protocol to work.

How public-key authentication works

Here's how it works. The actual process is more complicated than presented, but the following is essentially correct:

1. **You generate a public- and private-cryptographic-key pair.**

2. **Optionally, encrypt your private key with a pass phrase.**

3. **Place the public key in your remote user account.**

4. **Keep your private key on your local computer.**

5. **Use the OpenSSH client to connect to the remote SSH server.**

6. **The remote SSH server generates a random number and encrypts it with your public key.**

7. **The remote SSH server sends the encrypted random number to your OpenSSH client.**

8. **Your OpenSSH client decrypts the random number with your private key and sends the result back to the server.**

If the returned random number matches the original, you're authenticated because only the private key can decrypt what has been encrypted using the public key.

Creating a OpenSSH public- and private-key pair

Now, let's try a real-world example. Start by generating the public/private key-pair.

1. **Click the GNOME Applications menu and select Accessories⇨ GNOME Terminal.**

2. **Type the following and press the Enter key:**

   ```
   ssh-keygen -t rsa
   ```

   The `ssh-keygen` displays the *Generating public/private rsa key pair* message.

3. **Press the Enter key when you're prompted to enter a filename.**

4. **Type a pass phrase when prompted.**

   Longer pass phrases provide more protection. Use at least a 20-character pass phrase if you can. I recommend using a phrase you're familiar with. For instance, select a pass phrase like *I'm going down to south Park.*

The ssh-keygen utility displays a fingerprint of the key you just generated. Fingerprints identify your keys from fraudulent ones.

Configuring your remote account with your public key

After you create your private/public-key pair, you need to copy the public key to your remote user account and configure the account to use the public key. The public key should be placed in the `authorized_keys` file in the `.ssh` directory in your user account's home directory on the remote machine. Follow these steps:

1. **Type the following command and press the Enter key:**

   ```
   scp ~/.ssh/id_rsa.pub username@remotemachine
   ```

   The `scp` is another OpenSSH utility — Secure Copy — used to copy files from and to remote machines.

2. **Log in to the remote machine.**

   ```
   ssh username@remotemachine
   ```

3. **Create, if necessary, the .ssh directory.**

   ```
   mkdir .ssh
   ```

4. **Change the permissions on the .ssh directory.**

   ```
   chmod 700 .ssh
   ```

   This command gives total access to the owner (you) of the .ssh directory and denies all access to everyone else. OpenSSH requires that the files and directories it accesses have minimal access.

5. **Insert your public key into the authorized_keys file in the .ssh directory.**

   ```
   cat id_rsa.pub >> .ssh/authorized_keys
   ```

   Using the double greater-than symbols (>>) appends the contents of the id_rsa.pub file into the authorized_keys file if it already exists. Alternatively, this command creates the authorized_keys file if it doesn't exist and copies the contents of id_rsa.pub into it.

6. **Change the permissions on the authorized_keys file.**

   ```
   chmod 600 .ssh/authorized_keys
   ```

You can now use OpenSSH public-key authentication to log in to your remote user account.

Using public-key authentication to log in to your remote account

After you copy and configure your public key to the remote user account, you can use the key-pair to log into your remote account. Follow these steps:

1. **Type the following command in your local user account:**

   ```
   ssh username@remotemachine
   ```

   The OpenSSH client looks in the local .ssh directory for private keys. It will find the private key you just generated (id_rsa) and use it to authenticate with the remote SSH server. Alternatively, you explicitly specify what private key to use by using the -i keyname option: ssh -i id_rsa username@remotemachine.

2. **Type the private-key pass phrase when prompted.**

You're logged in to your user account on the remote machine and you didn't have to enter a password!

Two-factor authentication provides the most secure authentication method available. *Two-factor* means that you must provide two factors to gain access to an account. Generally, one factor is something you physically possess, and the second factor is something you know. Commercial two-factor systems provide a physical device such as a smart card or token that requires a password or personal identification number (PIN) to work. Anyone intent on surreptitiously gaining access to your account must first steal both factors.

The OpenSSH public-key system provides two-factor authentication. Someone must steal your private key and your pass phrase to break into your user account. Stealing those factors is easier than stealing a commercial one because, by default, you store your private key in your home directory on your computer. Anyone who breaks into your computer can potentially copy your key and use a key logger to read your pass phrase. However, you can further approximate commercial two-factor systems by keeping your private key on removable media like a USB memory stick. The article "Tighter SSH Security with Two-Factor Authentication," found at `http://interactive.linuxjournal.com/article/8957`, describes the process in more detail.

Using ssh-agent to Store Private Keys

OpenSSH public-key authentication is a great system, giving you two-factor authentication for free. However, using public-key authentication can become onerous if you have to frequently use it to log in to remote machines. You should use a long — at least 20 characters — pass phrase to secure your private key, and typing it for every authentication becomes difficult.

OpenSSH provides a solution in the form of a utility called ssh-agent. The ssh-agent utility lets you decrypt and cache one or more private keys. Your OpenSSH client then uses the cached private key to authenticate to SSH servers.

You use the OpenSSH utility ssh-add to decrypt and cache private keys with ssh-agent. Once cached, the OpenSSH client (ssh) communicates with ssh-agent via a UNIX socket, which is specified by the SSH_AUTH_SOCK environmental variable.

I show how this works by, you guessed it, example. In this example, I assume you've generated your public-private-key-pair and placed the public key in the `.ssh/authorized_keys` file in your remote user account, as described in the section, "Using Public-Private Key Authentication," in this appendix. Follow these steps:

1. **Click the GNOME Applications menu and choose Accessories⇨ GNOME Terminal.**

2. **Type the following and press the Enter key:**

   ```
   ssh-add ~/.ssh/id_rsa
   ```

3. **Type your private-key pass phrase when prompted.**

   ssh-agent tells you that it's added the key.

4. **Type `ssh-add -1` and you see the private key's fingerprint.**

   Ubuntu starts ssh-agent when you log in to your Ubuntu user account. However, if the ssh-agent fails to start or the process dies for any reason, you can still start one yourself. First, check to see if ssh-agent is running by typing `ssh-add` and pressing the Enter key. If the response is *Could not open a connection to your authentication agent,* you need to start a new one. In that case, type `eval ` ssh-agent`` (those are back-tics). This starts ssh-agent and sets the SSH_AUTH_SOCK environmental variable.

5. **Type the following to log in to your remote account:**

   ```
   ssh username@remotemachine
   ```

   For instance, I type `ssh paul@myisp.com` to log into my ISP account.

How does all this work? Here's a slightly simplified description of how the process works:

1. The OpenSSH client connects to the SSH server and asks the server to authenticate the user.

2. The SSH server generates a random number and encrypts it with your public key.

3. The SSH server sends the encrypted random number to your OpenSSH client.

4. Your OpenSSH client uses the value of the SSH_AUTH_SOCK environmental variable to identify the UNIX socket connected to the ssh-agent.

5. Your OpenSSH client sends the encrypted random number to ssh-agent through the UNIX socket identified by SSH_AUTH_SOCK.

6. The ssh-agent reads your previously decrypted private key to decrypt the random number.

7. The ssh-agent sends the decrypted random number back to your OpenSSH client.

8. The OpenSSH client sends the decrypted random number back to the SSH server.

9. The remote SSH server compares the decrypted random number — from the OpenSSH client — to the original and authenticates your connection if they match.

Your private key never left your Ubuntu workstation and yet it was used to authenticate your connection. You can use ssh-agent to authenticate indefinitely without having to re-enter your pass phrase. You can set life-times on the cached keys and also forward the authentication agent to other machines.

Creating an Encrypted Wireless Network Using OpenSSH

A VPN within an unencrypted wireless network makes it easier to use your Ubuntu computer on wireless networks.

Chapter 7 describes how to connect your Ubuntu computer to three types of wireless networks: unencrypted and encrypted ones using either WEP or WPA encryption. The great thing about using unencrypted wireless networks is they're very easy to use — Ubuntu can use more wireless network adapters without encryption than with. The bad thing about using unencrypted wireless networks, of course, is that they don't protect your information.

You need two pieces of equipment to make this network:

- ✔ **A second Wi-Fi access point (AP):** You attach the second AP to your primary AP. The second AP will accept unencrypted connections from your Ubuntu computer. I use an old 802.11b AP that I replaced with a faster 802.11g model as the second AP.

   Devices based on the 802.11b protocol communicate at speeds up to 11 Mbps (million-bits-per-second), while 802.11g models go up to 54 Mbps.

- ✔ **An Ubuntu computer with a wireless network adapter:** I assume this computer is a laptop.

- ✔ **An account on a Linux computer:** This computer is the VPN server. You forward all Web and e-mail communication from the second AP through a user account on the VPN server using OpenSSH. OpenSSH provides the forwarding capability and the encryption. You can use Ubuntu Linux as the VPN server, of course; however, the essential ingredient to making this system work is a computer that provides an SSH server.

When you have your equipment, you need to configure the following:

- ✔ **An SSH server on the VPN server.**

- ✔ **A user account on the VPN server.**

- ✔ **Generate a public-private-key-pair.**

   Don't use pass-phrase protection and place the public key in the .ssh/authorized_keys file in your account on the VPN server.

✓ **Accept unencrypted connections on the second AP.**

Don't specify WEP or WPA.

✓ **Route all outgoing communication from the second AP to the VPN Server.** Normally, you configure your AP to route outgoing communication to your ISP via a cable modem or DSL modem. (Actually, most modern APs do this automatically.) However, in this case, you must use the VPN server to provide a VPN to the Internet using OpenSSH.

Configuring the second AP to route all outgoing traffic through the VPN server prevents anyone who doesn't have your private key from using your unencrypted wireless network. Intruders can connect to your second AP but can't make use of your Internet connection; nor can they access your private network attached to your primary AP.

However, you'll be able to browse the Internet and get and send e-mail. Your work will also be fully encrypted, at a higher level than possible with WEP or WPA encryption, by using OpenSSH. You accomplish this by configuring your OpenSSH client on your Ubuntu laptop to forward such connections through your user account on the VPN server. All of your Web and e-mail communication will be encrypted and forwarded to their destinations by OpenSSH.

Configuring your second AP

The particulars involved with configuring your second AP depend on its make and model. You only need to configure how it gets its Internet interface connection, often referred to as the WAN (wide area network), how it gets its IP address, and where it sends outgoing packets.

The general process is as follows:

1. **Open Firefox and connect to your secondary AP.**

2. **Type the administrative account username and password.**

3. **Go to the menu that specifies how the WAN interface gets its IP address and change from dynamic (DHCP) to static.**

4. **Change the WAN interface IP address to an unused value on the primary AP.**

   For instance, my primary AP uses the network address space of 192.168.1.1 through 192.168.1.254. The primary AP's IP address defaults to 192.168.1.1, so I chose 192.168.1.254, which is easy to use and does not interfere with the DHCP addresses that the primary AP hands out to connecting computers.

5. **Change the default destination IP address to the address of your VPN server.**

All outgoing communications from the secondary AP will automatically be sent to your VPN server. This protects your AP from surreptitiously being used by intruders. Anyone who doesn't have your private key won't be able to use your wireless network, even though it's unencrypted.

6. **Save your changes and restart your secondary AP.**

Configuring your VPN server user account

To start using your wireless VPN, you need a Linux computer connected to your primary AP. The VPN server must be running an SSH server. You also need a user account on the VPN server.

1. **Connect your Ubuntu laptop computer to your primary AP using a wired Ethernet connection.**

   See Chapter 6 for more information about making such connections.

2. **Log in to your Ubuntu laptop user account.**

3. **Generate a public-private-key-pair using the following command:**

   ```
   ssh-keygen -t rsa -f key-vpn-fwd -C key-vpn-fwd
   ```

   This command is a variation of the one used in the section, "Using Public-Private Key Authentication," earlier in this chapter. In this case, I use the -f option in order to choose a descriptive filename. The -C option inserts the string key-vpn-fwd into the private-key file, which helps identify its purpose in the future.

4. **Press the Enter key when prompted to select a pass phrase.**

   In this case, create an unencrypted private key to automatically establish an SSH port-forwarding connection to the VPN server whenever you boot the Ubuntu laptop. The private key will remain safe on your Ubuntu computer as long as it isn't compromised. This is reasonable because anyone who breaks into your laptop can also steal your WEP or WPA keys.

   Make sure you protect both your private keys and your Ubuntu computer. Set minimal file permissions on your private keys — only the owner should be able to read the file. Update your Ubuntu/Debian packages whenever new ones become available. Use good passwords on your user account and protect them well. Also, use the advice given throughout this book on good system administration hygiene.

5. **Use the following command to copy your public key to your VPN server user account:**

   ```
   scp .ssh/id_rsa.pub username@vpnserver
   ```

6. **Log in to your user account on the VPN Server:**

```
ssh username@vpnserver
```

7. **Append the public key into the `authorized_keys` file in the `.ssh` directory in your VPN server user account.**

```
cat id_rsa.pub >> .ssh/authorized_keys
```

I assume you've protected the `authorized_keys` files as described in the section "Using Public-Private Key Authentication."

8. **Type the following command and press the Enter key:**

```
ssh -i .ssh/key-vpn -D 8888 username@vpnserver
```

For instance, I would type `ssh -i .ssh/key-vpn -D 8888 paul@vpnserver` to make the connection.

This command creates an SSH connection to the VPN server using dynamic port forwarding. I use static port forwarding in the "Using OpenSSH Port Forwarding" section in this chapter. However, dynamic port forwarding lets you create a Web proxy server using OpenSSH. I forward all Web traffic through this connection. The port 8888 is arbitrary; you can use any port number above 1024.

9. **Type the following command and press the Enter key:**

```
ssh -i key-vpn -L 1433:ispmail.com:143
        username@vpnserver
```

In my case, I would type `ssh -i .ssh/key-vpn -L 1433:mail.myisp.com:143 paul@vpnserver` to make the connection.

Here, I establish an SSH connection to provide static port forwarding that I use to receive messages. I use static rather than dynamic forwarding in this case because I want to connect to only one external machine to get my e-mail.

10. **Type the following command and press the Enter key:**

```
ssh -i key-vpn -L 2555:ispmail.com:25
        username@vpnserver
```

In my case, I would type `ssh -i .ssh/key-vpn -L 2555:mail.myisp.com:25 paul@vpnserver` to make the connection that lets me send messages.

I configured three OpenSSH connections that will let me browse the Internet plus send and receive e-mail.

Configuring Firefox and Thunderbird to use OpenSSH port forwarding

After you configure your wireless VPN, you can start securely using the Internet via your unencrypted, insecure wireless network. All you have to do is configure Firefox and Evolution to use it.

Configuring Firefox

Configuring Firefox requires you to use a proxy connection instead of a direct one to the Internet.

1. **Click the GNOME Applications menu and choose Internet⇨Firefox.**

   A Firefox window opens.

2. **Click the Edit menu and choose the Preferences option.**

   The Preferences dialog opens.

3. **Click the Advanced button and select the Network tab.**

   The Connections Setting dialog opens.

4. **Click the Manual Proxy Configuration radio button.**

5. **Type 127.0.0.1 in the SOCKS Host text box.**

6. **Type the dynamic port number you selected in the Port text box.**

   You specified the dynamic port number in Step 8 of the section "Configuring Your VPN Server User Account." For instance, I selected the dynamic port number 8888.

7. **Click the OK button.**

   Control returns to the Firefox Preferences dialog.

8. **Click the Close button.**

You can now make unencrypted connections from your Ubuntu laptop to the secondary AP and securely browse the Internet.

Configuring the Thunderbird e-mail client

To securely send and receive e-mail, you must configure Thunderbird to use OpenSSH static port forwarding.

Evolution doesn't let you change the port it uses to receive e-mail, so use Thunderbird.

Follow these steps:

1. **Click the GNOME Applications menu and select Internet⇨ Thunderbird Mail.**

   A Thunderbird window opens.

2. **Click the Edit menu and select the Account Settings option.**

   The Account Settings dialog opens.

3. **Choose the Server Setting menu option.**

4. **Type 127.0.0.1 in the Server Name text box (replacing any existing server information).**

5. **Type the static port number you selected in Step 9 in the "Configuring Your VPN Server User Account" section.**

   For example, I type the value of 1433.

6. **Click the Outgoing Server (SMTP) menu option.**

7. **Select your outgoing server and click the Edit button.**

   The SMTP Server dialog opens.

8. **Type 127.0.0.1 in the Server Name text box (replacing any existing value).**

9. **Type the static port number in the Port text box.**

   In my case, I enter the value of 2555.

10. **Click the OK button.**

    Control returns to the Account Settings dialog.

11. **Click the OK button.**

OpenSSH now provides a secure tunnel for incoming and outgoing e-mail messages. Your unencrypted wireless network provides high security using OpenSSH!

Appendix C

About the CD

This appendix describes what you get on the companion CD and the minimum computer configuration you need for Ubuntu Linux.

The companion *Ubuntu Linux For Dummies* CD contains the full Ubuntu Linux 6.10.

The companion CD contains most applications described in this book. However, you must download a few applications, such as Network Manager (Chapter 7), from the Internet. I describe where to find and how to download and install such applications.

System Requirements

To use the *Ubuntu Linux For Dummies* CD-ROM, make sure that your computer meets (or exceeds) these minimum requirements:

✔ An Intel-compatible 32-bit PC with a CD drive, an LCD display or multi-sync monitor, a keyboard, and a mouse. (The attached CD doesn't work with *64-bit* PCs. You can download a compatible CD for 64-bit PCs from www.ubuntu.org.)

For reasonable performance using the graphical GNOME Desktop and X Window System, I recommend at least 512MB, but you can get away with only 256MB of main memory.

✔ Enough hard drive space for your planned Ubuntu system. You have two options:

• *No hard disk space.* Yes, that's right, none! You can run Ubuntu Linux directly from CD. However, your computer won't remember your settings and your work when you shut down.

The instructions for booting the Ubuntu Linux operating system directly *(live)* from the CD are in Chapter 2.

• If you want to make a *permanent* Ubuntu Linux installation that remembers your settings and your files, you need at least *3GB* of hard disk space. I recommend at least *10GB* of unused disk space so you can store plenty of document and media files.

Instructions for permanently installing Ubuntu Linux to your hard drive are detailed in Chapters 3 and 4.

You can run Ubuntu Linux on older, slower equipment if you run in *text mode* (enter at the boot prompt). However, most of the instructions and capabilities in this book use graphical mode.

What You Find

The companion CD includes the full version of Ubuntu Linux and much more. In other words, it contains a ton of stuff, such as

- ✔ The GNOME Desktop graphical environment
- ✔ The rich, great-looking OpenOffice.org desktop productivity suite — word processor, spreadsheet, slide presentation program, and more
- ✔ Mozilla's powerful and cutting-edge Firefox browser
- ✔ The powerful, easy-to-use Evolution e-mail and calendaring client
- ✔ Many multimedia applications
- ✔ Numerous graphical tools
- ✔ System administration tools and utilities
- ✔ Network services
- ✔ Games

If You Have Problems with Your CD

We test the companion CD on as many computers and configurations as possible. Unfortunately, we can't test enough computers to ensure that our CD will work across the board.

Call the Wiley Product Technical Support phone number at 800-762-2974 if you have problems using the companion CD. Outside the United States, call 1-317-572-3994. Alternatively, browse www.wiley.com/techsupport — Wiley Product Technical support on the Internet — to obtain support. Wiley Publishing provides technical support for only physical manufacturing flaws in the Ubuntu Linux CD. You must contact the program's vendor or author for application-specific support.

Call 800-225-5945 to place additional orders or to request information about other Wiley products.

GNU General Public License

Version 2, June 1991
Copyright © 1989, 1991 Free Software Foundation, Inc.
59 Temple Place - Suite 330, Boston, MA 02111-1307, USA

Preamble

The licenses for most software are designed to take away your freedom to share and change it. By contrast, the GNU General Public License is intended to guarantee your freedom to share and change free software–to make sure the software is free for all its users. This General Public License applies to most of the Free Software Foundation's software and to any other program whose authors commit to using it. (Some other Free Software Foundation software is covered by the GNU Library General Public License instead.) You can apply it to your programs, too.

When we speak of free software, we are referring to freedom, not price. Our General Public Licenses are designed to make sure that you have the freedom to distribute copies of free software (and charge for this service if you wish), that you receive source code or can get it if you want it, that you can change the software or use pieces of it in new free programs; and that you know you can do these things.

To protect your rights, we need to make restrictions that forbid anyone to deny you these rights or to ask you to surrender the rights. These restrictions translate to certain responsibilities for you if you distribute copies of the software, or if you modify it.

For example, if you distribute copies of such a program, whether gratis or for a fee, you must give the recipients all the rights that you have. You must make sure that they, too, receive or can get the source code. And you must show them these terms so they know their rights.

We protect your rights with two steps: (1) copyright the software, and (2) offer you this license which gives you legal permission to copy, distribute and/or modify the software.

Also, for each author's protection and ours, we want to make certain that everyone understands that there is no warranty for this free software. If the software is modified by someone else and passed on, we want its recipients to know that what they have is not the original, so that any problems introduced by others will not reflect on the original authors' reputations.

Finally, any free program is threatened constantly by software patents. We wish to avoid the danger that redistributors of a free program will individually obtain patent licenses, in effect making the program proprietary. To prevent this, we have made it clear that any patent must be licensed for everyone's free use or not licensed at all.

The precise terms and conditions for copying, distribution and modification follow.

Terms and Conditions for Copying, Distribution and Modification

0. This License applies to any program or other work which contains a notice placed by the copyright holder saying it may be distributed under the terms of this General Public License. The "Program", below, refers to any such program or work, and a "work based on the Program" means either the Program or any derivative work under copyright law: that is to say, a work containing the Program or a portion of it, either verbatim or with modifications and/or translated into another language. (Hereinafter, translation is included without limitation in the term "modification".) Each licensee is addressed as "you".

    Activities other than copying, distribution and modification are not covered by this License; they are outside its scope. The act of running the Program is not restricted, and the output from the Program is covered only if its contents constitute a work based on the Program (independent of having been made by running the Program). Whether that is true depends on what the Program does.

1. You may copy and distribute verbatim copies of the Program's source code as you receive it, in any medium, provided that you conspicuously and appropriately publish on each copy an appropriate copyright notice and disclaimer of warranty; keep intact all the notices that refer to this License and to the absence of any warranty; and give any other recipients of the Program a copy of this License along with the Program.

    You may charge a fee for the physical act of transferring a copy, and you may at your option offer warranty protection in exchange for a fee.

2. You may modify your copy or copies of the Program or any portion of it, thus forming a work based on the Program, and copy and distribute such modifications or work under the terms of Section 1 above, provided that you also meet all of these conditions:

    a) You must cause the modified files to carry prominent notices stating that you changed the files and the date of any change.

    b) You must cause any work that you distribute or publish, that in whole or in part contains or is derived from the Program or any part thereof, to be licensed as a whole at no charge to all third parties under the terms of this License.

    c) If the modified program normally reads commands interactively when run, you must cause it, when started running for such interactive use in the most ordinary way, to print or display an announcement including an appropriate copyright notice and a notice that there is no warranty (or else, saying that you provide a warranty) and that users may redistribute the program under these conditions, and telling the user how to view a copy of this License. (Exception: if the Program itself is interactive but does not normally print such an announcement, your work based on the Program is not required to print an announcement.)

    These requirements apply to the modified work as a whole. If identifiable sections of that work are not derived from the Program, and can be reasonably considered independent and separate works in themselves, then this License, and its terms, do not apply to those sections when you distribute them as separate works. But when you distribute the same sections as part of a whole which is a work based on the Program, the distribution of the whole must be on the terms of this License, whose permissions for other licensees extend to the entire whole, and thus to each and every part regardless of who wrote it.

Thus, it is not the intent of this section to claim rights or contest your rights to work written entirely by you; rather, the intent is to exercise the right to control the distribution of derivative or collective works based on the Program.

In addition, mere aggregation of another work not based on the Program with the Program (or with a work based on the Program) on a volume of a storage or distribution medium does not bring the other work under the scope of this License.

3. You may copy and distribute the Program (or a work based on it, under Section 2) in object code or executable form under the terms of Sections 1 and 2 above provided that you also do one of the following:

    a) Accompany it with the complete corresponding machine-readable source code, which must be distributed under the terms of Sections 1 and 2 above on a medium customarily used for software interchange; or,

    b) Accompany it with a written offer, valid for at least three years, to give any third party, for a charge no more than your cost of physically performing source distribution, a complete machine-readable copy of the corresponding source code, to be distributed under the terms of Sections 1 and 2 above on a medium customarily used for software interchange; or,

    c) Accompany it with the information you received as to the offer to distribute corresponding source code. (This alternative is allowed only for noncommercial distribution and only if you received the program in object code or executable form with such an offer, in accord with Subsection b above.)

    The source code for a work means the preferred form of the work for making modifications to it. For an executable work, complete source code means all the source code for all modules it contains, plus any associated interface definition files, plus the scripts used to control compilation and installation of the executable. However, as a special exception, the source code distributed need not include anything that is normally distributed (in either source or binary form) with the major components (compiler, kernel, and so on) of the operating system on which the executable runs, unless that component itself accompanies the executable.

    If distribution of executable or object code is made by offering access to copy from a designated place, then offering equivalent access to copy the source code from the same place counts as distribution of the source code, even though third parties are not compelled to copy the source along with the object code.

4. You may not copy, modify, sublicense, or distribute the Program except as expressly provided under this License. Any attempt otherwise to copy, modify, sublicense or distribute the Program is void, and will automatically terminate your rights under this License. However, parties who have received copies, or rights, from you under this License will not have their licenses terminated so long as such parties remain in full compliance.

5. You are not required to accept this License, since you have not signed it. However, nothing else grants you permission to modify or distribute the Program or its derivative works. These actions are prohibited by law if you do not accept this License. Therefore, by modifying or distributing the Program (or any work based on the Program), you indicate your acceptance of this License to do so, and all its terms and conditions for copying, distributing or modifying the Program or works based on it.

6. Each time you redistribute the Program (or any work based on the Program), the recipient automatically receives a license from the original licensor to copy, distribute or modify the Program subject to these terms and conditions. You may not impose any further restrictions on the recipients' exercise of the rights granted herein. You are not responsible for enforcing compliance by third parties to this License.

7. If, as a consequence of a court judgment or allegation of patent infringement or for any other reason (not limited to patent issues), conditions are imposed on you (whether by court order, agreement or otherwise) that contradict the conditions of this License, they do not excuse you from the conditions of this License. If you cannot distribute so as to satisfy simultaneously your obligations under this License and any other pertinent obligations, then as a consequence you may not distribute the Program at all. For example, if a patent license would not permit royalty-free redistribution of the Program by all those who receive copies directly or indirectly through you, then the only way you could satisfy both it and this License would be to refrain entirely from distribution of the Program.

    If any portion of this section is held invalid or unenforceable under any particular circumstance, the balance of the section is intended to apply and the section as a whole is intended to apply in other circumstances.

    It is not the purpose of this section to induce you to infringe any patents or other property right claims or to contest validity of any such claims; this section has the sole purpose of protecting the integrity of the free software distribution system, which is implemented by public license practices. Many people have made generous contributions to the wide range of software distributed through that system in reliance on consistent application of that system; it is up to the author/donor to decide if he or she is willing to distribute software through any other system and a licensee cannot impose that choice.

    This section is intended to make thoroughly clear what is believed to be a consequence of the rest of this License.

8. If the distribution and/or use of the Program is restricted in certain countries either by patents or by copyrighted interfaces, the original copyright holder who places the Program under this License may add an explicit geographical distribution limitation excluding those countries, so that distribution is permitted only in or among countries not thus excluded. In such case, this License incorporates the limitation as if written in the body of this License.

9. The Free Software Foundation may publish revised and/or new versions of the General Public License from time to time. Such new versions will be similar in spirit to the present version, but may differ in detail to address new problems or concerns.

    Each version is given a distinguishing version number. If the Program specifies a version number of this License which applies to it and "any later version", you have the option of following the terms and conditions either of that version or of any later version published by the Free Software Foundation. If the Program does not specify a version number of this License, you may choose any version ever published by the Free Software Foundation.

10. If you wish to incorporate parts of the Program into other free programs whose distribution conditions are different, write to the author to ask for permission. For software which is copyrighted by the Free Software Foundation, write to the Free Software Foundation; we sometimes make exceptions for this. Our decision will be guided by the two goals of preserving the free status of all derivatives of our free software and of promoting the sharing and reuse of software generally.

NO WARRANTY

11. BECAUSE THE PROGRAM IS LICENSED FREE OF CHARGE, THERE IS NO WARRANTY FOR THE PROGRAM, TO THE EXTENT PERMITTED BY APPLICABLE LAW. EXCEPT WHEN OTHERWISE STATED IN WRITING THE COPYRIGHT HOLDERS AND/OR OTHER PARTIES PROVIDE THE PROGRAM "AS IS" WITHOUT WARRANTY OF ANY KIND, EITHER EXPRESSED OR IMPLIED, INCLUDING, BUT NOT LIMITED TO, THE IMPLIED WARRANTIES OF MERCHANTABILITY AND FITNESS FOR A PARTICULAR PURPOSE. THE ENTIRE RISK AS TO THE QUALITY AND PERFORMANCE OF THE PROGRAM IS WITH YOU. SHOULD THE PROGRAM PROVE DEFECTIVE, YOU ASSUME THE COST OF ALL NECESSARY SERVICING, REPAIR OR CORRECTION.

12. IN NO EVENT UNLESS REQUIRED BY APPLICABLE LAW OR AGREED TO IN WRITING WILL ANY COPYRIGHT HOLDER, OR ANY OTHER PARTY WHO MAY MODIFY AND/OR REDISTRIBUTE THE PROGRAM AS PERMITTED ABOVE, BE LIABLE TO YOU FOR DAMAGES, INCLUDING ANY GENERAL, SPECIAL, INCIDENTAL OR CONSEQUENTIAL DAMAGES ARISING OUT OF THE USE OR INABILITY TO USE THE PROGRAM (INCLUDING BUT NOT LIMITED TO LOSS OF DATA OR DATA BEING RENDERED INACCURATE OR LOSSES SUSTAINED BY YOU OR THIRD PARTIES OR A FAILURE OF THE PROGRAM TO OPERATE WITH ANY OTHER PROGRAMS), EVEN IF SUCH HOLDER OR OTHER PARTY HAS BEEN ADVISED OF THE POSSIBILITY OF SUCH DAMAGES.

END OF TERMS AND CONDITIONS

Index

Notes

Notes

SINESS, CAREERS & PERSONAL FINANCE

0-7645-9847-3

0-7645-2431-3

Also available:
- Business Plans Kit For Dummies
  0-7645-9794-9
- Economics For Dummies
  0-7645-5726-2
- Grant Writing For Dummies
  0-7645-8416-2
- Home Buying For Dummies
  0-7645-5331-3
- Managing For Dummies
  0-7645-1771-6
- Marketing For Dummies
  0-7645-5600-2
- Personal Finance For Dummies
  0-7645-2590-5*
- Resumes For Dummies
  0-7645-5471-9
- Selling For Dummies
  0-7645-5363-1
- Six Sigma For Dummies
  0-7645-6798-5
- Small Business Kit For Dummies
  0-7645-5984-2
- Starting an eBay Business For Dummies
  0-7645-6924-4
- Your Dream Career For Dummies
  0-7645-9795-7

ME & BUSINESS COMPUTER BASICS

0-470-05432-8

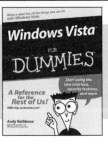

0-471-75421-8

Also available:
- Cleaning Windows Vista For Dummies
  0-471-78293-9
- Excel 2007 For Dummies
  0-470-03737-7
- Mac OS X Tiger For Dummies
  0-7645-7675-5
- MacBook For Dummies
  0-470-04859-X
- Macs For Dummies
  0-470-04849-2
- Office 2007 For Dummies
  0-470-00923-3
- Outlook 2007 For Dummies
  0-470-03830-6
- PCs For Dummies
  0-7645-8958-X
- Salesforce.com For Dummies
  0-470-04893-X
- Upgrading & Fixing Laptops For Dummies
  0-7645-8959-8
- Word 2007 For Dummies
  0-470-03658-3
- Quicken 2007 For Dummies
  0-470-04600-7

OD, HOME, GARDEN, HOBBIES, MUSIC & PETS

0-7645-8404-9

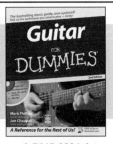

0-7645-9904-6

Also available:
- Candy Making For Dummies
  0-7645-9734-5
- Card Games For Dummies
  0-7645-9910-0
- Crocheting For Dummies
  0-7645-4151-X
- Dog Training For Dummies
  0-7645-8418-9
- Healthy Carb Cookbook For Dummies
  0-7645-8476-6
- Home Maintenance For Dummies
  0-7645-5215-5
- Horses For Dummies
  0-7645-9797-3
- Jewelry Making & Beading For Dummies
  0-7645-2571-9
- Orchids For Dummies
  0-7645-6759-4
- Puppies For Dummies
  0-7645-5255-4
- Rock Guitar For Dummies
  0-7645-5356-9
- Sewing For Dummies
  0-7645-6847-7
- Singing For Dummies
  0-7645-2475-5

ERNET & DIGITAL MEDIA

0-470-04529-9

0-470-04894-8

Also available:
- Blogging For Dummies
  0-471-77084-1
- Digital Photography For Dummies
  0-7645-9802-3
- Digital Photography All-in-One Desk Reference For Dummies
  0-470-03743-1
- Digital SLR Cameras and Photography For Dummies
  0-7645-9803-1
- eBay Business All-in-One Desk Reference For Dummies
  0-7645-8438-3
- HDTV For Dummies
  0-470-09673-X
- Home Entertainment PCs For Dummies
  0-470-05523-5
- MySpace For Dummies
  0-470-09529-6
- Search Engine Optimization For Dummies
  0-471-97998-8
- Skype For Dummies
  0-470-04891-3
- The Internet For Dummies
  0-7645-8996-2
- Wiring Your Digital Home For Dummies
  0-471-91830-X

rate Canadian edition also available

rate U.K. edition also available

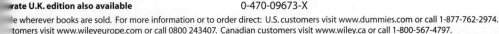

WILEY

SPORTS, FITNESS, PARENTING, RELIGION & SPIRITUALITY

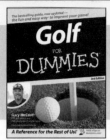

0-471-76871-5

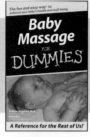

0-7645-7841-3

Also available:
- Catholicism For Dummies
  0-7645-5391-7
- Exercise Balls For Dummies
  0-7645-5623-1
- Fitness For Dummies
  0-7645-7851-0
- Football For Dummies
  0-7645-3936-1
- Judaism For Dummies
  0-7645-5299-6
- Potty Training For Dummies
  0-7645-5417-4
- Buddhism For Dummies
  0-7645-5359-3

- Pregnancy For Dummies
  0-7645-4483-7 †
- Ten Minute Tone-Ups For Dummie
  0-7645-7207-5
- NASCAR For Dummies
  0-7645-7681-X
- Religion For Dummies
  0-7645-5264-3
- Soccer For Dummies
  0-7645-5229-5
- Women in the Bible For Dummies
  0-7645-8475-8

TRAVEL

0-7645-7749-2

0-7645-6945-7

Also available:
- Alaska For Dummies
  0-7645-7746-8
- Cruise Vacations For Dummies
  0-7645-6941-4
- England For Dummies
  0-7645-4276-1
- Europe For Dummies
  0-7645-7529-5
- Germany For Dummies
  0-7645-7823-5
- Hawaii For Dummies
  0-7645-7402-7

- Italy For Dummies
  0-7645-7386-1
- Las Vegas For Dummies
  0-7645-7382-9
- London For Dummies
  0-7645-4277-X
- Paris For Dummies
  0-7645-7630-5
- RV Vacations For Dummies
  0-7645-4442-X
- Walt Disney World & Orlando
  For Dummies
  0-7645-9660-8

GRAPHICS, DESIGN & WEB DEVELOPMENT

0-7645-8815-X

0-7645-9571-7

Also available:
- 3D Game Animation For Dummies
  0-7645-8789-7
- AutoCAD 2006 For Dummies
  0-7645-8925-3
- Building a Web Site For Dummies
  0-7645-7144-3
- Creating Web Pages For Dummies
  0-470-08030-2
- Creating Web Pages All-in-One Desk
  Reference For Dummies
  0-7645-4345-8
- Dreamweaver 8 For Dummies
  0-7645-9649-7

- InDesign CS2 For Dummies
  0-7645-9572-5
- Macromedia Flash 8 For Dummie
  0-7645-9691-8
- Photoshop CS2 and Digital
  Photography For Dummies
  0-7645-9580-6
- Photoshop Elements 4 For Dumm
  0-471-77483-9
- Syndicating Web Sites with RSS F
  For Dummies
  0-7645-8848-6
- Yahoo! SiteBuilder For Dummies
  0-7645-9800-7

NETWORKING, SECURITY, PROGRAMMING & DATABASES

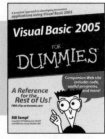

0-7645-7728-X

0-471-74940-0

Also available:
- Access 2007 For Dummies
  0-470-04612-0
- ASP.NET 2 For Dummies
  0-7645-7907-X
- C# 2005 For Dummies
  0-7645-9704-3
- Hacking For Dummies
  0-470-05235-X
- Hacking Wireless Networks
  For Dummies
  0-7645-9730-2
- Java For Dummies
  0-470-08716-1

- Microsoft SQL Server 2005 For Dur
  0-7645-7755-7
- Networking All-in-One Desk Refe
  For Dummies
  0-7645-9939-9
- Preventing Identity Theft For Dum
  0-7645-7336-5
- Telecom For Dummies
  0-471-77085-X
- Visual Studio 2005 All-in-One De
  Reference For Dummies
  0-7645-9775-2
- XML For Dummies
  0-7645-8845-1

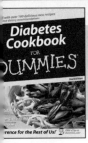

0-7645-8450-2

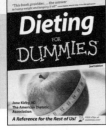

0-7645-4149-8

Also available:

Bipolar Disorder For Dummies
0-7645-8451-0

Chemotherapy and Radiation
For Dummies
0-7645-7832-4

Controlling Cholesterol For Dummies
0-7645-5440-9

Diabetes For Dummies
0-7645-6820-5* †

Divorce For Dummies
0-7645-8417-0 †

Fibromyalgia For Dummies
0-7645-5441-7

Low-Calorie Dieting For Dummies
0-7645-9905-4

Meditation For Dummies
0-471-77774-9

Osteoporosis For Dummies
0-7645-7621-6

Overcoming Anxiety For Dummies
0-7645-5447-6

Reiki For Dummies
0-7645-9907-0

Stress Management For Dummies
0-7645-5144-2

CATION, HISTORY, REFERENCE & TEST PREPARATION

0-7645-8381-6

0-7645-9554-7

Also available:

The ACT For Dummies
0-7645-9652-7

Algebra For Dummies
0-7645-5325-9

Algebra Workbook For Dummies
0-7645-8467-7

Astronomy For Dummies
0-7645-8465-0

Calculus For Dummies
0-7645-2498-4

Chemistry For Dummies
0-7645-5430-1

Forensics For Dummies
0-7645-5580-4

Freemasons For Dummies
0-7645-9796-5

French For Dummies
0-7645-5193-0

Geometry For Dummies
0-7645-5324-0

Organic Chemistry I For Dummies
0-7645-6902-3

The SAT I For Dummies
0-7645-7193-1

Spanish For Dummies
0-7645-5194-9

Statistics For Dummies
0-7645-5423-9

Get smart @ dummies.com®

- **Find a full list of Dummies titles**
- **Look into loads of FREE on-site articles**
- **Sign up for FREE eTips e-mailed to you weekly**
- **See what other products carry the Dummies name**
- **Shop directly from the Dummies bookstore**
- **Enter to win new prizes every month!**

ate Canadian edition also available
ate U.K. edition also available

wherever books are sold. For more information or to order direct: U.S. customers visit www.dummies.com or call 1-877-762-2974.
omers visit www.wileyeurope.com or call 0800 243407. Canadian customers visit www.wiley.ca or call 1-800-567-4797.